QUEER RICANS

CULTURAL STUDIES OF THE AMERICAS

George Yúdice, Jean Franco, and Juan Flores, series editors

For more titles in the series, see page 244.

QUEER RICANS

Cultures and Sexualities
in the Diaspora

LAWRENCE LA FOUNTAIN–STOKES

Cultural Studies of the Americas 23

 University of Minnesota Press
Minneapolis • London

For information on previously published material reprinted in this book, see the Publication History on page 225.

Published by the University of Minnesota Press
111 Third Avenue South, Suite 290
Minneapolis, MN 55401-2520
http://www.upress.umn.edu

Library of Congress Cataloging-in-Publication Data

La Fountain–Stokes, Lawrence M. (Lawrence Martin), 1968-
  Queer Ricans : cultures and sexualities in the diaspora / Lawrence La Fountain–Stokes.
    p.   cm. – (Cultural studies of the Americas ; 23)
  Includes bibliographical references and index.
  ISBN 978-0-8166-4091-1 (hc : alk. paper) – ISBN 978-0-8166-4092-8 (pb : alk. paper)
  1. Minority gays – United States. 2. Puerto Ricans – United States – Social life and customs.
I. Title.   II. Title: Cultures and sexualities in the diaspora.
HQ76.3.U5L3 2009
306.76'6089687295073 – dc22   2009006991

To my parents, Mona and Don La Fountain,
and in loving memory of my maternal grandmother,
Carmen Giménez de la Rosa, vda. de Stokes

Contents

Introduction

On Queer Diasporas and Puerto Rican Migration Histories

S EXUALITY IS A KEY FACTOR shaping and defining Puerto Rican migration to the United States.[1] It is as relevant as economic, political,
and social factors. Its impact on immigrant experience is as significant as
race, sex, gender, class, physical and mental health, education, religion,
and ability or disability. The longstanding, historical refusal to acknowledge the centrality of sexuality to migration is rooted in prejudice and
ignorance, as well as in conservative, reactionary, sexist, misogynist, and
homophobic politics. The purpose of *Queer Ricans: Cultures and Sexualities in the Diaspora* is to challenge this and transform Puerto Rican
migration studies paradigms by showing how attitudes toward stigmatized forms of same-sex sexuality and gender variance provoke and
affect migration, and how artists, writers, filmmakers, dancers, choreographers, and performers have documented and discussed this fact. I
seek to show how this experience has had a historical, gendered, and geo-
spatial dimension, that is to say, how it has changed from the late 1960s
until the first decade of the 2000s; how it is affected by gender; and how
it varies according to where the individual artists live, be it, for example,
New York, New Jersey, Philadelphia, Chicago, or San Francisco. I also
explore the differences between queer first-generation migrants, which
is to say, people born in Puerto Rico who came to the United States as
adults, and queer second-generation migrants, referring to those born in
the United States of Puerto Rican parents, specifically the way that varying models of assimilation or integration into American society affect
individual lives.

Persecution or intolerance of individuals who engage in same-sex sexuality or show gender divergence leads some but not all lesbian, gay,
bisexual, and transgender (LGBT) people to want to leave the place

where they live, or to feel that they must leave in order to survive.[2] This can entail moving from one neighborhood to another, from one town or city to another (what is commonly referred to as internal migration), or from one country to another (international migration). In the case of Puerto Rico, it can also mean temporarily or permanently moving to the metropole, that is to say, to the United States, which constitutes a form of colonial migration.[3] Puerto Rican queer migration to the United States has to do with the colonial links between the two countries since the end of the Spanish–Cuban–American War of 1898, the two countries' inter-linked economies, the facility of travel, and the legacy of imperialism; it also has to do with the small size of the island, issues of unemployment, underemployment, and economic stagnation, and the fact that there is only one major metropolitan area, that of San Juan. Sexuality need not necessarily be the primary motivation; it can simply be a factor, one among many considerations. Obviously, the most dramatic cases (and those that garner the most attention) have to do with violent expulsion, which can come from the family or the community. Resistance to migration is often unacknowledged and not seen as such; in other words, "not migrating" is not acknowledged as an act of resistance to a specific dominant logic, which it is.

Frame of Analysis, Methodology, and Approach

The goals of this book are to trace, document, and analyze the links or relationship between queer identities and practices (understood in the most expansive ways) and Puerto Rican migration as they developed since the 1960s and are represented or discussed in cultural productions. As such, the key terms guiding my inquiry are "queer sexuality," "culture," and "migration," all of these in a transnational or translocal Puerto Rican diasporic context, especially in the United States. To understand the general phenomenon of Puerto Rican queer migration, I focus on a very limited number of Puerto Rican, Nuyorican, Chicago Rican, Philly Rican, CaliRican, and DiaspoRican cultural manifestations by diverse artists and writers, many of them autobiographical — literary, audio-visual, and performative — and analyze these in a migration studies framework, to see what they reveal about queer diasporic experience.

My approach employs careful discussion of artistic texts in relation to their authors and contexts. I offer extensive biographical information in some cases with the understanding that this is integral for a full comprehension and appreciation of the works and of the social phenomena they portray. All of the artists and cultural productions that I discuss are very well known and highly respected in what are for the most part very rarefied circles; these works have never been discussed or compared in a broader framework and, in general, with some important exceptions, are not familiar to mainstream audiences. In some cases, such as those of dance-theater and performance art, I have attended shows with limited runs, have had access to video recordings that are not in common circulation, and have been able to transcribe and notate performances for which there were no written scripts.[4] I also consulted diverse libraries and archives in Puerto Rico and the United States[5] and had extensive conversations with some of the artists I write about, complementing my possibilities for analysis. The work that I put into researching this book might not be immediately apparent to people who are not aware of the difficulties of these processes and of the novelty and specific demands of my comparative approach.

My use of the term "queer" in *Queer Ricans* references the cultural shifts and academic and theoretical developments, notably in the English-language world, that have expanded or transformed the study of LGBT experience, focused as they were on specific identities or individuals, to a broader critique of society and a demand for the recognition of the workings of power over sexuality at large.[6] The word "queer" itself carries a very specific charge of disruption; its use signifies the reappropriation of an insult and its transformation into something new and different.[7] I should point out that I do not use the term solely in opposition to or as a negation of the conceptual universe represented in the acronym LGBT, but as a complement, as I am not interested in dismissing the contributions of LGBT studies or of LGBT identities to our current understanding of society. In fact, one of the motivating factors for this study is to bring together and highlight previous scholarly contributions on Puerto Rican queer/LGBT studies that have allowed me to carry out my work.

At the same time, I am painfully aware of the bind or limitation of using "queer" and LGBT as stand-ins for practices, identities, and experiences that are much more complex and diffuse, and that at times have very distinct, idiosyncratic, vernacular specificities captured in Spanish-language words such as *pato, pata, maricón, loca, marimacha, marimacho, vestida,* and *bugarrón,* as well as in English-language terms and expressions such as "butch," "femme," and "on the down-low."[8] I would much prefer to use the highly stigmatized term *pato,* for example, for a (usually effeminate) male homosexual, which has very particular cultural resonances and an explosive semantic charge; I have chosen not to do so for the sake of intelligibility and simplification and to benefit from the supposed "neutrality" or "objectivity" of a more internationally recognized term such as "gay," which many understand to be less offensive and more modern.[9]

This book is not a sociological or anthropological or ethnographic study of the experience of queer or LGBT Puerto Ricans, although such a book would be a valuable contribution, and in fact social science methodologies and findings will illuminate and give credence to my argument, which is significantly informed by Latin American and U.S. Latina/o social science literature. It is also not a historical analysis of queer Puerto Rican migration, another necessary project, although at times my arguments will be organized or couched in a historical framework. Nor is it an encyclopedia or a literary/cultural history of all LGBT Puerto Rican artists and writers. It is, however, an effort to see how sexuality has been a constitutive element in shaping Puerto Rican migration principally (but not exclusively) to the United States, and how different artists have represented or publicly articulated this issue.

This book seeks to validate the lives and experiences of queer and LGBT Puerto Ricans on the island and elsewhere, and also seeks to critically interrogate dominant notions about what it means to be a Puerto Rican and an American and to be part of a global queer diaspora, in the context of U.S. imperialism. *Queer Ricans* is the first book to explicitly address Puerto Rican queer culture and migration from an academic and scholarly perspective, to bring together a focus on men and women, and to clearly announce itself as such in its title.[10] In order to challenge migration studies paradigms that systematically exclude concerns about nontraditional or divergent gender expressions and sexualities, I establish a dialogue with Latina/o, American, Latin American, transnational, critical race, ethnic, queer, and feminist and women's studies, as well as with those focusing on literature, film, performance, and visual cultures. I offer close readings of the cultural texts that comprise my queer Puerto Rican archive and critical methodologies that can help us to understand many different Puerto Rican (and non–Puerto Rican) cultural productions. While the Puerto Rican case is quite specific, the experience of queer migration is (dare I say) universal, or at the very least is becoming every day more and more common in many different locations around the globe, as a by now large and growing body of research has shown.

The careful analysis of cultural texts that comment on or relate to Puerto Rican queer migration serves to map out the intersections of migration, culture, and sexuality. By the term "culture," I wish to refer to a wide variety of phenomena, including both the more general anthropological definitions of culture as the central or core beliefs and interactions that mark a particular community of people, as well as the more specific usages of culture (and especially "cultural productions") as those referring to high culture, mass culture, and popular culture, specifically to literature, film, dance, theater, and performance, among other arts.[11] In effect, in this book I would like to account for the general, as when we say, "Puerto Rican culture is intolerant (or rather, what is more true, ambivalent) about homosexuality," in which what we mean is culture as society, the mores and values and customs of that society, as well as the particular, as when we refer to the specificity of a certain work of art, say René Marqués's novel *La mirada* (The look) or his essay "El puertorriqueño dócil" (The docile Puerto Rican).

Cultural analysis is privileged in my work with the understanding that cultural means of expression, in addition to reflecting an individual's thoughts and mastery of craft, also form an integral part of and contribute to a community's self-definition and allow for discussions of prevalent fundamental issues that the group is confronting. Cultural expressions provide important insights that may not be gleaned from statistical data, which for the most part is not available. There is a critical mass of Puerto Rican cultural productions that address the question of migration and homosexuality, and these provide comprehensive and heterogeneous information. In addition to analyzing their aesthetic values and worth, it is my intention to use cultural forms as sources of knowledge but also (when possible) to understand or imagine how these cultural productions are used or could be used by individuals and within the group or community to negotiate and/or enforce specific viewpoints or to develop strategies of resistance; in other words — following the philosopher Michel de Certeau's lead — to always allow for a multiplicity of possible interpretations and relationships, unforeseeable and uncontrollable. Understandably, there are diasporic Puerto Rican cultural productions that oppose or condemn homosexuality, as well as ones that defend or exalt it; some of the texts and events that we will study are widely known, while others are more obscure or have had limited circulation. Not all cultural productions that address this topic are necessarily well-crafted, technically proficient, or aesthetically pleasing;

in this book, I will focus on works that do meet certain standards and that in my judgment represent a happy marriage of content and form.

While serious discussion of the fundamental link between present-day Puerto Rican homosexualities and the circular, two-way migration of Puerto Ricans (and Americans) to and from the United States has only been very recent, the research of numerous scholars has served to establish a critical mass of theoretically informed knowledge about Puerto Rican queer and LGBT experience, laying the essential groundwork for my analysis.[12] These contributions constitute what I would identify as "Puerto Rican queer studies" (or perhaps "queer Puerto Rican studies"), a field that is in obvious dialogue with and indebted to broader lesbian and gay studies and queer theory as these fields are articulated in hegemonic centers of knowledge, in dominant U.S. academia but also elsewhere (notably in Latin America), as well as to feminism, race, and ethnic studies, and an enormous diversity of specific disciplines.[13] Puerto Rican queer studies share a strong link with other antihegemonic critical queer studies projects such as those discussed by E. Patrick Johnson and Roderick A. Ferguson, which build on the indispensable work of U.S. Third World feminism, especially as articulated by the Chicana lesbians Gloria Anzaldúa, Cherríe Moraga, and Chela Sandoval.[14] My conception of "Puerto Rican queer studies" (a phrase that perhaps one day will be as meaningful as "French feminism," "Chicana feminism," or "Black queer studies") integrates social science and humanities contributions (and I hope, in the future, exact and natural sciences) as methodologies and knowledges that enable us to practice what Sarita See and José Quiroga have called, on different occasions, a "critical hermeneutics." To my knowledge, there has been no systematic attempt to look at these contributions as a whole and in full dialogue with each other, and that is, perhaps, one of the main contributions of this book.

Because of its specific historical and cultural situation in terms of colonialism and migration, Puerto Rican society and culture offer a unique and fascinating example that simultaneously reflects development and underdevelopment; nationalism, nation-building, and statelessness; colonialism and postcolonialism; competing ethnic, racial, religious, and class identifications; heterogeneity and homogeneity; tradition and modernity. Puerto Rican queer studies bring to broader lesbian and gay and (Anglo-European) queer studies a very specific disciplinary and conceptual intersectionality, a reality located between the national and international, local and global, autochthonous and foreign, insular yet simultaneously *transfronterizo*: a space between the fragment and the whole. I will proceed to discuss these particularities in some detail in the following sections for, as I hope to show, Puerto Rican queer studies are a crucial component for understanding U.S., Latin American, and Caribbean realities, and by their paradigmatic role are useful to understand many other colonial–metropolitan, migratory, and diasporic situations.

Is Puerto Rico a Particularly Homophobic Place (More Than the United States, for Example)?

It is not an understatement to affirm that divergent sexualities (notably same-sex attractions and interactions) and alternative sex and gender practices such as cross-dressing and prosthetic, hormonal, and surgical body transformations have historically been and still are sources of contention, mistrust, and provocation in Puerto Rico, censored by the state (i.e., the government), by many churches, by the medical establishment, and by ordinary individuals. It is also true that Puerto Rico is not unique in its homophobia or more homophobic than many other countries in Latin America or than the United States, for that matter, although at the present moment the island does have an above-average level of daily violence affecting the entire population and alarming murder rates for gay men.[15] Puerto Rico shares many attributes with the United States, especially given its colonial relationship as a nonincorporated, semi-autonomous territory or commonwealth that is subjected to the U.S. Constitution and Bill of Rights and to U.S. federal laws and agencies. Some of these common attributes include a lengthy history of lesbian and gay activism dating to the 1970s, LGBT pride parades since 1991, and highly contested processes of legal reform. In fact, it can be argued that Puerto Rican homophobia and gay liberation are in some ways a result of the island's colonial ties to the United States, in other words, that Americans have exported some forms of homophobia to Puerto Rico, as well as the socially progressive impetus to combat it.[16] For example, the act of sodomy was first criminalized in Puerto Rico in 1902, shortly after the U.S. invasion of 1898, when the island was under a classic formal colonial regime, yet activist-led initiatives similar to those occurring across the United States (and across the globe) have resulted in national discussions and public congressional hearings in 2007 about sections of the civil code that pertain to family life, suggesting possible future recognition of same-sex couples and their rights to joint custody of children and to inheritance.[17]

Numerous diverse cultures have come together on the island (or more accurately, the archipelago) of Puerto Rico — and now, as a result of the diaspora, at different locations around the world — to constitute what we can call, following Benedict Anderson, the Puerto Rican "imagined nation." Many of these cultures have historically seen homosexuality as an undesirable or inappropriate behavior and for the most part have not accepted it as a valid or serious expression of identity; when recognized, it has often been seen as a joke or as a threat and dealt with through violence, insult, silence, police arrests, and/or ostracism.[18] Puerto Rico has historically been a predominantly Catholic country whose legacy includes the persecution of sodomites during the Inquisition, where conservative Evangelical Christian churches and preachers similar to those in the United States have recently made enormous political strides (as have more progressive, progay Protestant churches), and where police-sponsored massive arrests and entrapment of men who have (or are perceived or imagined as wanting to have) sex in public rest rooms and on beaches still occur.[19]

Same-sex sexual attractions and practices, as well as identities based upon these, have existed in Puerto Rico in similar ways to those of the United States and of many Latin American societies: as an essential, phantasmatic, and abject Other or necessary marginal figure in the construction of masculinity and femininity, as a common yet stigmatized reality, as well as an unnamable and often ignored silence. The marginalization or stigmatization that queers experience is structurally similar to the oppression women, blacks, immigrants, handicapped people, and other "minority" groups are subjected to, even while the nature of each of these is manifested differently and serves different purposes for those who enforce them; then again, as the sociologist Elizabeth Crespo Kebler has argued in her important article " 'The Infamous Crime against Nature,' " the situation of Puerto Rican lesbians (notably their invisibility, as an unnamable, unimaginable abject) is directly tied to the heterosexual matrix that rules over all women's gender and sex experience,[20] and we could think of relationships linking other forms of oppressions within a more complex, grid-like accounting of the workings of hegemonic power.

Puerto Rican sexualities are a living, mutable phenomenon, open to general currents but also demonstrating certain specific traits. Social and historical processes involving the juxtaposition or layering of indigenous, African, and Southern European (predominantly Judeo-Christian but also Muslim) practices and beliefs during centuries of colonization produced complex sexual ideologies that are still not fully understood. American colonization introduced yet another level of complexity. Large influxes of Latin American and Caribbean immigrants, especially from Cuba and the Dominican Republic, and the dramatic migration of Puerto Ricans to the United States (and their return migration back home) have also contributed to transforming and shaping Puerto Rican sexual cultures.

Until very recently, general social intolerance of homosexuality, lesbianism, bisexuality, and transgenderedness in Puerto Rico has entailed specific expectations, conventions, and patterns of behavior, at least as far as urban middle-class and some upper-class individuals are concerned. These conventions and behaviors include secrecy or nondisclosure of personal matters in family, professional, and social environments (homosexuality, lesbianism, and bisexuality are tolerated as long as they are not disclosed or are negotiated strictly as an "open secret" or *secreto a voces/secreto abierto*) and, at the opposite end of the spectrum, voluntary, highly encouraged, or even forced migration.[21] It is generally recognized that poor, working-class, and rural communities have different paradigms and levels of tolerance for gender deviance, especially for effeminate men who behave like women (*locas*); these vary location by location, which makes it risky to make generalizations.[22]

Homosexualities and the State

Social discourses on sexual difference in both Puerto Rico and the United States have traditionally (even after the historic 1969 Stonewall revolt) talked about nonnormative sexual orientation as a form of deviant behavior against which the national population needs protection. In Puerto Rico, homosexuality has been viewed at different moments during the twentieth century as a threat to the national character.[23] As I mentioned earlier, the act of sodomy became illegal in 1902, when the Puerto Rican Penal Code was altered to more closely follow North American models, specifically, that of California; the 1974 reform of the code extended the definition of sodomy, which previously only referred to men, to include acts between women.[24] It was only in 2003 that the act was decriminalized in Puerto Rico, barely three days before the Supreme Court decision of *Lawrence v. Texas* eliminated this law in the United States.[25] Many activists in Puerto Rico saw this three-day precedent as an important affirmation of autonomy and anticolonialism, but others have argued that it was simply a performative gesture enacted to avoid the embarrassment of acknowledging prejudiced social views or lack of modernity.[26]

Homosexuality, and especially gay liberation, has at times been seen as imported or inflated by virtue of the island's colonial relationship with the United States: openly gay, militant homosexuals and other LGBT individuals are seen as emulating foreign attitudes, posing a menace from the outside, and not necessarily behaving as Puerto Ricans are expected to (that is to say, in accordance with what is problematically construed as "authentic" or "true" with regard to Puerto Rican values and culture).[27] This understanding parallels discourses in other Latin American countries, where the prevalence of homosexuality (and other "unsociable" behavior) at the beginning of the twentieth century was attributed, as Jorge Salessi has shown for Argentina, to immigration.[28]

Social discourses that posit the foreign provenance or "unnaturalness" of homosexuality have often been accompanied by social measures that seek to confine or expel homosexuals, be it by placing them in institutions of social control or by actually forcing them out of the national borders. As the historians and philosophers George Mosse and Michel Foucault have famously discussed, modern understandings of homosexuality underwent a profound shift in many European countries in the mid- to late nineteenth century, as homosexuality came to be viewed as an identity and not as an act or conduct; older procedures of homosexual persecution were transformed at this time, and incarceration and psychiatric treatment became commonplace. Historically, the most severe and extreme cases of attempts at expulsion have included the Nazi policies of extermination, which sought to rid German and, more broadly, European society not only of Jews, Gypsies, Jehovah's Witnesses, and "lumpen" criminals but also of homosexuals.[29] Another example of expulsion is that of the post-1959 revolutionary Cuban government, which after initial efforts of "reforming" homosexuals through forced work camps known as UMAPs (Unidades Militares de Ayuda a la Producción, or Military Units to Aid Production) deported thousands of homosexuals, such as Reinaldo Arenas, along with other "undesirables" in 1980 through the port of Mariel.[30] Similar labor-reeducation camps are believed to have existed in Trinidad and Tobago and the Dominican Republic. Such draconian methods have never been employed in Puerto Rico, but the massive, government-sponsored migratory waves have at times been a convenient way to send undesired subjects away to the United States, including a good number of LGBT and gender-discordant individuals.

What Is the Relation between
Puerto Rican Queer Diasporas and Global Contexts?

While economic and political motivations for Puerto Rican migration have been widely recognized, seldom have other social motivations, like sexual orientation (and more specifically, homosexuality) been acknowledged as causal factors or received the careful scrutiny they deserve.[31] This omission is part and parcel of a more general absence of an LGBT/queer analysis of Puerto Rican society, but also corresponds to the ways in which leading national and international migration scholars have completely ignored the question of nonhegemonic sexualities.[32] In fact, as the scholar Steven Seideman has shown, many social scientists have faced open hostility and entrenched resistance when trying to introduce queer sexuality parameters as valid categories of analysis that go beyond studies of "deviance" or social marginality.

Remarkably, the last decade of the twentieth century witnessed a veritable explosion of studies on the topic of transnational queer migration.[33] In the 1990s, sexuality and questions of divergent gender expression and sexual orientation came to be more broadly acknowledged as causal factors for national (internal) and international (cross-border) migration — what Irene Sosa has termed "sexual exile" and Manolo Guzmán refers to as "sexile" — and were also recognized as important variables affecting immigrant experience.[34] These physical movements or displacements entail meaningful numbers of people on a global scale and, in the case of lesbian, gay, bisexual, and transgender individuals, are now referred to as "Queer Diasporas," as Cindy Patton and Benigno Sánchez-Eppler's eponymous volume indicates. This groundbreaking research has also included Martin Manalansan's work on Filipino migrants, Gayatri Gopinath's work on South Asians, David Eng's meditations on Asian America, Oliva Espín's work on Cuban lesbians, Héctor Carrillo's work on Mexicans, Susana Peña's articles on gay Cubans in Miami, Carlos Decena's work on Dominicans in New York, and important anthologies such as *Passing Lines* (2005), *Queer Globalizations* (2002), and *Queer Migrations* (2005).[35] My book shares intersections with these projects, yet poses intrinsically different questions, as the Puerto Rican context of colonial migration necessarily implies a different focus.

The persecution of individuals for reasons of nonnormative sexual practices or identities and the particular difficulties produced by their localized, autochthonous manifestations or by health-related causes such as HIV and AIDS are now documented by international nongovernmental organizations such as Amnesty International, Human Rights Watch, and the International Gay and Lesbian Human Rights Commission (IGLHRC) and have joined catastrophic natural and man-made phenomena (war, political repression, religious intolerance), economic necessity, and personal aspirations as conditions recognized to affect migration.

Why Go to the United States
When We All Know How Homophobic It Is?

The fact that so many diasporic queer subjects choose to come to the United States is quite remarkable, given this country's history of exclusionary policies and current hostility toward recognizing LGBT civil rights. In her landmark book *Entry Denied: Controlling Sexuality at the Border* (2002), Eithne Luibhéid lucidly shows how issues of sexuality have determined who can and who cannot get into the United States, and the horrifying experiences some individuals (especially women) have faced while trying to cross the border. Given the current political climate, it should come as no surprise to learn that gay Americans (especially those involved in transnational relationships) are actually migrating to other countries such as Canada, as well as leaving states perceived to be more homophobic and moving to ones perceived as more friendly, or which have instituted pro-LGBT measures such as gay marriage, civil unions, domestic partnership rights, and gay adoption.[36]

In the United States, immigration laws that prohibited the entrance of people on the basis of ideology, race, behavior, or handicaps technically forbade homosexuals, specifically from 1917 to 1990, under the category of "moral turpitude."[37] While the effects of the law were often more ideological than practical, there are documented cases of exclusion, as well as of deportation.[38] These laws did not apply to most Puerto Ricans, who received U.S. citizenship in 1917, but are still indicative of the ideas held about who should and who should not be allowed to enter the country.[39]

Generalized intolerance of homosexuality and increased awareness and organization within the lesbian, gay, bisexual, and transgender community in the United States have led, especially since World War II, to massive geographic displacements, notably toward large urban enclaves on both coasts, notably San Francisco and New York, as well as to many other large and mid-size cities; gay migration to suburbs and rural areas is a much more recent phenomenon.[40] In the case of Puerto Rico, as well as that of many Latin American countries, displacements have occurred first to urban locations within the countries themselves and second, in those places where there are feasible opportunities for international migration, to other countries such as Australia, Brazil, Canada, Mexico, the United States, and select countries in Western Europe. These displacements occur in the context of social policies such as laws against sodomy in the home countries as well as a result of social intolerance, discrimination, harassment, and persecution. The "threat" or option of migration affects those who remain as much as those who leave, especially those who have relatives and friends who have left and who have considered the option of migrating themselves.

U.S. citizenship has allowed Puerto Ricans to partake in what is referred to as the "air bridge" or "air bus," by which individuals may freely move back and forth from the island to the United States; this has been especially important for those affected by HIV and AIDS, who travel for medical and family reasons. The "air bus," or *guagua aérea,* taking up the metaphor used by the writer Luis Rafael Sánchez, also facilitates general patterns of circular migration, a constant displacement of gays and lesbians and other queer subjects who have experienced living on both the island and in the United States and who at different moments may settle in one or the other place.

Several points bear final consideration: individuals who participate in same-sex intercourse may migrate to the United States or another country for reasons other than those of sexual orientation; not all individuals who identify as homosexual (or LGBT) or engage in same-sex intercourse migrate or leave their countries of origin, and it is important to try to understand why this is so; the existence of a visible gay community in a country does not contradict the perceived or real necessity of specific individuals to migrate. Sadly, it has become increasingly apparent that LGBT migration to the United States does not necessarily ensure safety (particularly for working-class and trans subjects), as numerous, well-publicized murders remind us.

The experience of first-generation queer Puerto Rican immigrants varies according to a number of factors, including where they settle; what their contact with the diasporic Puerto Rican and the North American LGBT community is; what their race, class, gender, age, self-presentation, educational background, political orientation, command of the English language, mental health, and HIV and AIDS status is; the terms under which they migrated; the degree to which they maintain ties to their family and community of origin in Puerto Rico; and the ways they identify themselves with regard to their sexuality. In some cases, apparently quite similar individuals can have very different experiences and perspectives.

Second- and third-generation Puerto Rican LGBT immigrants often have concerns different from those of their first-generation peers. These include different experiences with acculturation, varying relations to other U.S. ethnic and racial communities, loss of Spanish in favor of English and Spanglish, uncertainty about cultural baggage, and rejection by island-born Puerto Ricans. All generations face problems of discrimination. At the same time, the links and shared experiences of second- and third-generation LGBT Puerto Ricans with African Americans (observed most clearly in the investment in African American politics and youth culture) are generally stronger than for first-generation immigrants, especially for those who grow up in urban centers. The involvement of all of these immigrants within their communities (be it the diasporic Puerto Rican community or the LGBT community or both) often requires careful negotiations and can be a source of tension. Primary and secondary allegiances on the basis of different aspects of identification can strain an individual's energy but, as Bob Cant has observed in a broader context, can also have creative results.

What Is Queer Rican Culture?

Queer Rican culture is many things, entailing myriad cultural forms. It is a daily, lived practice as much as the production of objects for consumption or collection. It is an attitude, a pose, a shared understanding, and also a vastly understudied field. It is a space that shows the intersection of Puerto Ricanness, migration, and queer genders and sexualities.

Literary and autobiographical sources have, for a long time, shown how emigration has served both as a regulatory measure and a liberatory strategy in Puerto Rico with regard to nonnormative sexualities; at the very least, having narratives set outside Puerto Rico seems to facilitate certain types of representation, but also presents very particular forms of anxiety. Bernardo Vega's memoirs, as it has been amply noted, mention how this well-known Puerto Rican tobacco worker, socialist labor leader, and diasporic community pioneer threw his prized wristwatch overboard as he neared New York City in 1916, after hearing rumors that he might be considered effeminate for wearing it; he later learned that watches similar to his were extremely popular.[41] As early as the 1920s, José I. de Diego Padró presented a Cuban bisexual sadist in New

York as the best friend of the Puerto Rican protagonist in his monolithic novel *En babia*.[42] Other well-known authors who write in Spanish, such as Pedro Juan Soto, José Luis Vivas Maldonado, Emilio Díaz Valcárcel, Luis Rafael Sánchez, and Magali García Ramis, have also included such accounts in their work.[43] García Ramis's *Felices días, tío Sergio* (Happy days, Uncle Sergio, 1986) is an especially interesting case, as this novel presents back-and-forth migration of a gay man (that of the title's character, Uncle Sergio), but also portrays a proto-lesbian protagonist (Lidia) who resists leaving the island, even if she dreams of running away with Sophia Loren to Italy or New York.[44]

English-language literary portrayals have been mixed. Widely recognized diasporic Puerto Rican cultural productions written during the 1960s and 1970s, such as those of Piri Thomas, Pedro Pietri, and Miguel Piñero, did not have a gay liberationist bent.[45] Much more nuanced depictions appear in the work of Nicholasa Mohr, a writer characterized by her sensitivity to matters of gender and sexuality.[46] More recent portrayals by authors such as Judith Ortiz Cofer, Abraham Rodríguez Jr., and Ernesto Quiñónez have unfortunately tended toward the representation of queer identity as a form of social stigma.[47]

In general, it is not until openly, self-identified gay and lesbian cultural producers begin to document and explore their migration or "sexile" in the 1970s and 1980s that more insightful, contestatory voices come to the fore, at least among island-born artists who write in Spanish. Perhaps the two paradigmatic figures of this are the now deceased writer Manuel Ramos Otero, lost to AIDS in 1990, who will be the focus of chapter 2, and Luz María Umpierre, the focus of chapter 3; other writers from this period include Víctor Fragoso (who died of AIDS in 1982), Nemir Matos-Cintrón, Carmen de Monteflores, Carlos Rodríguez-Matos, and Alfredo Villanueva-Collado (who lives with HIV/AIDS). More recent first-generation writers who write in Spanish include Daniel Torres, Angel Lozada, Moisés Agosto (who has now returned to Puerto Rico), and Benito Pastoriza Iyodo, while others such as Aldo Alvarez, Carlos Mock, and J. Delgado-Figueroa write predominantly in English, as does the Chicago-based performer/podcaster Fausto Fernós.

There is a danger in having an exclusive focus on literature as far as tracing a historical (or even generational) model of queer Rican culture: filmmaking, performance, and activism actually antecede gay liberationist literary portrayals. Appearing in the 1960s and early 1970s, "1.5" and second-generation trans activists and performers such as Sylvia Rivera, Holly Woodlawn, Mario Móntez (née René Rivera), and the (first-generation, island-born) underground filmmaker José Rodríguez-Soltero, many of whom engage in what could be termed, following José Esteban Muñoz, as "disidentificatory" political or artistic representations, actually predate "open" first-generation literary voices but are only recently being reclaimed as Puerto Rican.[48] The cases of Woodlawn and Móntez are especially complex, as Frances Negrón-Muntaner has observed in *Boricua Pop,* because they are more often known for their association with gay, white, avant-garde artists such as Andy Warhol, Jack Smith, and Charles Ludlam rather than for their own talent and originality; Negrón-Muntaner does not mention Rodríguez-Soltero, who formed an important part of this circle and can be seen as an *auteur* of the status of his Anglo colleagues.[49] Of course, Sylvia Rivera's activist/political "performance," as a Stonewall veteran, Gay Liberation Front militant, Young Lords member, and trans activist, is of quite a different nature from that of individuals in the world of the arts yet is similar in the ways in which she constructed a public persona, one that served to advance a collective desire for political rights.[50]

There is now a significant number of second-generation gay, lesbian, and bisexual Nuyoricans or, to quote Mariposa (María Fernández), "DiaspoRicans," whose work reflects the dramatically different experience of being born and raised Puerto Rican in the United States; this work is predominantly in English or Spanglish and reflects much closer attachments to sites in the United States (particularly diasporic Puerto Rican communities) and generally less interest or concern with the island of Puerto Rico itself. These second-generation artists include filmmaker Rose Troche and writer, performer, and cartoonist Erika López (whom I will discuss in chapter 4); dancer/choreographer Arthur Avilés and his first-cousin Elizabeth Marrero (the focus of chapter 5); the playwrights Janis Astor del Valle, Milton Díaz, Charles Rice-González, and Edwin Sánchez; the writer and activist Robert Vázquez-Pacheco; the L.A.-based performance artist Marcus Kuiland-Nazario; the writer Charlie Vázquez; and poets or spoken word artists like Rane Arroyo, Mariposa, Ingrid/Ignacio Rivera, and Emanuel Xavier.

Structure of the Book

This book follows a historical (chronological), spatial, and generational model as a means to show different processes and transformations. It starts in the 1960s, moves through the 1970s and 1980s, and ends with a discussion of works from the 1990s and the first decade of the

2000s. Commencing in Puerto Rico, it moves to New York and then to Philadelphia, New Jersey, Chicago, and San Francisco, before returning to the Bronx. In generational terms, it focuses initially on a writer who has lived mostly in Puerto Rico but also in Spain and New York (Luis Rafael Sánchez), then on first-generation immigrants to the United States (Manuel Ramos Otero, Luz María Umpierre, Frances Negrón-Muntaner), and finally on second-generation artists born in the United States (Rose Troche, Erika López, Arthur Avilés, and Elizabeth Marrero). This generational model is in many ways indebted to and in implicit dialogue with similar models proposed by Nicolás Kanellos, Gustavo Pérez Firmat, and very especially Juan Flores, who has also analyzed the different stages and moments of diasporic Puerto Rican cultural production in a historical context.[51]

In chapter 1, I focus on Luis Rafael Sánchez's "¡Jum!" (1966) as a paradigmatic case of the violent expulsion of a queer Puerto Rican subject. This short story portrays the persecution and harassment that an effeminate black man is subjected to by his community, culminating in his death. While this story was written in the 1960s, its central motif will be repeated in a wide assortment of cultural productions, including René Marqués's *La mirada* (1976), Frances Negrón-Muntaner's *Brincando el charco: Portrait of a Puerto Rican* (1994), and Angel Lozada's *La patografía* (1998). Actual or self-imposed expulsion from the social collective (the family, the nation) is at the core of much of twentieth-century queer Rican migration, or at least of its leading cultural imaginings, even if some queer cultural representations such as Magali García Ramis's *Felices días, tío Sergio* and Antonio Martorell's *La piel de la memoria* (Memory's tattoo) also show selective cases of resistance. "¡Jum!" is especially important as an artistic statement that bears witness to inhumane violence; its discussion also allows for a nuanced focus on the centrality of race, specifically blackness, in Puerto Rico.

Queer men and women's migration experiences can be quite different and change over time, as I will show in chapters 2 and 3. This becomes evident when we explore two paradigmatic cases of Puerto Rican writers who came to the United States in the late 1960s and early 1970s: Manuel Ramos Otero, who migrated to New York in 1968, and Luz María Umpierre, who migrated to Philadelphia in 1974. As first-generation exiles who left Puerto Rico explicitly because of their sexual orientation, Ramos Otero and Umpierre had to choose how to incorporate themselves into new communities in the United States, and they quite literally chose opposite paths, as their literary production demonstrates. Both had to negotiate identification with the largely homophobic diasporic Puerto Rican community at the same time that they negotiated racist dominant Anglo-American, English-language culture and their ties to the lesbian and gay and feminist communities; these ties and identifications changed over time, as the artists became more comfortable or established in their new identities as diasporic queer subjects. In both cases, we see a desire to reconcile sexual, national, and ethnic identities, and a progression or evolution of experiences. Sex and gender differences can be said to have impacted their reception in the United States, their bonds, and their community involvements.

Queer Puerto Rican artists who came of age in Puerto Rico and in the United States in the 1980s and 1990s faced a quite different panorama. This is strikingly apparent when we analyze the lives and cultural productions of Frances Negrón-Muntaner (who was born on the island in 1966 and came to the United States in 1986), Rose Troche (born in Chicago in 1964), and Erika López (born in New York City in 1968), which I do in chapter 4. Negrón-Muntaner is a first-generation migrant who was openly lesbian on the island before she left, and who came to the United States to further her education; Claudia Marín, the protagonist of Negrón-Muntaner's best-known film, *Brincando el charco,* is portrayed as leaving Puerto Rico because of her family's rejection. Negrón-Muntaner (and her character Claudia Marín) settled in a Philadelphia that was in many ways quite different from (but in important ways similar to) the one that Umpierre found when she arrived in the 1970s.

Unlike Negrón-Muntaner, Rose Troche and Erika López were both born and raised in the United States. Troche experienced frequent moves, albeit she lived mostly in predominantly white suburban areas and in Chicago, where she later attended college and graduate school, while López grew up in Massachusetts and in a predominantly white suburb in southern New Jersey, where she was raised by two lesbian women, later moving to Philadelphia to attend art school and then to California. As the mixed-race daughter of a German-American lesbian mother and a black diasporic Puerto Rican father, López faced particular challenges and experiences. Because she is a second-generation Puerto Rican who was not born on the island and who does not speak Spanish, her perspective and experiences differ considerably from those of Ramos Otero, Umpierre, and Negrón-Muntaner. Troche also experienced alienation and cultural isolation, living in environments where there were few if any Puerto Ricans. Yet Negrón-Muntaner, Troche, and López do share things in common in that they favor feminist viewpoints and visual means of representation, those being filmmaking and cartoons, alongside their writing and López's performance work.

Second-generation queer Puerto Rican artists and cultural producers engage with issues of sexuality and national/ethnic identity in very different ways from first-generation migrants, having in large part to do with their different life experiences and issues. Greater distance from Puerto Rico, from the Spanish language, and from traditional and contemporary culture on the island is counterbalanced by closeness to different communities in the United States, to the English language, and to other experiences. Erika López's and Rose Troche's cases are interesting given their initial lack of contact with Latina/o communities and their closeness to the queer spaces of San Francisco and Chicago, respectively.

In the case of New York–based Arthur Avilés and Elizabeth Marrero, whose work I discuss in chapter 5, issues of poverty and proximity to the Puerto Rican and African American communities in the Bronx lead to a very different type of cultural engagement. Avilés's and Marrero's work is also different because they are performing artists who directly engage their working-class communities and have sought to create alternative spaces. Even between the two of them there are important differences: Avilés (closer to Erika López) does not know Spanish, while Marrero was brought up bilingual and bicultural. Avilés's and Marrero's postmodern fairytale dance-theater pieces such as *Arturella* and *Maéva de Oz* allow them to envision utopian spaces of integration and transformation that illustrate the rich possibilities of being queer and Rican in America in the twenty-first century.

Chapter 1

The Persecution
of Difference

IN ORDER TO FULLY UNDERSTAND QUEER MIGRATION, it is useful to acknowledge the profound violence and intolerance that marks some (but not all) people's lives, most notably those of individuals whose divergent sexual practices or gender identities provoke widespread criticism and censure.[1] That this is the case should come as no surprise, as daily ritualized performances of gender and sexuality are one of the most common spaces for the negotiation and establishment of social and cultural norms, of what is perceived or understood to be adequate, acceptable, or desired.[2] These performances generally entail the enactment of heterosexual virile manhood and feminine womanhood, in a context where the enforcement of dominant norms often occurs through violence.

While Puerto Rican culture is based on quite rigid notions of appropriate behavior for men and women, it is also a flexible system that can allow for what would seem to be egregious contradictions. These occur at times at liminal moments such as carnivals (for example, the Feast of Santiago Apóstol in Loíza), when many social conventions are broken, but also in everyday life.[3] Male-to-female transvestites, masculine women, and effeminate men are ubiquitous in all Puerto Rican towns and diasporic neighborhoods, yet they are also the frequent object of derision and even attacks. Prescriptions against male effeminacy and female masculinity do not work to simply eliminate gender-variance or trans practices and identities, but rather stigmatize this behavior and give it a specific meaning.[4] In fact, in this configuration, the social performance of effeminate manhood is *necessary* for other men's successful enactment of virile masculinity to work, as it is performed in perfect counterpoint. To put it simply, in this relational system, there can be no *macho* if there is no *loca* or *maricón*, perhaps in the way that there can be no virgin if there is no whore.[5] This system, with its arbitrary

1

and ever-changing rules and intrinsic violence, leads some individuals to want to migrate in order to safeguard their lives.

This ambivalence and inconsistency is at the heart of Luis Rafael Sánchez's short story "¡Jum!" (1966), translated by Rose M. Sevillano as "Hum!" (1997). This remarkably brief, synthetic text by one of the most widely revered Puerto Rican authors of the twentieth century is emblematic of Puerto Rican homophobia and how it leads to migration, specifically as the end result of malicious gossip (*chismes*) that turn into physical and emotional violence. "¡Jum!" presents the story of a black effeminate man who never speaks in the entire narration and who is ultimately led to his death by a murderous, intolerant mob composed of his formerly affable neighbors; it is the story of a failed attempt to leave. The story's emotional intensity and technical sophistication have led it to be recognized as a masterpiece by many Puerto Rican literary critics, including Jossianna Arroyo, Arnaldo Cruz-Malavé, and Agnes Lugo-Ortiz; it has gained the status of a "foundational fiction," that is to say, critics and readers have seen it as a landmark or defining moment, particularly reflective of a 1960s pre-Stonewall moment.[6]

My analysis of "¡Jum!" will serve to elucidate archetypal forms of homophobic or antihomosexual collective social violence in a very specific, racially marked environment, and will also demand an exploration of the particularities of Puerto Rican and Afro-Diasporic racial dynamics. As Alfredo Villanueva-Collado has also observed, Sánchez's representation of the persecution of difference functions as a narrative model or metanarrative that reappears in other literary works by Puerto Rican authors. Given the paucity of published analyses of black Puerto Rican homosexualities, I will also draw from the rich bibliography describing issues of black sexualities in the United States and elsewhere. My analysis will shed light on the concepts of gossip, silence, and voice, and on the role of artists and intellectuals in denouncing situations of social injustice. Moreover, it will draw attention to migration as a potential strategy for liberation, albeit one that can generate a ferocious backlash.

Sánchez's story forms part of his collection *En cuerpo de camisa* (In shirt sleeves), a volume that, as many critics have observed, focuses on outcasts and marginal figures in Puerto Rican society.[7] While immediate public response to the book was somewhat limited, the author's later publishing successes — (most notably the release of *La guaracha del Macho Camacho* (Macho Camacho's beat) in 1976) — provoked retrospective attention to his earlier production; for example, Luis Molina

Casanova's feature-length film *La guagua aérea* (The air bus, 1993), based on a celebrated fictional "essay" or meditation by Sánchez, included two stories from *En cuerpo de camisa* ("La maroma" and "Tiene la noche una raíz") as interpolated episodes.[8] Numerous critics have emphasized the author's use of orality in these stories, a narrative and stylistic innovation that would continue to appear in later literary works.[9] The fact that Sánchez is a semicloseted gay author who is *mulato* in a country where the literary establishment has historically been rather racist and sexist (not to mention outwardly homophobic) is also of special importance; critics have also analyzed the veiled and not-so-veiled mentions of homosexuality in his other works, specifically in his two novels, *La guaracha del Macho Camacho* and *La importancia de llamarse Daniel Santos* (The importance of being Daniel Santos), where the author clearly jokes about the fact that he is gay and in the closet.[10]

One of Sánchez's stylistic achievements in "¡Jum!" is to effectively show how gossip is one of the social tools used to control those who diverge from the norm. The story begins precisely by signaling the dissemination of murmurs: *El murmureo verdereaba por los galillos* (The whispering traveled from mouth to mouth).[11] This gossiping is about *el hijo de Trinidad* (Trinidad's son), a nameless subject who will be identified throughout the story only by his family relation.[12] In fact, the name Trinidad — literally meaning "Trinity" — is used for men and, especially, women and could thus refer to either the character's father or mother, or could also indicate a surname (as in the case of the well-known boxer Tito Trinidad). In the Christological sense, the name "the son of Trinity" can be read as the equivalent of Jesus, as the child who forms the Holy Trinity along with God the Father and the Holy Ghost. The idea of Trinidad's son as martyr will be further expanded throughout Sánchez's text.

The second sentence of the story has no subject or main verb (or rather, it is implicit: *decían* [people were saying]), and begins with the relative pronoun *que*: "Que el hijo de Trinidad se prensaba los fondillos hasta asfixiar el nalgatorio" (That Trinidad's son was tightening his buttocks until he suffocated his entire rear).[13] The directness (and "anonymity") of the grammatical structure emphasizes the immediacy and perversion of gossip, as well as its specifically social character. The style or syntax also reflects the clause's status as gossip by omitting any designation of the identity of the gossiper(s). What we have here is not the use of gossip as a gendered, class-specific tool of resistance, as the literary scholar Patricia Meyer Spacks has argued in her classic

Gossip (1985), or as *tretas del débil* (feints or tactics of the weak), as cultural critic Josefina Ludmer has called the subterfuges that subaltern subjects engage in in order to survive. What we have here is the more recognized, malicious use of gossip as a way to discipline unruly subjects and create a general negative social reaction: gossip as a form of ostracism and persecution, in the very specific context of a critique of gender performance.

The double mention of the buttocks (first referred to as *los fondillos* and then as *el nalgatorio*) serves as a hyperbolical, self-referential code for male homosexuality, strictly understood as effeminacy: Trinidad's son (it is suggested) is the kind that "takes it up the butt." This association can be made as a result of the primacy of the buttocks as a site of (effeminate) homosexual identification in Latin America: as many scholars have argued, under traditional Latin American (and Mediterranean) paradigms of masculinity it is predominantly the "passive" or receptive partner engaging in anal sex who is stigmatized and considered to be "homosexual," akin to a woman.[14] While theorists such as Guy Hocquenghem and Leo Bersani insist on the primacy of the anus in Western European and North American social constructions of male homosexuality — for the first, as a site of liberation; for the second, as a site of death, specifically in the context of AIDS — in Latin America, its centrality extends to the entire gluteal region in a hetero- and homosexual matrix, where the buttocks and hips acquire hypersexualized connotations and greater socially recognized erotic valence.

What does it mean for people to say "[t]hat Trinidad's son was tightening his buttocks until he suffocated his entire rear"? The salacious comment suggests specific bodily practices or a specific form of self-awareness or anxiety that can be contrasted to the more generalized male practice of public cupping or fondling of the genitals. The critic Efraín Barradas has argued that *nalgatorio* (the place of the buttocks) was not a word in current usage at the time this story appeared in 1966, but rather a neologism created by Sánchez from the base root *nalgas* and the suffix *-orio,* which serves to intensify its meaning.[15] However, the word had already appeared in 1949 in the Cuban writer Alejo Carpentier's novel *El reino de este mundo,* where it also carried connotations of femininity and of women's bodies; perhaps in the Puerto Rican context of the 1960s the word stuck out as unusual.[16] The centrality of the butt within Puerto Rican culture and identity, already a hallmark of Luis Palés Matos's now canonical poem "Majestad negra" (Black majesty, 1937), will subsequently be developed by numerous writers and cultural critics, including Edgardo Rodríguez Juliá in his urban chronicle *Una noche con Iris Chacón* (A night with Iris Chacón), Manuel Ramos Otero in his essay "De la colonización a la culonización" (From colonization to assification), and Frances Negrón-Muntaner in her essay "Jennifer's Butt," part of *Boricua Pop*, where she discusses Jennifer López's celebrity and the publicity generated by her derrière.[17]

Most significantly, Sánchez's association of the butt with the effeminateness of a *black* man reinforces particular tropes of racialized identification more commonly identified with women: the sexualized reduction of the body to the rear end — one that the subject is described as trying to suffocate, i.e., minimize or control.[18] As the extremely important, formerly closeted, now deceased, Puerto Rican bisexual scholar Isabelo Zenón Cruz commented in his wide-ranging analysis of black culture and racism in Puerto Rico, curiously titled *Narciso descubre su trasero* (Narcissus discovers his rear, 1974–75), black physiognomy is commonly reduced to a series of "distinctive" traits (including skin, hair, nose, lips, hips, buttocks, and even smell) that are repeatedly overcompensated in all physical descriptions.[19] Here the buttocks become a marker not only of sex, gender, and age or stage of physical development (puberty and adulthood), but also of race, or more concretely, of racialization, which is to say, the process by which the concept of "race" becomes embodied on a subject as a result of prejudiced social views that seek to mark and establish difference.[20]

Why does Narcissus have to discover his *trasero*? According to Zenón Cruz, the racism that is institutionalized by the dominant white classes has made black subjects believe they are inferior; the sight of the face is denied to a subject in such a state of oppression. The author begins a section titled "El bulto es del negro, el hontanar del blanco" (The burden is of the black man, the spring of the white man) by quoting himself in an epigraph:

> Submitted to a humiliating process of alienation, of a criminal estrangement from our life as a people, the black man, new Narcissus, instead of looking for himself, rejects himself, for he can't find his beauty anywhere; for he doesn't see himself in the distorted mirror that white man has organized for him. He does not find his countenance, but rather his rear.[21]

He then begins:

> We have shown to exhaustion in the first two chapters that the black Puerto Rican has been cruelly alienated from Puerto Ricanness. Wounded, humiliated, rejected to the point of nausea, he has learned to despise himself. The

> false image that the white man has created of him is more real than his own breathing. The physical and spiritual *bulto* [burden] of the black man reflects in the distorting *hontanar* [spring] that the cunning colonizing interests of white men have laid at his feet. In that fountain he discovers his rear, not his face.[22]

Thus, according to Zenón Cruz, the black subject's identification with or recognition of his rear end is not positive (and the author does in fact seem to be privileging a male subject); it is the result of a profoundly flawed series of social relations that dehumanize the individual. In this conception, the butt becomes the negation of true identity. Zenón Cruz's metaphorization employs traditional Western definitions and hierarchies of the body, privileging the face ("mirror of the soul") and "denigrating" (making black) the lower body, the site of sexual and excretory functions. The masculine overtones of this are evident, as the butt is seen as a sign of feminization and castration; in the case of patriarchal, heterosexist appraisals of women, the butt is not a degraded part of the body, but rather a central erogenous zone.

Zenón Cruz's discussion of the butt acquires more nuances or significance in his analysis of the treatment of that part of the body in Puerto Rican literature, particularly in poetry.[23] He extensively quotes the Cuban anthropologist Fernando Ortiz's praise for Afro-Antillean poems such as those of Luis Palés Matos that thematize women's hips (which he understands to often be an euphemism for or extension of the buttocks) as well as the butt itself. Zenón Cruz, who quite clearly lacks a radical feminist grounding, is quick to point out that identification of the black female body with that region should not be discarded simply to counter a prevalent stereotype; he does not believe that the black body needs to be desexualized in order to correct racist claims. Yet part of Zenón Cruz's "open-mindedness" may be read as a general disregard for the problem of female objectification; this explains why he can agree with Ortiz's passages, which are blatantly sexist.[24]

While it would initially seem that, according to Zenón Cruz, Trinidad's son's association with the butt can only be negative, something to be overcome (as the butt is the negation of the face, which is "true" identity) one would think that the reconsideration of the female gluteal region might allow new valorizations. This is highly suspect in light of Zenón Cruz's observations on male homosexuality, which, in agreement with the Martinican intellectual Frantz Fanon, are presented as a product of the subjugation of black individuals. They can also be seen as a form of internalized homophobia, given Zenón Cruz's tortuous relationship to his own sexuality as a married man with children who nevertheless had public liaisons with men; the author never discusses his personal experiences in his book. Zenón Cruz does not analyze "¡Jum!" but he significantly alludes to it, in passing, in a section of his book entitled "The Black Homosexual in White Society." In this section, he also cites a study by Antonio Martínez Rosario based on an extremely reduced sample of three informants (one "passive" black homosexual and one "active" and one "passive" white homosexual); Martínez Rosario observes that the dominant stereotype is that black men are hypermasculine and thus will play the "dominant," "active," or insertive role in sexual intercourse, a widely held popular view.[25] Zenón Cruz ultimately defers to Fanon as the greatest authority on homosexuality in the black community, a problematic gesture given that, as the black gay British filmmaker Isaac Julien and others have argued, Fanon's views on the matter were profoundly homophobic.

All ambiguity regarding the intent of the second sentence of Sánchez's "¡Jum!" is immediately clarified by the next sentence of the story: "Que era ave rarísima asentando vacación en mar y tierra" ("That he was a queer bird taking a vacation on land and sea").[26] While the designation *ave rara* (from the Latin *rara avis,* meaning rare bird) refers to eccentric behavior, something akin to a modernist oddity (i.e., a strange or unusual person), in the Caribbean the use of the nomenclature of birds (*pájaros* in Cuba and the Dominican Republic, *patos,* or ducks, in Puerto Rico) commonly refers to homosexuals; this animal metaphor has a stigmatized charge.[27]

Trinidad's son is accused of being vain (a typical form of criticism made against women and male homosexuals), of spending undue attention (for a man) on his appearance. Yet there are important motivations for this overvaluation of personal visual projection: as the gay Argentine anthropologist and poet Néstor Perlongher comments in *O negócio do michê* (Male prostitution in São Paulo, 1987), *a deriva homossexual* (gay cruising) relies on the reading of surfaces, on marking the body in an effort to signal specific meanings that for the most part will not be articulated verbally in public; in the Cuban writer Severo Sarduy's elaboration of an aesthetics of the Baroque (under which the figure of the trompe-l'oeil and the man-becoming-woman are privileged), surface is everything. It is under these conditions that Trinidad's son wears *tréboles* (green clover), green being a color associated with inappropriate sexuality (*viejo verde,* for example), and specifically with homosexuals in

Puerto Rico, especially when worn on Thursdays;[28] it also explains why he wore *encajillo* (lace), a signal of male vanity or of femininity.

Trinidad's son's "difference" marks him visually not only through specific details but through the general demeanor of his appearance, one that can be read through the lens of class. He did not follow his community's general pattern: his life, previous to the marked ascendancy of the taunts that occurs in the story, seemed "unregimented" according to the community's standards, as this accusation shows: "That he would don his Sunday best even when it was Monday or Tuesday."[29] This complaint can be read as one referring to vanity but also to *nomadology,* especially if we extend the term from its geographic connotations (displacement through space) and employ it to define or categorize a temporal dislocation of instituted practices, as the philosophers Gilles Deleuze and Félix Guattari argue in their treatise of that name. Wearing one's Sunday best at other times, at all times, indicates noncompliance with specific ideas of appropriate conduct. To what material conditions does this comment allude? It can either mean that Trinidad's son spent undue amounts on clothes; that all his clothes were of exceptional quality (or at least appeared to be so); or that he dressed with an elegance that marked him as different from the rest of the working-class community. Since no mention is made in the story as to the character's employment, it is not clear if his clothing was related to his work. Yet his sartorial practice indicates his participation in an alternative community: perhaps that of dandies or any other groups defined by obsessive care in appearance, where different norms of propriety are followed.[30]

Comments on the character's clothing are accompanied by criticisms against his use of make-up, an engagement with specific cosmetic practices associated with femininity. These are contrasted to the black male's supposed hypermasculinity, a trait that Zenón Cruz points to as a recurrent trope of identification. Significantly, it is at this moment when Trinidad's son's blackness is first mentioned — he is constructed in an oppositional manner, as a feminine and not virile man, a "failure":

> — ¡Que se perfuma con Com Tu Mi!
> — ¡Que se pone carbón en las cejas!
> — ¡Que es mariquita fiestera!
> — ¡Que los negros son muy machos!
> — ¡Y no están con ñeñeñés!
> (L. R. Sánchez, "¡Jum!" 56)

> "He reeks of Com Tu Mi perfume!"
> "He puts on eyeliner!"
> "He's a party-going sissy!"
> "Black men are very manly!"
> "They aren't sissies!"
>   (L. R. Sánchez, "Hum!" 132)

At this moment, the question of black masculinity warrants further examination.

Why is it that black men are expected to be extremely virile? Historically, as a result of patterns established during centuries of African slavery in the Americas, as well as the general cultural formations that establish gender roles under a patriarchal heterosexist order under which all men are assumed to have irrepressible sexual urges, black men have come to be seen as a sexual threat to white "womanhood" as well as a political and social threat to white males; as the essayist Calvin Hernton notes, their demonization has allowed for more severe practices of control and violence as deterrent for any possible infringement of social codes.[31] The "purity" of the white race (what we could also define as the maintenance of white supremacy as an economic and political regime) has been historically understood to be contingent upon the sacrosanct preservation of white womanhood's virginity and, after marriage, her moral rectitude; black men's physical strength, often a result of rigorous labor demands, and sexual desires (socially sanctioned as the general condition of men in a patriarchal society) make them a threat.

The fact that white male slave owners were consensually and nonconsensually engaging in sexual intercourse or rape of black female slaves, who would bear their children and contribute to the formation of a *mestizo* (or *mulato*) society was somehow not considered as a threat to whiteness in the same widespread manner. In Puerto Rico, racist discourse found an officially sanctioned spokesperson in the figure of university professor Antonio S. Pedreira who, in his 1934 classic essay *Insularismo,* showed a profound discomfort with any "mixing" of the races, a "fusion" that he believed created general "confusion," one of the supposed causes of the island's crisis. It will not be until the 1970s when citizen activism and the intellectual and theoretical contributions of people such as Zenón Cruz and José Luis González in his landmark *El país de cuatro pisos* (The four-storeyed country) more successfully challenge these views.[32]

The external projection of black hypermasculinity is countered within black communities by a reversal, that is, the reading of hypermasculinity as a strategy of resistance and defense. The black male must be strong in this context, as it is argued that the future and well-being of the "race" depend on it. This explains the profoundly conservative nature of many black organizations in the United States, especially those that have a religious, bourgeois, or nationalist character.[33] Over the last two decades, black gay scholars and artists such as Roderick Ferguson, Phillip Brian Harper, E. Patrick Johnson, Dwight A. McBride, Marlon Riggs, and Robert F. Reid-Pharr have responded critically to these expectations, discussing the detrimental effects of black male homophobia and proposing new conceptualizations that can overcome this bias. In Puerto Rico, the black gay dancer, choreographer, and performance artist Javier Cardona has offered an open indictment of racism as well as a veiled critique of homophobia in his performance *You Don't Look Like* (1997) as well as a celebration of men's dancing bodies and a critique of heterosexism in *Ah mén!* (2004), while the writer Mayra Santos-Febres has offered a nuanced portrayal of black male-to-female transvestism in *Sirena Selena vestida de pena* (2000), a novel that became a major international publishing success and has received extensive and very positive critical reception.[34]

In "¡Jum!" Trinidad's son is accused of being effeminate precisely in this context of hypermasculinity. As such, his gender performance is not merely a failure with regard to his gender, but is also perceived as a denial of the responsibility the collective has placed (and feels it is forced to place, by external imposition) on its men to "uphold" (or "uplift") the race. Interestingly enough, the black lesbian poet, writer, and activist Cheryl Clarke has argued that this prejudice is not shared in the same way by all poor and working-class black communities in the United States, which at times might be more tolerant of gender and sexual difference (41). This is clearly not the case in Sánchez's text.

As we have seen, the community's negative appraisal of Trinidad's son is immediately established in the very first paragraph of Sánchez's story. The whole town is gossiping about and against him, at all hours of day and night. The very title of the story ("Hum!") expresses the indignation and hostility, the open contempt they have for him and that they will articulate verbally. As Agnes Lugo-Ortiz has remarked, those critics such as Julio Ortega who have analyzed the function of orality in Sánchez's work have always praised it as a device of popular incorporation and have rarely if ever noted the clearly negative connotations that it has in this text.[35]

The community's men act in unison, as a collectivity that feels socially legitimated and justified in its teasing and taunting. The narrator describes the scene: "Los hombres, ya seguros del relajo, lo esperaban por el cocal para aporrearlo a voces" (The men, already sure of their game, would wait by the coconut grove to attack him with words).[36] In this case, the particular word usage emphasizes linkages of masculinity and violence: *aporrear* (to hit with a stick); *aporrearlo a voces,* a metaphoric description of aggression, one in which the symbolic violence of words and their ability to inflict harm is recognized.[37] Thus, the men employ a series of insults, which comprise rather imaginative yet malicious linguistic derivations of current slang: *pato* (duck = fag) also becomes *patito* (duckling = little fag), *pateto* (similar to *patético,* pathetic), and *patuleco* (person with a physical deformity of the legs or feet, also meaning fag); *loca* (mad woman = fag) is also *loqueta;* and *marica* (Mary = fag) also engenders *maricastro* and *mariquita* (ladybug = fag).[38]

The women also participate in the harassment, but their taunts are different, not abject or bestial but rather profoundly gendered: they call him *madamo* (female madam) and *mujercita* (little woman), terms that ridicule Trinidad's son by feminizing him and highlighting his gender divergence.[39] The depiction of the community's behavior emphasizes how women can and do participate in this oppression and in the maintenance of specific social structures as much as men. As the French sociologist Pierre Bourdieu observed (in a broader context), communities in general are set on maintaining the *habitus* or particular order that defines them, which in this case prohibits male effeminacy; for that reason, repression is not a prerogative of the men but rather a collective affair.

The result of all this taunting is that Trinidad's son "locked himself up in his miserable house to live out a lonely existence."[40] If, as Perlongher and Hocquenghem have noted, the marginalization of homosexuality tends to create social systems in which subjects move to the street and to other public spaces to engage in their milieu, the character's withdrawal signals a double and especially disturbing separation: from his immediate community (the black neighborhood) and from important spaces of homosexual/homosocial exchange.

The protagonist's seclusion in his modest house does nothing to stop the verbal attacks: as we have seen, it provokes a series of accusations concerning the adequate gender performance of a black man, turning him into a pariah and outcast. After the protagonist becomes secluded, the community refuses to offer its services, as *La Ochoteco* stops cooking for him, Perdolesia stops doing his laundry, and the barber stops cutting his hair. To add insult to injury, his exclusion is signaled physically, as his neighbor Eneas Cruz purchased wire to set up a fence.[41]

Thus, what initially could be understood as a strategic retreat to the privacy and security of his home goes on to become more like an isolated imprisonment, as all forms of social support are cut off, social networks being an essential key to survival. The protagonist's nomadic capacity, already limited by a self-imposed containment, is further reduced, at least in a symbolic manner, by his neighbor's aggressive gesture. Fences, as August Wilson's play by that name reminds us, serve not only to keep out but also to keep in, and in this case, this double gesture of containment and rejection is imposed upon Trinidad's son against his will. It is only a matter of time until, much as during other historical periods of repression, the external controls that limit mobility act to expel and ultimately to (try to) eliminate difference.

"Hum!" is constructed by alternating the narrator's description of what is happening to the protagonist with citations of the taunts enunciated by the community. As Agnes Lugo-Ortiz has observed, the protagonist remains silent as well as nameless throughout the story: his version is never offered and is unknown to us. It would seem that Sánchez, as a black, closeted homosexual writer and intellectual, had an intuition of the dilemma of speech, of what Trinidad's son's self-disclosure or voice would mean in terms of the production of subjectivity as an oppressed individual. In this sense, there comes to mind Josefina Ludmer's discussion in her previously mentioned essay "Tretas del débil" of the rather complex negotiations of "saying" (*decir*) and "knowing" (*saber*) and their negative permutations, as demonstrated in the Mexican nun Sor Juana Inés de la Cruz's "Response to Sor Filotea." Historical, marginal, or oppressed subjects (particularly women, in Ludmer's analysis) can be painfully aware of the meanings of silence and speech, of what one can and cannot say, of what it means to speak. Sánchez's story, written before the historic 1969 Stonewall revolt, noticeably partakes of a different logic of resistance (or resignation) to oppression, that of a *parable* in which the protagonist's sacrifice is meant to teach readers (the community) a lesson, which we could summarize as follows: "See, that's why we are forced to leave: because you make it impossible for us to live in peace, and lead us to our deaths."

Gayatri Spivak's meditation in "Can the Subaltern Speak?" and her negative conclusion, that they cannot, specifically when talking about deceased subaltern subjects of history such as women who died and left no written account of their experiences, also illuminates the complexity of the predicament of silence and speech. In her well-known provocative essay, the U.S-based Indian Marxist feminist invites us to reflect on the possibilities that marginal subjects have for public (historical) articulation, that is to say, to convey their experience in their own words, or rather, for us to recuperate that experience when those subjects have died and left no written record. At times, when such voices do not exist, artists will invent them or try to imagine what they would sound like. Queer Puerto Rican migration narratives are marked by the knowledge that some people never made it: never jumped the puddle (i.e., the Atlantic Ocean), were never even allowed to leave.

Sánchez, it would seem, or at the very least the narrator of his story, would be in agreement with Spivak, with the notion that it is the postcolonial, queer-of-color artist or intellectual who can speak for the dead, for silent ones who have died, and at best attempt an approximation (a deconstruction, Spivak would say) of the historical situation of specific individuals and complex social phenomena: in Spivak's case, of Hindu widow burning; in Sánchez's, of black homosexual persecution; in both cases, under the specific situation of colonialism, be it British or American. What we have here are communal rituals of violence that reestablish the dominant order, and in which the personal volition of the subject is uncertain, seeming to entail a wish or an obligation to die.

The situation of marginality produced by racial difference in "¡Jum!" (that is, being black in a white-dominant racist society) does not foster understanding or tolerance of other marginal identities or solidarity among the marginalized, but rather makes the community more vigilant against difference, something that performance scholar José Esteban Muñoz will explain in *Disidentifications* by referring to Antonio Gramsci's notions on the contradictory ideologies that oppressed people in fact demonstrate in real life.[42] In the context of "Hum!" marginalized blacks are portrayed as unable to tolerate the presence of Trinidad's son. It appears as though the community has decided in unison that he is no longer one of its members. The social pressures exerted against him, reminiscent in their extreme nature of the severity and strength of the punishments imposed by the classical Greek tragedy's chorus, indicate a will to annihilate rather than reform. There is no indication in the story that the community believed it could change Trinidad's son's behavior through its harassment. The ostracism and violence of their actions rather indicates a will to destruction.

Under these circumstances, the protagonist decides to do what any sensible person would do, which is to leave. Rather than accepting this information with relief, the community is outraged and understands that it is being betrayed. Once again, a new wave of gossip begins, this time accusing the protagonist of wanting to be white:

> El murmureo florecía por los galillos. Que el hijo de Trinidad se marchaba porque despreciaba los negros. Que se iba a fiestar con los blancos porque era un pelafustán. Y que se había puesto flaaacooo para tener el talle de avispa. En cada esquina, los hombres se vestían la lengua con navajas.
> —¡Que el hijo de Trinidad es negro reblanquiao!
> —¡Que el hijo de Trinidad es negro acasinao!
> —¡Que el hijo de Trinidad es negro almidonao!
> Las mujeres, entre amén y amén, sacaban el minuto para susurrar:
> —¡Mal ejemplo!
> —¡Indecente!
> —¡Puerco!
> —¡Que es un cochino!
> —¡Que es dos cochinos!
> —¡Que es tres cochinos! (L. R. Sánchez, "¡Jum!" 56–57)

> The whispering flew from mouth to mouth. That Trinidad's son was leaving because he despised dark-skinned men. That he was going to party with the whites because he was a good-for-nothing. And that he had gotten *skiiiiny* so he could be slender like a wasp. In every corner the men would fling knives from their mouths:
> "Trinidad's son is a bleached nigger."
> "Trinidad's son is a good for nothing nigger!"
> "Trinidad's son is a stiff nigger!"
> The women, between one Amen and the next, took a minute to whisper.
> "A bad example!"
> "Gross!"
> "Swine!"
> "He's a pig!"
> "He's two pigs!"
> "He's three pigs!" (Sánchez, "Hum!" 132–33)

Both women and men participate equally in harassing him. The women's attacks are represented as especially hypocritical since they come shrouded in religious prayer ("between one Amen and the next").[43] We also notice a continuation of the process of bestialization (comparing him to a pig) already begun with the references to *patos*.

It is interesting that it is only when Trinidad's son gives signs of departing that he is accused of being a traitor. While earlier taunts brought up the question of black maleness and singled him out for not follow-ing correct behavior, they did not identify white culture as the source of his "deviance." However, once word is out that he plans to leave, both accusations are associated. His effeminateness can be read as something foreign to the community, something that is not "natural" to it but rather comes from the outside (or so they would like to believe, and are ready to kill to defend).

The community's association of homosexuality and whiteness is syn-thesized in a cry from the crowd: "¡El hijo de Trinidad / de la pasa estirá / es marica na más!" ("Trinidad's son with his straightened kinky hair is nothing but a fag!").[44] The reference to "relaxed" or straightened hair is used by the mutinous group as a marker of a denial of blackness, some-what oblivious to the fact that a great number of black Puerto Rican women (as well as some men) in fact do engage in that cosmetic practice and that, as Isar Godreau argues, this should not be seen as a sign of an individual's negation of racial identity; the noted black British critic Kobena Mercer has also discussed the problematics of black hair as a sign of "purity" and identity.[45] It is perhaps Trinidad's son's gendered transgression (as hair straightening is seen as a predominantly female activity) that marks this as more anomalous. The reduction of Trinidad's son to an exclusive trait (to being a *marica,* or fag) is the culmination of a process of dissociation, by which that element can be "purged" from the community.

The conclusion of the story is tragic. Trinidad's son's nighttime at-tempt to escape is thwarted, as the community has been spying on him; they accost him immediately in the anonymity of the dark. It is at this mo-ment that the verbal attacks become physical; the crowd is soon joined by a pack of dogs. The similarity between these two groupings suggests the community members are hardly distinguishable from animals in their viciousness and savagery. Sánchez bestializes the oppressor in the same way that he had portrayed them bestializing their victim. At this mo-ment, the son of Trinidad literally becomes Christ-like, persecuted by the masses, fulfilling the meaning of his name: "Extendidos los brazos como cruces . . . la sangre calentando por la carne . . . El dolor abierto en la noche sin ojos" ("His arms stretched like a cross . . . The blood curdled through his skin . . . The opened wound in the blind night").[46] The repe-tition of insults in sets of three further serves to emphasize the religious connotations perceived from the very start in the protagonist's name: the divine trilogy of Christian belief, as well as the threesome formed by Jesus and the two thieves at the moment of the crucifixion. This queer

Christological symbolization will reappear in later Puerto Rican works, including René Marqués's novel *La mirada* (1976), during the rape scene in prison, as well as in Angel Lozada's *La patografía* (1998), where a young child becomes a duck and is eventually killed by an angry mob in Mayagüez, and in Emanuel Xavier's novel *Christ-Like* (1999).[47]

Unlike the story of the crucifixion (and more akin to that of Moses and the fleeing Israelites in Egypt), in "Hum!" Trinidad's son finally makes it to an unnamed river that delimits the boundaries of the community. In opposition to Julia de Burgos's "Río Grande de Loíza" (1938), that supposedly "manly" river that separates the historically black settlement of Loíza Aldea from its neighboring vicinities and is celebrated in one of the *mulata* Puerto Rican poet's most famous lyrical compositions, this one is feminized and rendered deadly. The protagonist's arrival at the water (also an important trope in African American and Afro-Caribbean narratives) does not solve his problems, as the taunts continue, the crowd screaming "¡Mariquita!" (fairy) three times. Trinidad's son encounters the water, which seems to offer some kind of solace, as it goes from initially being very cold to the touch, to then become *tibia, más tibia, más tibia* (the warm water, warmer, warmer), perhaps akin to the maternal womb.[48] The narrator emphasizes how the taunting voices become weaker in the distance, are harder to hear, and become fragmented.

The story ends with the drowning of Trinidad's son, graphically represented on the page (as Lugo-Ortiz has commented):

> Entonces, que no vuel-va, que no vuel-va, que no vuel-va, el hijo de Trinidad
> glu...
> que
> glu...
> no
> glu...
> vuelva
> glu...
> se
> glu...
> hundió. (Sánchez, "¡Jum!" 60)

> Then, don't come back, don't come back, don't come back, son of Trinidad.
> gloop...
> do
> gloop...
> not
> gloop...
> come back

> gloop...
> he
> gloop...
> sank. (Sánchez, "Hum!" 135)

Much like in the tragic end of the Chilean José Donoso's novel *El lugar sin límites* (Hell has no limits, published in 1966, the same year as "Hum!"), the homosexual subject, an abject figure that does not enjoy respect even in death, is eliminated to insure the normativity of the community, to eliminate the presence and conduct of an individual who does not conform to standard dominant practices.[49] As in Donoso's work (and in the Mexican director Arturo Ripstein's 1977 cinematographic representation of that novel, with a script by Manuel Puig), the presence of dogs, water, night, and the violent persecution by a mob serve to characterize the fury unleashed as a result of homophobia against an effeminate man.[50] Trinidad's son's attempt to escape, and thus move on to other realities, is curtailed by the violence of a community unwilling to accept difference, even beyond the narrow bounds of its geographic location. Sánchez's narration is a ruthless and brutal depiction of the cruelty and hatred to which homosexual (or gender dissonant) subjects are subjected to as a result of their conduct. Those critics that describe Trinidad's son's death as "suicide" seriously miss the incriminating implications of "¡Jum!"[51]

Yet what is lacking in Sánchez's text is a discussion or fuller recognition of the complex negotiations of sexuality and male effeminacy that Latin American cultures in fact often engage in — for example, the fact that Trinidad's son did live in that community at all, or that La Manuela (Donoso's protagonist) for many years led a relatively "visible" or "open" life, running (and owning) her own brothel in a small, rural town. La Manuela's murder is the result of a tragic mistake — openly kissing Pancho, her male object of affection — and as such violating the complex code of in/visibility that allows for her existence. Of course, this murder indicates the subjacent violence that undergirds the entire system, and how fragile and fickle the social order is. But to deny its other dimensions — the actual space of possibility — is to seriously misread and underestimate the very particular and unique "social contract" that is portrayed.

There is an eminent risk in placing "¡Jum!" at the beginning of this book, in claiming or seeing it as a "paradigmatic" or foundational fiction. This risk has to do with the tendency to reify Puerto Rican (and

Latin American) culture (and specifically black culture) as especially intolerant. Why not highlight Carlos Alberto Fonseca's lyrical poem "En voz baja ... Para un efebo" (Sotto voce: For an ephebe, 1942), identified by Carlos Rodríguez-Matos and José Olmo Olmo as the first openly homoerotic poem in Puerto Rican letters, as Arnaldo Cruz-Malavé has also pointed out?[52]

I have started with "¡Jum!" because of chronology (1966) and because of the way its foundational myth (the desire to escape from persecution juxtaposed to ultimate annihilation) is taken up or repeats itself in other authors' work (René Marqués, Angel Lozada, and even to a limited extent in Frances Negrón-Muntaner's film *Brincando el charco*), and also seems to be contested or rewritten (with a more positive conclusion) in texts such as Carmen Lugo Filippi's short story "Milagros, calle Mercurio" (Milagros, Mercury Street, 1980), a story of the unspoken attraction between two women, set in the southern Puerto Rican city of Ponce.[53] The impact of "¡Jum!" is also verified by the significant critical attention it has received. It is one of many possible starting points — one that evidently needs discussion; perhaps one that will ultimately be overcome. The fact that the story's author, Luis Rafael Sánchez himself, has been able to lead a successful transatlantic (New York–San Juan) life (and that as such, "Hum!" is evidently not his *own* story, although perhaps one of his nightmares), also helps us to put things into perspective. "Hum!" perhaps responds best to the drama and passion of myth, of ancient, classical stories — tales that capture our attention precisely because of their display of raw emotion and violence — which unfortunately seem to repeat themselves in our day and age. Perhaps "Hum!" is more like a scream in the night, or a moment of profound clarity, provoked by lightning, that allows deep knowledge in its sudden revelation: that of the potential for inflicting horror that all of humanity possesses. What is clear, however, is that "Hum!" is a story about migration: about a young effeminate black man's understanding that he must leave, and his community's violent denial of that option for liberty.

Chapter 2

Autobiographical Writing and Shifting Migrant Experience

> I couldn't stand the repressive atmosphere
> of Puerto Rico. I had realized that New
> York was a city where I could live without
> feeling persecuted all the time. In Puerto
> Rico, I felt too much persecution because
> of the openness of my sexuality.
>
> — Manuel Ramos Otero,
> interview with Marithelma Costa

FOR SOME GAY MEN, Puerto Rico is (or has been, at specific historical moments) a space of impossibility, frustration, and fear, a situation that has led to migration, especially to New York. Such is the case of Manuel Ramos Otero, widely heralded as the most important openly gay Puerto Rican writer of the twentieth century, who left Puerto Rico in 1968 explicitly because of his sexuality and the discrimination he experienced.[1] Unlike more recognized and celebrated closeted writers such as René Marqués and Luis Rafael Sánchez, Ramos Otero always thematized his experiences and publicly acknowledged his homosexuality, a posture that brought him ostracism and censorship. He would go on to live in New York for nearly twenty-two years, until shortly before his death from AIDS-related illnesses in 1990.

Ramos Otero's life and writings are profoundly illustrative of some of the experiences of first-generation gay Puerto Rican migrants to the United States, particularly (but not exclusively) those of college-educated, middle-class men who, motivated to a great extent by the persecution, repression, or discomfort they felt on account of their sexual orientation, left their homeland in the 1960s and 1970s. This group would also include other openly gay male Puerto Rican writers such as Víctor F. Fragoso, Carlos Rodríguez-Matos, Alberto Sandoval-Sánchez, and Alfredo Villanueva-Collado.[2] Ramos Otero is less well known than other exiled queer Latin American generational peers such as Reinaldo Arenas, Severo Sarduy, and Manuel Puig, who all became consecrated precisely in the 1960s and 1970s, or than queer Chicano novelists such as John Rechy and Arturo Islas, yet it can be argued that his contribution to Latin American, Caribbean, U.S. Latino, and, specifically, Puerto Rican letters, is unprecedented.[3] Ramos Otero's penchant for "minor" genres such as the short story, poetry, the experimental novel, and the essay, and his location as an openly queer Puerto Rican author in New York in the 1970s and 1980s who wrote in Spanish is quite likely the principal reason for the general disregard for his work outside of mostly Puerto Rican literary circles, where he is widely revered and championed, at least by more progressive critics.[4] In fact, following the model proposed by Gilles Deleuze and Félix Guattari in their book on Kafka, we can argue that Ramos Otero contributed mostly toward the articulation of a *minor literature,* a very innovative, valuable, aesthetically successful and critical oeuvre with political implications that is nevertheless not appreciated or well received, a point the New York–based Spanish poet and critic Dionisio Cañas also makes.[5] This work is overlooked in Latin America because of the peripheral status of Puerto Rico; marginalized in the United States because of the author's racialized, subaltern, or colonial Puerto Ricanness and Spanish-language use; belittled in the Caribbean because of the author's homosexuality and exile up north; and looked upon with suspicion everywhere because of his openly militant gay liberationist and feminist politics.

The analysis of a series of Ramos Otero's short stories, poems, and essays will allow us to chart some of the different moments of his migratory experience, to explore his relationship to writing as disguised or distorted confession or personal mythmaking, and to theorize on the importance he attributed to his personal distance from Puerto Rico as an emancipatory position, which is to say, exile as a necessary step for self-liberation. For the author, dislocation was an essential element that permitted the elaboration of his work and his comment on the homeland.[6] A close reading of Ramos Otero's essay on the exiled gay Spanish poet Luis Cernuda will show the Puerto Rican author's vision on the interrelated nature of solitude, margination, and art. I will argue that Ramos Otero's comments on Cernuda are equally applicable to himself, and that in fact he is conducting what I call "autobiography-by-critical-projection," that is to say, a writing about the self that occurs simultaneously with the act of writing about (an)other.

After establishing the centrality of autobiography and exile to Ramos Otero's writing project and aesthetic vision, I will go on to analyze select short stories and poems that will illustrate the shifts in Ramos Otero's perceptions of himself and of New York and Puerto Rico. I will show how there is a marked evolution or change from his first collection of short stories, *Concierto de metal para un recuerdo y otras orgías de soledad* (Metal concert for a remembrance and other orgies of solitude, 1971), to *El cuento de la Mujer del Mar* (The story of the woman of the sea, 1979) and *Página en blanco y staccato* (Blank page and staccato, 1987), as well as his posthumous book of poems, *Invitación al Polvo* (Invitation to the dust, 1991). Specifically, I will show how Ramos Otero goes from a position of vague resistance to geographic specificity (stories set in a floating yet unspecified space of Puerto Rico and New York) to an engagement with the concrete gay geography of New York (Christopher Street), the geography of memory (the island of Puerto Rico), and the geography of the Puerto Rican diaspora in New York and elsewhere. These geographic engagements obviously also entail profound psychological and community dimensions, as they indicate ties to diverse populations, communities, languages, and cultures.

Important literary critics such as Juan G. Gelpí and Arnaldo Cruz-Malavé have also pointed to these shifts in Ramos Otero's work. Gelpí has described them as "a dramatization of stages of the experience of migration and exile."[7] For Gelpí, the first stage is marked by "the insolence and solipsism" of the characters and by the constant digressions in the text, which the critic understands to be the result of the shock of migration.[8] Gelpí argues that these tensions are transformed in Ramos Otero's later production, where Ramos Otero shows a marked interest in naming specific locations, part of "an oscillation between the place of origin and the space of exile," what the critic identifies as "a fundamental gesture of exile literature: to name, to invoke the place of origin by means of words."[9]

Gelpí also comments on how the discontinuity of exile is mediated and softened in Ramos Otero's work starting with *The Story of the Woman of the Sea* through the notion of stories as collections of voices, for example that of the storyteller and his lover, Angelo, or those of the poets Luis Palés Matos and Julia de Burgos. The same can be said of *Blank Page and Staccato,* for example, the voices of researchers, island writers and

Puerto Rican immigrants to Hawai'i in the story "Vivir del cuento" and the spirits of the dead in "La otra isla de Puerto Rico." Gelpí will argue that the greatest innovation of Ramos Otero's third collection of short stories will be to present these disparate voices, to "give them voice" so to speak, by carefully engaging with Puerto Rican history as "a history of migrations, displacements, and exiles" and privileging oral accounts as opposed to the conservative written register. Here the storyteller becomes "an oral historian, a spiritual medium of voices, whom dominant society has labeled as a liar."[10] This analysis goes totally against the argument of the literary critic Aurea María Sotomayor, who feels that Ramos Otero's writing becomes more and more distanced from Puerto Rico as time goes by.[11] Gelpí's analysis is closer to that of Arnaldo Cruz-Malavé, who has also seen "Hollywood Memorabilia," "The Story of the Woman of the Sea," and "Blank Page and Staccato" (the three stories I will most closely be analyzing) as moments in which Ramos Otero partakes in what Gayatri Spivak has identified as a moment of deconstruction, that of *displacement*.[12] My analysis will ultimately show how exile and migration are not fixed or static realities but rather processes that change as time goes by.

Luis Cernuda as "Mask," or the Logic of Autobiography by Critical Projection

As a young, somewhat marginalized queer diasporic writer seeking to establish himself in the world, Ramos Otero actively worked to identify and celebrate (and at times critique) a series of predecessors: a corpus including both gay writers and well-established Latin American and European figures, as well as other "marginal" or noncanonical Puerto Rican authors, whom he felt linked to in some way.[13] One of the clearest examples of this is in a series of poems entitled "Epitafios" (Epitaphs) in *El libro de la muerte* (The book of death, 1985), which includes verses dedicated to Federico García Lorca, Oscar Wilde, Tennessee Williams, and René Marqués, among others.[14] This corpus would, on the one hand, substantiate and give critical weight to his endeavor and, on the other, serve to establish a metaphorical dialogue through his writing, one that reelaborated Puerto Rican culture and expanded its links to other literary traditions in the world.[15] Of the authors he engaged, none received as much careful critical attention as the exiled Spanish poet Luis Cernuda, who was born in 1902 and died in 1963, and who should be seen as one of Ramos Otero's most important literary precursors.

Ramos Otero's essay on this poet was published in 1988 in the Puerto Rican journal *Cupey* in Spanish. To my knowledge, no critic except Wilfredo Hernández has remarked on the striking parallels between Cernuda's life (such as presented in this essay) and that of Ramos Otero.[16] "The Ethics of Margination in the Poetry of Luis Cernuda" can be read as Ramos Otero's elaboration of a poetics of biographical criticism that is particularly suited not only to the Spaniard but also to himself; it is the defense of a Romantic reading of the artist as outsider who constructs his universe in opposition to a hostile and nonunderstanding world. My critical effort will seek to link this essay on Cernuda to Ramos Otero's other works, such as those he addressed in a piece of self-reflexive literary criticism titled "Ficción e historia: Texto y pretexto de la autobiografía" (Fiction and history: Text and pretext of autobiography). In that short essay, published shortly after his death, he invited precisely this type of interpretation, stressing the interlinked nature of his life and writing: "I believe that, ultimately, the only thing I have ever done since I took up writing has been the translation of autobiography" (23).

Why autobiography? What is it about narrating the story of the self that seems so attractive? In her landmark analysis of the Latin American autobiographical tradition, Sylvia Molloy has remarked upon the "dominant"/hegemonic model, in which (heterosexual, white) male statesmen recount their lives as *grand récit,* highlighting their contributions to the nation, or their centrality in political and other social processes that are usually taken to constitute "History" with a capital H. Molloy juxtaposes this model to an alternate one, one in which the stories of relatively subaltern or marginal subjects such as blacks, émigrés, women, and homosexuals articulate their location and experience. Robert Richmond Ellis, in his two books on gay Hispanic autobiography, has also signaled the vital importance of this genre for queer writers in Spain and the Americas.

Autobiography and autobiographical fiction, of course, are privileged genres in queer U.S. and Latina/o narratives: from the strongly autobiographic origins of John Rechy's *City of Night,* Piri Thomas's autobiographic recollections in *Down These Mean Streets,* to Nicholasa Mohr's personal reimaginings in *Nilda,* Judith Ortiz Cofer's *The Line of the Sun,* Julia Alvarez's novels and essays, and Esmeralda Santiago's autobiographical trilogy of memoirs, *When I Was a Puerto Rican, Almost a Woman,* and *The Turkish Lover.*[17] Queer Chicana/o authors such as Gloria Anzaldúa, Cherríe Moraga, and Richard Rodríguez have also found the autobiographical essay a rich source of inspiration, as a genre responsive to their expressive needs.

Autobiographically inspired fiction accomplishes many things: a referentiality to the self, a simultaneous grounding in experiential reality and social/communal/national history, and a space for the free flight of imagination and for creative expression. While autobiography can also be seen as a straightjacket or prison, for authors such as Ramos Otero it represents an enabling strategy, full of possibility. To conduct autobiographical projection as a form of literary criticism is to challenge norms, mix genres, and surreptitiously stake out a location of creative subversion and affirmation. This is especially the case in a notoriously conservative context such as that of Puerto Rico, where leading writers such as José Luis González were publicly disparaging Ramos Otero for his autobiographical bent.[18]

Ramos Otero's life holds interesting parallels to that of Cernuda. The Puerto Rican author, whose full given name was Jesús Manuel Ramos Otero, was born in 1948 in Manatí, a small town located on the northern coast of the island.[19] After completing a bachelor's degree in social sciences at the University of Puerto Rico at Río Piedras, Ramos Otero migrated in December of 1968 to New York, where he would live for most of his adult life. While he had already won at least one literary prize and published some short stories before leaving, all of his books (including four collections of short stories, a novel, and two volumes of poetry) appeared after his departure, some posthumously. Most of the author's work was completed in the United States, although he vigorously participated in the island's intellectual and cultural scene, publishing and reading his work there during his frequent visits. He also established his own (short-lived) publishing house in New York, El libro viaje (The Book Trip), which produced, among other things, his only novel, the highly experimental *La novelabingo* (The bingo novel, 1976).[20] The poet, short-story writer, novelist, and performer returned home to Puerto Rico in 1990, where he died from AIDS-related complications at the age of forty-two, surrounded by relatives and many of the island's most respected literary figures.

I substantiate my claim of what I call Ramos Otero's "autobiography-by-critical-projection" by noting the elements that he highlights regarding Cernuda: the Spaniard's vocation as a poet; his homosexuality; his perpetual exile; his insistence on the themes of love, death, and loneliness; his idea of writing as resistance and social critique; and as a brilliant final touch, Cernuda's link to Puerto Rico, where Cernuda's father was born during the later period of Spanish colonial domination. For our present discussion, my task will not be so much to ascertain the accuracy or merit of Ramos Otero's critical work, but rather to trace his analytical moves and see how they serve his own interests in relation to his own life and literary production. Cernuda presents a fascinating case of a person engaged in a transoceanic circuit of exile (Spain, France, England, the United States, and finally Mexico) that is profoundly different from that of Ramos Otero (Puerto Rico, New York), but that maintains an intrinsic circum-Atlantic link. And Ramos Otero, as poet/scholar, will in fact construct an image or representation of Cernuda that will serve as a "mask" or "persona" of himself, much as his narrators and protagonists do in his own literary production.

Early in "The Ethics of Margination," Ramos Otero quotes a passage from Cernuda's essay "Historial de un libro" (History of a book), which he presents as emblematic of the poet's general position on writing. As Cernuda states, "whatever people censure, cultivate, for that is the real you."[21] Ramos Otero goes on to clarify that censure is not the same as mere critique; the former action suggests that the writing subject is in a position of opposition to the dominant power structures, which then attempt to assert their control over the writer's production, that is to say, over his or her work of art.

Ramos Otero believes that Cernuda's rebellious or antiauthoritarian position stems principally from a double margination: that which he experiences as a poet (the object of scorn and ridicule at the time) as well (and perhaps even more dramatically) as a homosexual. According to Ramos Otero, it is the latter difference that informs Cernuda's relation to the written word; his sensibility as a poet is directly linked to the persecution he experiences because of his sexuality. As Ramos Otero writes, "Cernuda is aware that the biting edge of censure awaits him at the other side of his poetic and human endeavor, for as a homosexual, he had already perceived this in the moral and traditional rigidity of Spanish society" ("La ética" 17). Thus, according to this reading, for Cernuda, poetry and sexuality go hand in hand, much as they did for Ramos Otero; we see the formation of a double margination that brings forth a particular *visión inusitada* (unusual vision) that allows for access to *la verdad del mundo* (the truth of the world, "La ética" 20).

This understanding of a queer, exalted poetic "double consciousness" (to borrow W. E. B. Du Bois's phrase) can be seen as similar to the "border/mestiza sensibility" of the radical Chicana theorist and writer Gloria Anzaldúa, who argues in her 1987 classic *Borderlands/*

La frontera that marginal figures share *la facultad,* that is to say, "the capacity to see in surface phenomena the meaning of deeper realities, to see the deep structure below the surface" (60) and who will also argue that art making, and specifically writing, are essential and necessary processes for survival, especially for marginalized people. This is a sentiment that will be echoed by Ana Castillo in her *Massacre of the Dreamers* in her elaboration of what she calls Xicana (or Mexic Amerindian) "poetics of conscientización" (consciousness-raising, 163–79), and that the lesbian Puerto Rican poet Luz María Umpierre also defends in *The Margarita Poems.*

In the case of Ramos Otero's depiction of Cernuda, the result of being a poet and a homosexual will be shame and, more importantly, loneliness (*soledad*); both identities are shrouded in secrecy (17). At the same time, people who are attuned to perceive this difference will be able to recognize themselves and establish links of solidarity. This is an important motif that Ramos Otero's generational peer Magali García Ramis explores in her landmark novel *Felices días, tío Sergio* (Happy days, Uncle Sergio, 1986), where she writes: "Adults never suspect, or want to imagine that there exist intimate and extremely strong ties between their children and prohibited people. But children, from the time they are small, know, intuit, and recognize themselves among the prohibited ones, if it is within them to be like that when they grow up."[22]

For Ramos Otero, Cernuda's vision stems from his marginality and his confrontation with a stultified social order. Ramos Otero will locate Cernuda precisely at the edge of social experience: "his poetic vocation always occurs in the margin and comes from the margin, from the border between the truths that feed his desire for liberation from an existence stuck in tradition" ("La ética" 19). This margin, both symbolic and physical, provoked as it is by exile, is the space where Cernuda's (and Ramos Otero's) critique can be best elaborated; a startlingly similar or parallel elaboration to that of Anzaldúa, also mirroring Silviano Santiago's notions of a "space in-between" and Homi Bhabha's "Third Space."[23] For all of these thinkers, the interstitial space of the outsider who negotiates the fringe as a member/nonmember is a space of possibility, knowledge, and creativity, even if it is also marked as a space of physical and emotional pain. This is also the space of knowledge at the core of queer theory's epistemological project, the claim that sexual and gender difference can create not only otherness but also clarity and understanding that is threatened or lost by assimilation and normalization.[24] It is precisely this consciousness of the critical nature of the margin that leads Cernuda (and Ramos Otero)[25] to criticize the well-known poet Federico García Lorca's closeted, trepidatious behavior, marked by a constant appeal to propriety, specifically as conveyed in his "Ode to Walt Whitman," where Lorca degrades "maricas" (effeminate men) and exalts manliness.

Ramos Otero identifies the writing of *Los placeres prohibidos,* Cernuda's most explicit book, as a turning point in his production, a violent rupture with the dominant Christian morality: "It is with this book … that his loneliness as a man and a poet will become even more intense and will provoke, from then on, his total margination" ("La ética" 21). This loneliness or margination perhaps corresponds to how Ramos Otero felt in 1975 after the scandal produced by the publication of his own short story about female prostitution and interracial relations, "La última plena que bailó Luberza" (Luberza's last dance), in issue 7 of the 1970s Puerto Rican alternative literary and cultural journal *Zona de carga y descarga,* along with Rosario Ferré's "Cuando las mujeres quieren a los hombres" (When women love men) as well as by the boycott of "Historia ejemplar del esclavo y el señor" (Exemplary story of the slave and the master), a story about gay sadomasochism that appeared in issue 8; these events, documented by Ramos Otero's co-conspirator Rosario Ferré, are among the most notorious scandals in Puerto Rican literary history, which, as Gelpí has shown, was being fiercely contested in the 1970s.[26] A reading public needs to be created, Ramos Otero constantly says in reference to Cernuda, and in his own case, this public did not (for the most part) exist.

Another important confluence of the Puerto Rican critic's ideas with his perception of the Spanish poet's sentiment occurs when Ramos Otero states that for Cernuda, the only possibility of a loved one is in the poem itself. Following Octavio Paz's analysis of Cernuda (but with a different interpretation), Ramos Otero comments:

> I also wonder if one can talk of the loved one in Cernuda's poetry or if the loved one exists to inhabit the poem and the poem is the only body of the beloved. It seems as though the loved one is banned in real life, and it is only through poetry that this prohibited pleasure can become concrete, and as such, be sublimated. ("La ética" 23)

This idea will approximate Ramos Otero's own elaboration of *el hombre de papel* (the man of paper), that of the idealized figure of the lover that exists only on the written page as a poetic creation, a trope Daniel Torres has carefully analyzed.[27] At another moment, Ramos Otero comments on Cernuda's *Invocaciones*:

> It is perhaps this same alliance between man and poet that does not allow for a lover who does not understand this pact, this *coraza* [armor] that protects the man and the poet, the always persecuted. This is why he is able to realize with the death of a formerly beloved man that the desire for life becomes concrete only through death. ("La ética" 24)

This is a remarkable series of comments in light of Ramos Otero's own literary production. The series of short stories and poems that I will analyze *all* show a profound meditation on the possibility of love and the construction of a desired figure as a *writerly* phenomenon; they are also obsessed with death. In Ramos Otero's work, he insistently, almost obsessively, plays with the fictive quality of the story and its relation to the emotional dynamics between the characters. The Puerto Rican author constantly withholds the possibility of "real" love and affection by emphasizing the relation of these to the imagination of the lover in his depiction of the loved one. And, since death is no further away in writing than the simple will or desire of the author, Ramos Otero will repeatedly kill his characters or have them die or run off and disappear, allowing the author/narrator to return to his original state of solitude.

Stage One: *Concierto de metal para un recuerdo y otras orgías de soledad* (1971)

Ramos Otero's "Hollywood Memorabilia," from his first collection *Metal Concert for a Remembrance and Other Orgies of Solitude,* is one of the most representative stories of Ramos Otero's initial phase of exile, of his early production in New York.[28] As Juan G. Gelpí has argued, Ramos Otero's writings from this period are distinguished, above all else, by the first-person narration and by the narrator's and/or protagonist's essential loneliness that becomes manifest through violence against the reader: "Solitary young men, who have emigrated to New York City, frequently defend themselves from the experience of *shock* provoked by the big city by using verbal aggression. The narrator of 'Hollywood Memorabilia' would be an exemplary case of this type of provocation to the reader" (*Literatura y paternalismo* 139). The stories in this first book are also marked by the general lack of specificity regarding geographic location and occasionally by the lack of identification of the gender of the protagonist/narrator characters.[29]

While Gelpí goes no further in his analysis, his indication is a useful if somewhat misleading start. It is useful because loneliness and disorientation are indeed characteristic traits of the characters in *Metal Concert*. Yet it is slightly misleading, because "Hollywood Memorabilia" is in fact the only story definitely set in New York, as well as the only one with an openly homosexual narrator/protagonist (some of the other stories also strongly suggest this, but are ultimately ambiguous).

"Hollywood Memorabilia" is particularly indicative of some of the practices that Ramos Otero would continue in his later writing: those of presenting a gay Puerto Rican writer in New York as central character, narrator, and protagonist, and of writing metaliterary fiction in which the characters in the story often allude to the "fictional" nature of the texts and their ability to create and destroy in this imaginary world. As is often the case, the narrator/protagonist shares autobiographical elements with the author; Arnaldo Cruz-Malavé and Dionisio Cañas have emphasized that these should be seen as projections or *personae* of the writer (what Jossianna Arroyo refers to as *máscaras*, or masks), and not simply as straightforward depictions.[30]

Metal Concert, which includes stories from before and after Ramos Otero migrated, shows the spatial passage of his migration; "Alrededor del mundo con la Señorita Mambresi" (Around the world with Miss Mambresi), which is part of this collection, illustrates his presentiment that if he didn't migrate, he would be doomed to solitude and a perhaps even deeper sadness.

"Around the World with Miss Mambresi" is a remarkably explicit story that discusses matters of repressed female sexuality and their compensation or sublimation through erotic fantasies and self-gratification. It is the story of the loneliness and sexual frustration of a thirty-seven-year-old, middle-class woman, as narrated by her younger brother; he imagines her distracting herself with the memory of her past love interests (curiously named Paul, Lambert, Manuel, and Enrique), none of whom she has had sex with; with the daily rituals of an old-style bourgeoisie (playing the piano, eating pastries, attending concerts at the Casals Festival, and attending family funerals); with never-fulfilled fantasies of leaving her home; and even with masturbation. The narrator insists that he will not reproduce and be caught in her predicament; he will alter this fate by emigrating somewhere, anywhere:

> I finish my studies of sociology at the university and I feel that I begin my life because I change place, I march off to Austria or Chicago and possibly

> to Philadelphia and I think it will be different, that my youthful suffering
> and ignorance will end, having observed Miss Mabresi's eyes with great at-
> tention, to find the casual exhaustion of she who awaits death after savoring
> an éclair.... And I leave without saying goodbye because I fear staying and
> waiting even longer, uniting with her in her limitless wait. (*Concierto de
> metal* 75)

It is interesting that, among the places he mentions where he would like
to go (including Philadelphia, spelled in English in the original) and the
ones he later claims to visit (Ceylon, St. Petersburg, and black Africa),
there is no mention of New York.[31] "Around the World with Miss Mambresi" is a clear indictment of the stultifying effects of a closed, narrow,
bourgeois society upon some of its members. The need to emigrate (consistently referred to as travel) has nothing to do in this case with the
socioeconomic factors that had been leading to major social upheaval in
Puerto Rico since the 1940s and that were documented in works such as
René Marqués's *La carreta* (The oxcart, 1952), but rather to a desire for
self-emancipation and liberty.[32] It also does not have to do with social intolerance for homosexuality, a subject that will be openly addressed only
in Ramos Otero's last (and posthumously) published book, *Invitación al
polvo* (Invitation to the dust).

In "Hollywood Memorabilia," the protagonist/narrator has finished
his studies and moved to New York City. He is twenty-three years old
and works in the afternoons as a social science research assistant and
in the evenings as a film projectionist, in addition to being an aspiring
filmmaker and an author — a category he contrasts sharply to that of
"writer," which he likens to being a newspaper journalist. He is also
wont to grandiose philosophizing and egomania: in fact, the story begins
with his statement "I am God" (*Concierto de metal* 77), which is partly
a reflection of his awareness of the power of invention that an author
has. The protagonist is convinced that he will die at the age of thirty, a
morbid assertion he insistently repeats throughout the story, perhaps the
sign of depression.

As Gelpí has remarked, a distinguishing trait of this and of other
narrations from this early volume are their emphasis on solitude and
loneliness, as indicated by the book's title, ...*y otras orgías de soledad*
(and other orgies of solitude). In "Hollywood Memorabilia," the protagonist describes his relationship with three men: one from high school
(Angel Antonio, who is compared to the male protagonist of *Gone with
the Wind*) and two he meets in New York, John and Paul, the second
described as slightly reminiscent of James Dean, "but the one from *East*

of Eden and not the one from *Rebel without a Cause*" (*Concierto de metal* 80). They are all portrayed as sharing some physical features, most notably their blondish/brown hair. The three in fact become a type of composite or sum ("Angel-John-Paul"), a life trajectory marked by substitutions and lack, as well as "characters" for the "author"/narrator to play with in his imagination. The protagonist currently has no relationship with any of these men, although he thinks of them constantly and believes that Paul might visit him at some time. He seems to know or be friends with no one else in New York.

Given this state of unattachment, the protagonist/narrator's main relationship is to storytelling (specifically self-analysis), to cinema (specifically gay camp classics of Hollywood's Golden Age, but also to all old Hollywood films from the 1930s and 1940s), and to mostly white screen divas such as Greta Garbo, Rita Hayworth, Vivien Leigh, Joan Crawford, Marilyn Monroe, Mae West, and Ava Gardner, who become his central points of reference. He also believes or fantasizes that his body is disintegrating and being projected on screen, where he is becoming a character in the films he shows, an element that moves this story in the direction of science fiction or fantasy, particularly of the type explored by Argentine authors such as Adolfo Bioy Casares, Jorge Luis Borges, and Julio Cortázar. The cinematographic displacement and obsession of "Hollywood Memorabilia" also appears in later Puerto Rican texts such as García Ramis's *Happy Days, Uncle Sergio* and Antonio Martorell's *La piel de la memoria* (Memory's tattoo), as well as of the work of other Latin American writers such as Manuel Puig, who was also inspired by the Spanish/Mexican Rita Hayworth (née Rita Cansino) in his *Betrayed by Rita Hayworth* (1968). In fact, Ramos Otero has commented elsewhere on his childhood habit of spending long amounts of time at the movie theater in Manatí.[33]

If the nameless narrator/protagonist's Platonic experience in high school with Angel Antonio can be taken as indicative of the possibilities of homosexual relationships or encounters in the narrator's place of origin (which we assume is Puerto Rico), this experience is limited to daydreaming. The narrator's attraction to Angel Antonio is mediated by film: the protagonist feels he is Scarlett O'Hara from *Gone with the Wind* while the object of his affection is Ashley Wilkes. Strangely enough, Ramos Otero's depiction of homosexuality in Puerto Rico does not include scenes of sex, unlike René Marqués's slightly later portrayal in *La mirada* (1976); yet, one could argue that it is precisely Ramos

Otero's daring openly gay writing subject that inspires or allows the much older Marqués to be explicitly erotic.

In contrast to the sterility of Puerto Rico, New York becomes a space where late evening walks lead to sexual encounters and relationships; the protagonist meets both Paul and John after leaving the movie theater, as he was going home after work. Yet even here there is a dichotomy between the actual physical exchanges and the cerebral meditations on film, that is to say, the protagonist's fantasies of being a glamorous female film character or screen diva, and reenacting or experiencing their death scenes. The protagonist's actual exchanges with men such as John and Paul seem rather common or simple: inviting them over to his apartment for coffee or tea; having lunch or dinner; having John move in, which is not discussed in detail; having sex.

In "Hollywood Memorabilia" we can observe a negotiation of multiple physical and imaginary spaces: crowded subways where a woman talks of Israel's military aggression against its neighbors; abandoned, dark, late-night desolate streets that lead to sexual encounters; and the multiple spaces of the movie theater, including the auditorium, the visual and material space of its screen, the solitary projection booth, and the imaginary or mental space of filmic representation, predicated on a camp sensibility. These multiple locations are resolved in narration or writing: the scene of writing will allow for their constant intersection, as reminiscing conjures or brings forth the men's and the film diva's memories.

There is little difference in "Hollywood Memorabilia" between experiential reality and the one created by feelings in the mind, as the protagonist seems to not want to distinguish between the two, to mix freely, to confuse painful memory with longing and authorial flourishes:

> For I do not distinguish if I want to live every day as if it was the last; if Angel Antonio is the same as Illusion of Life Angel Antonio (in other words I want to know if the illusion ends when it is filled with traits, if Angel is the end of the illusion for being the created illusion). (*Concierto de metal* 80)

The life of the individual is a sum of memories borrowed from favorite films: "I write my life that is a remembrance of emotions reconstructed through Rita Hayworth in *Gilda,* Gloria Swanson in *Sunset Boulevard,* etcetera, etcetera!" (*Concierto de metal* 83–84). While emigration (travel) was presented as a necessary, life-giving measure in "Around the World with Miss Mambresi," the move to New York seems to focus around an obsession with or drive toward death. New York has brought about sexual relationships with men, but it has not done away with the protagonist's solitude. Thus his desire for a tragic, climactic, early end.

Stage Two: *El cuento de la Mujer del Mar* (1979)

Ramos Otero's second collection of short stories includes an eponymous narration that is representative of a second moment of emigrant/exilic production. This story, "El cuento de la Mujer del Mar" (The story of the woman of the sea), focuses on the relationship between a nameless, unemployed homosexual Puerto Rican writer (*el cuentero,* or story-teller), who is the narrator of the story, and Angelo, his Italian-American boyfriend, a formerly married man whose wife left him for an Irish policeman. Angelo is an X-ray technician from New Jersey alternately referred to as *el enano neapolitano* (the Neapolitan dwarf), perhaps because he measured only 5′ 8″, short in comparison to Ramos Otero's six feet plus, and as "Polifemo" (Polyphemus), the Cyclops described by Homer in the *Odyssey,* because of Angelo's one immobile eye. This pairing (that of a dwarf Polyphemus) is paradoxical, as Cyclops were giants; if Angelo is Polifemo, this would make the narrator/storyteller into Odysseus or Ulysses, although in his storytelling he is actually closer to Penelope, or perhaps to Homer himself.

The narrator's relationship with Angelo is sustained by their mutual storytelling, a type of queer immigrant reenactment of *The 1001 Nights,* in which the Puerto Rican becomes a new Scheherazade in a dark room of the Hotel Christopher in New York.[34] This narrative romantic structure (maintaining emotional and affective ties through storytelling) is also similar to that engaged by the imprisoned character of Molina in Manuel Puig's *The Kiss of the Spider Woman* (1976) and by Diego in Tomás Gutiérrez Alea and Juan Carlos Tabío's film *Strawberry and Chocolate* (1993), which have become gay Latin American classics. Angelo and the narrator's relationship is also nourished by their travel (physical and metaphorical, i.e., hallucinogenic, or even through the hotel mirror à la Lewis Carroll's *Through the Looking-Glass*), by sex (specifically by their never successful search for another man for a threesome), and by their alcohol and drug use. It is, faithful to the Indo-Persian/Arabic literary precedent, a story of night, like John Rechy's *City of Night,* of nocturnal, marginal beings, and of storytelling as a means of life, to ward off death.[35] Their storytelling involves differing versions of the story of the Woman from the Sea: in the case of the Puerto Rican, her name is Palmira Parés, "la Mujer del Mar," a dark-skinned fictional character based on the poet Julia de Burgos, who is counterposed to "Filimelé," a *mulata* character and poetic muse of the renowned poet Luis Palés Matos, who called her Filí-Melé in a cycle of poems dedicated to her; this fictional character has also inspired other Puerto Rican poets such as María Arrillaga (*Yo soy Filí Melé*) and Iván Silén (*Los poemas de Filí-Melé*).[36] Ramos Otero's Filimelé is presented as the lover of Palmira Parés or "la mujer de la Mujer del Mar" (the woman of the woman of the sea).[37] In the case of Angelo, it is the story of his Italian grandmother, Vicenza Vitale, "la Donna del Mare."

"The Story of the Woman of the Sea" can be seen as a "fictional" literary or metacritical essay, in which the narrator cum literary critic articulates his views on Palmira Parés as a shadow or projection of Julia de Burgos, although he will constantly state that he is literally "inventing" her (Parés) as a strategy to keep his love with Angelo alive. (For example, Julia de Burgos is not known to have had lesbian relationships and died in 1953 of alcoholism and not in 1954 of a drug overdose, as it is portrayed here.) Parés's last name can also be seen as a play on or feminization of Palés, particularly given the regional Puerto Rican phonetic interchangeability of the letters *l* and *r* (albeit usually in word- and syllable-final positions).[38] The narrator of "The Story of the Woman of the Sea" will constitute himself in relation to Parés (her character and her reappearing ghost, which returns repeatedly after her death in 1954), much as the narrator protagonist of Ramos Otero's "Inventario mitológico del cuento" (Mythical inventory of the story, also in this collection) constitutes himself as the mirror inverse of the writer Julio Cortázar.[39] The demise of the relationship between Palmira Parés and Filimelé in 1939, in turn, will be mirrored by the separation of the storyteller and Angelo in what seems to be 1970s New York.

The first noticeable difference between this story and those of *Metal Concert* is the emphasis on geographical specificity, a trait that, as we observed, was largely absent from the earlier writing. Not only is the main thread of this narration squarely set in New York City and, more specifically, on Christopher Street, at the time the main axis of its gay neighborhood, but there are also a number of additional important spatial locations (Manatí, San Juan, New Jersey, Italy, Montreal), where the parallel narrations take place and to where the narrator and Angelo travel. This geographical identification is a significant change in Ramos Otero's writing, especially relevant with regard to his relation to space and to his condition as an exilic subject. The initial resistance to specificity yields to a very concrete effort to map locations that are significant:

a web of loci that the writer, nomad-like, inhabits both in his literary work and in his travels and writing. The need to specify fixed points also grows as the writer detaches himself from the naturalized site of origin, the place of repulsion or rejection (Puerto Rico) and begins to establish himself in New York.

Another significant change in this second stage is the opening toward linguistic plurality: while the story is predominantly written in Spanish, there are important passages in English and occasional sprinklings of Italian, both of these always presented as citations of Angelo's speech. The protagonist mentions that his exchanges with Angelo are in broken street English ("amándonos en la zona de un inglés callejero," 101), indicating that it is this language that enables the two immigrants to communicate and to tell each other their tales.[40] The fact that it is street language indicates that it is colloquial, not a highly erudite or traditionally literary one. Yet while the protagonist might be using English in his relationship, he never uses it in the story itself to transmit his feelings or ideas, as this is always done in Spanish.[41]

A noticeable continuity with previous stories is the author's obsession with the theme of loneliness (*soledad*) and death. This is at the core of the parallel narrations of "The Woman of the Sea," particularly Palmira Parés, whose life is presented as one of almost uninterrupted solitude, except for her sojourn with Filimelé, and of the narrator's relationship with Angelo, which does not seem to generate much except occasional sex, some companionship, and the very narration itself, and whose main purpose seems to be to ward off loneliness. Love is presented as something unattainable, and the lovers will continuously worry about its demise, which will predictably occur on New Year's Eve, as the affair is destined to end after one thousand nights, i.e., three years. Their preternatural anxiety will limit their ability to enjoy the time they do spend together. Loneliness is also insistently associated with the experience of exile.

Space, that is to say, the physical geography the characters inhabit, is central to the development of "The Story of the Woman of the Sea." The explicit focus on New York City and Christopher Street in this story is important both because it places immigrant Puerto Ricans (or rather, *one* immigrant Puerto Rican) at its core and because it presents that space, constantly compared to Old San Juan, as one of desolation and loneliness, producing something akin to claustrophobia. We could also argue that there are several metaliterary spaces, including Arabia (as an Orientalist narrative projection or referent) and the time/mindspace of drugs, although these occupy a more abstract and less tangible dimension.

Puerto Rican immigrants have been present in New York City since the second half of the nineteenth century and continued (and have continued) to come during the entire twentieth and early twenty-first centuries. Early immigrants included cigar workers and political exiles, and later ones were most often laborers and former countryside inhabitants, although there have also always been middle- and upper-class migrants.[42] The communities that became established as successive migrations came to the city produced varying cultural texts that documented their experiences and allowed for the exploration of myriad realities. For the most part, this was a collective endeavor, or one shared with the community. There are exceptions to this, for example Julia de Burgos's "Farewell in Welfare Island" (1953), written in New York during the last year of the poet's life, which presents a hauntingly desolate image of solitude. Ramos Otero's story, which showcases a Puerto Rican immigrant totally isolated from the Puerto Rican community in the city, can be read as sign that, just as on the island, the national community was (or perhaps was perceived as being, or the author chose to portray it as being) not especially willing to embrace members of differing sexualities, or that the author/narrator character was a *poète maudit* or bohemian marginal who purposefully chose to frequent other spaces.[43] In fact, earlier immigrant Puerto Rican narratives, such as José Luis Vivas Maldonado's story "La última la paga el diablo," Emilio Díaz Valcárcel's *Harlem todos los días,* or Piri Thomas's *Down These Mean Streets* do not present especially tolerant or accepting viewpoints of homosexuality. Then again, perhaps one could think of the storyteller as an openly queer, island-born counterpart to the bisexual, drug-using poet and playwright Miguel Piñero, a central character of the 1970s Nuyorican literary scene, whose experiences have been cinematographically portrayed by León Ichaso in his biopic *Piñero* (2001). Both Ramos Otero and Piñero relished the space of the margin and the pleasure of shocking the complacent middle-class; both are remembered with mixed feelings as difficult if brilliant people.

While New York City has had a variety of areas that have served as meeting places for the LGBT population, where communities have sprung up at different moments, none of these have been as important as Greenwich Village.[44] The effective consolidation of the Village as a modern-day "gay space" (at the very least in the community's imaginary) occurred as a result of the Stonewall Revolt of 1969, in which the participation of Latina and African American drag queens was an essential (if often downplayed) component. The riots on Christopher Street at Sheridan Square (corner of Seventh Avenue) strengthened and consolidated a much longer tradition of struggle for basic rights against police harassment and social vilification. To this day, Christopher Street holds a significant number of gay establishments, including bars, stores, cafés, and restaurants, although its centrality has diminished with the ascendancy of other gay neighborhoods such as Chelsea and Hell's Kitchen in the 1990s and 2000s.[45]

"The Story of the Woman of the Sea" is firmly located in 1970s Village territory. The narrator even gives the specific coordinates of Christopher Street, marking its location in the city as well as its relation to the story itself. His description, however, does not partake of a glorious mythification of it as a site of resistance and affirmation, but rather makes it into an "invisible" world — *la otra ciudad, invisible* (90) — decayed and polluted, as if reflecting in its very own physical constitution the marginality to which it is relegated, or the moral perdition with which it is associated.[46] If the story is a mirror, as is repeatedly emphasized, it is a mirror of that gay space: "The street begins at Greenwich Avenue (the latitude of smoke) and ends in the black waters of the Hudson River, in the abandoned piers, in the mirror of a room in the Hotel Christopher" (*El cuento de la Mujer del Mar* 103). This sleazy, run-down hotel — an essentially transitory space, as Gelpí has observed — will be the site for most of the story's narration, alongside other places on the street, such as the stoops of buildings and the piers, as well as dark clandestine bars.[47] In fact, there is never any mention of other people in any of these spaces; there are no references of other parts of New York; and the characters never leave — besides the "trips" their drug use can facilitate — except for a trip to Montreal and possibly (although most unlikely) to Manatí.

In this story, New York City is generally referred to as being in ruins ("New York ya estaba en ruinas," 100) or as a cemetery for exiled people ("La ciudad era entonces un cementerio de exilados," 104). This is similar to the representation of the gay space: the piers, for example, are not only abandoned (*abandonados*) but also infested with termites (*apolillados,* 91); the waters of Hudson River are dark, not simply because it is night, but we can assume with contamination. The lovers' wanderings around Christopher Street and the nearby piers are also strangely desolate, as if they never encountered anyone, as if the area were a ghost town.

Images of New York as a city in ruins were common during the 1970s, a period of great social unrest, white middle-class abandonment and flight to the suburbs, landlord dereliction, urban riots, high crime rates, and neighborhood burnouts, especially in Loisaida and the Bronx and other cities such as Newark and Detroit. It was the heyday of the notorious street and subway graffiti, a different type of diasporic cultural production, associated with emerging hip-hop culture that can in fact be seen as an effort to reclaim the city and assert its humanity.[48] Films such as *Taxi Driver* (1976) and the controversial *Fort Apache: The Bronx* (1981) served to construct and disseminate views of New York City as an urban wasteland, as well as of Puerto Rican migrants as violent, unruly people mired in poverty (à la *West Side Story*); documentaries such as the agit-prop film *El pueblo se levanta* (1971), Jerry Masucci and the Fania All-Stars' music concert *Our Latin Thing* (1972), and Marci Reaven and Beni Matías's *The Heart of Loisaida* (1979) attempt to counteract this negative portrayal and in fact show diasporic Puerto Ricans as proud people with a vibrant cultural life and a sense of community, struggling to gain control of their buildings and neighborhoods, akin to the effort spearheaded by the Young Lords, which included the participation of the radical street drag queen and activist Sylvia Rivera, by street posses such as the Harlem Renigades and the Dynamite Brothers, by vibrant salsa musicians, and by poets such as Miguel Algarín and other members of the Nuyorican Poets Café.[49]

What is odd or unusual about Ramos Otero's description of the city in ruins is that there is no mention of this; it is as though the ruins he is referring to are of a completely different nature, having to do with the state of his relationship and perhaps with the neglect or abandon of the West Village at that time, before its more recent gentrification. The area of the piers, for example, which is also central in the writings of other gay authors such as David Wojnarowicz, had been very busy for many decades before becoming abandoned in the 1960s and 1970s, when New York City lost most of its industrial and manufacturing base to other parts of the country (and eventually, other countries) with a cheaper labor force.[50] It can also be seen as the embrace of a decadent positionality reminiscent of French poets such as Rimbaud, Verlaine, and Baudelaire, a viewpoint that would find its most faithful inheritor in the heavily tattooed contemporary Puerto Rican rock musician Robi "Dräco" Rosa (of ex-Menudo fame); this nostalgia for decay is also similar to René Marqués's affectations for Old San Juan, and to Tennessee Williams's portrayal of the South, especially of New Orleans. Ramos Otero's negative views coincide with Reinaldo Arenas's less-than-glowing portrayal of 1980s New York in his autobiography *Before Night Falls* (1992), particularly his critique of sexual relations between men.

Is there a connection between Ramos Otero's insistent depiction of exile as the domain of solitude and his (partial) exclusion (be it self-imposed or socially enforced) from the Puerto Rican community in New York? The author was in fact quite involved in Latina/o theater in New York and taught Puerto Rican studies at various universities, which suggests that his life and the "autobiographical" self-projection he presents are not always in synchrony.[51] Is his insistence on solitude also possibly related to the fact that the North American gay community has traditionally excluded people of color from its ranks and offered them at best a lukewarm reception? This is certainly the case of someone like Sylvia Rivera, as Martin Duberman has documented.[52]

It is unclear why there is no mention in Ramos Otero's early texts of alternative community-building among other Puerto Ricans, Latinos, or queers of color (something that, as I mentioned, he was doing at this time); the protagonist's links with a fellow immigrant of working-class extraction signals the ways this occurred at an individual level. It might also have to do with the pensive, inward, or alienating experiences of certain drug-taking practices, shared by the two characters but not portrayed as collective endeavor, perhaps closer to a *Sid and Nancy* (Sid Vicious and Nancy Spungen) type of relationship, particularly to their heroin addiction and to her murder in 1978 in Room 100 of the Chelsea Hotel in New York. For Ramos Otero, the marginal, sex-radical gay world and the diasporic Puerto Rican world do not seem to mix.

In "The Story of the Woman of the Sea," exile not only describes an actual physical displacement from a place of origin; it is also used as a grounding metaphor for love and intimate relationships and for the very process of writing, similar to what we had seen in the essay on Cernuda; the story also constantly alludes to the *Odyssey*, specifically to Penelope's longing for her husband, Ulysses, refracted through the lens of melodrama, and to the storyteller and Angelo's trips, as well as those of Palmira Parés and Vicenza Vitale, as reenactments of Ulysses' displacements: the characters travel in search of a past that is essential to their present love relationship. It is no coincidence that Ulysses' trip back to Ithaca, after being freed by the nymph Calypso, also took three years — the same amount of time Ramos Otero's story is supposed to span — although Ulysses was estranged from his spouse for two decades. Ramos Otero's narrator elaborates a somewhat classical theory of love in which there is a mutual, reciprocal belonging to each other; one partner *becomes* the other in this totalizing exchange, ultimately marked by solitude and abjection. Discontinuity with everything, submission to another's will, and degradation turn love into a form of exile and a space of writing, as we can see in the following passage:

> Then, one exiles oneself in love as in cities. Everything is as old as the sun. But the city and exile are older than the moon and the night. The zone of exile is the same territory of solitude. And one learns the submission of the other. I kiss the Italian anus of the Neapolitan dwarf. It is terrible to be a storyteller to not die assassinated by the stabs of solitude. We are one another's man, inevitably. The beauty and the beast at the same time. (*El cuento de la Mujer del Mar* 103).

There are several things we can say, depending on whether we consider Ramos Otero's position (perhaps unfairly) as grandiloquent philosophizing, part of the dramatic persona he attempted to construct for himself, or as a classical citation of earlier codes of love or perhaps even of avant-garde aesthetics à la Jean Cocteau or even like Jean Genet.

The idea of *exilarse en el amor* (exiling oneself in love) implies a necessary abandon and intensity, as if one were unable to love without totally plunging into it, immersing oneself fully. Love is seen as the only possible remedy for the solitude of exile. There is no mention in "The Story of the Woman of the Sea" of any other type of meaningful relationship, such as with friends, a religious, cultural, social, or political cause, or a community. The radical exilic subject imagines himself as if in a vacuum. It is from this position of sexual marginality that Ramos Otero constructs the solitary character of his protagonist, one that thus appears shocking to a bourgeois mentality. His scatological mention of rimming (*beso el ano italiano*) posits elements of male homoerotic practices considered abject by mainstream society, specifying conducts of degradation and submission engaged in for their erotic and transgressive thrill and for their potential for pleasure and intimacy. The relationship is also predicated on the characters' drug consumption, as I have mentioned, which included marijuana, angel dust, cocaine, and heroin. Finally, the notion of love and solitude as linked to death (suggested by the mention of assassination) links this conceptualization of love to the tradition that Denis de Rougemont (*Love in the Western World*) and Georges Bataille (*Erotism: Death and Sensuality*) identify for the West.

Before concluding my comments on this story, it should be noted that the narration of the life and the critical appraisal of the (fictional) poet Palmira Parés occupies an extensive segment of its pages; the narrator's life parallels hers in many respects. By tracing and valorizing the life and work of Julia de Burgos (albeit in a fictionalized and distorted way) and incorporating diverse references to Luis Palés Matos, Ramos Otero effectively places his experience in a wider context of margination and of better recognized (national) literary production, similar to what we had argued in relation to Cernuda. The narrator's experience is mirrored in his narration of Palmira Parés, a key figure of solitude and abjection, whose tragic death from a heroin overdose à la Janis Joplin serves to propitiate the narrator's (literary) "murder" of his boyfriend Angelo; the narrator is described at the end as having bloody hands and sensing the smell of a cadaver. This scenario can also be seen as a misreading, as the fulfillment of the Persian king Shahryar's threat to kill the storyteller Scheherazade (Shahrzad), which in fact does not occur in *The 1001 Nights,* where the two live happily ever after.

"The Story of the Woman of the Sea" ends in a complete consummation of solitude. And just as in "Hollywood Memorabilia," the storyteller's relationship to his lover is marked by coming and going; by a desire to keep the extinguishing flames of love alive; by the notion that love is a "fiction" of sorts, a crafted narrative that is partially created by those who participate in it. Yet this story is also a "labyrinth" with its own minotaur, one in which the storyteller feels that the story (the text or narrative itself) has control over its characters and its own logic, and that as such, there is nothing he can do but follow its commands and designs. The story, ultimately, gives the storyteller the same type of emotional closure that death gives to all (or at least, most) lives.

Stage Three: *Página en blanco y staccato* (1987)

The five narrations included in *Blank Page and Staccato* are illustrative of a third, quite different moment of exile/migrant experience. These stories show a profound engagement with the history of the Puerto Rican migration, familiarity with the different geographic spaces they occupy (both in New York and other places) and with other migrations such as the black and Caribbean diaspora. They are also marked by a common central figure, a gay Puerto Rican writer (a self-projection of the author) who lives in New York, and who intervenes in disparate narrations in different ways.

The first of these stories, "La otra isla de Puerto Rico" (The other island of Puerto Rico), presents the death of a queer Puerto Rican man in Greece, Don José Usbaldo Olmo Olmo, a clear allusion to the gay Puerto Rican independent scholar and collector José Olmo Olmo, who resides in New York and was close friends with Ramos Otero.[53] The Hellenic setting can also be seen as a homage to the poet Constantine Cavafy, also celebrated by Ramos Otero in *El libro de la muerte* (59–60), and as an extension of the Homeric references discussed previously. This story is especially important for its validation of oral history as an alternative source of information (specifically on revolutionary struggles) that counters dominant, institutionalized versions, and in its emphasis on New York as another version of Puerto Rico, as indicated by the title. Here José Usbaldo's sister, doña Liboria Olmo Olmo, is presented as an unlikely expert on Puerto Rican history: "She would speak just as easily of the Nationalist Revolt...as of the Puerto Rican cigar rollers who had emigrated to New York since the last years of the previous century, later on establishing the bases of El Barrio" (*Página en blanco* 15). This type of comment is of value considering the omission from most national histories of migration as a significant historic event and of women as official historians.

One of the stories that doña Liboria will tell is that of Marie Cafolé, a revolutionary figure who is rumored to be her mother and was believed to be a runaway or maroon slave. What interests me, besides Marie's heroic stature, is her migratory history: "originally from Senegal and later on from the Canary Islands, and Martinique, and Haiti, and Puerto Rico, and from so many other places, until her disappearance in New York at the beginning of this century" (*Página en blanco* 18). Just as Ramos Otero had presented Palmira Parés's (Julia de Burgos's) migration as a valuable antecedent, here he will highlight the historical experience provoked by the African slave trade in the Americas, and the subsequent travel among the diverse islands of the Caribbean. This history will also form part of the background of Milagros Candelas and Sam Fat, characters from "Página en blanco y staccato" that I will carefully examine later on.

The last aspect of this story that I would like to highlight is the description of different migrants' links and relations to Puerto Rico, as well as the issue of whom Ramos Otero's intended audience is. While the Puerto Rican author emphasizes the need for the migration to be accounted for and recognized in official (island) discourses, he also distinguishes between the many experiences and attachments that the diasporic community holds:

> We are amidst the others of the other island of Puerto Rico, more than one million unexamined photos in the emigrant archives. We have been arriving here for a very long time, coming from the other one, and you know it. Some

wander about with long-expired images of coffee plantations, sugar fields, and tobacco farms.... Others have buried too many dead here and it's not worthwhile for them to think about Puerto Rico, where things are going so poorly.... There are many that do not know where the other island is. (*Página en blanco* 20–21)

Ramos Otero highlights two extremes of emigrant mentality in this categorization. One is a nostalgic longing for the countryside they abandoned, one that has disappeared or been dramatically transformed as a result of processes of modernization. At the other extreme are those whose lives have been consumed by the migratory experience and have nothing to return to, or those who for some reason have not had any direct contact with Puerto Rico. This would be, most clearly, the case of emigrants who left as children or who were born in the United States.

Who is Ramos Otero addressing in his story? Who is this *ustedes* (the formal, plural "you") referred to above? As the critic Dionisio Cañas has observed, it seems that the author is predominantly writing for an audience that is not necessarily in New York, that is most likely in Puerto Rico, or that is made up of exiled immigrants like himself. Ramos Otero has stated elsewhere (in his interview with Marithelma Costa): "Escribo para todo el que pueda leerme" (I write for everyone who can read me) and further clarified that his ideal average reader is Puerto Rican;[54] given the historic lack of translations of his work (as of 2009, only three of his more than thirty-four stories have appeared in English),[55] this ultimately implies a predominantly Caribbean, Spanish-reading island audience. This is further suggested by another statement: "The 'writer'...looks at words, ordered in a believable sequence for the paper (*and for you, who have always seen and felt the barrier of a sea, without having seen yourselves reflected in the mirror of exile*)" (quoted in Costa 22, italics mine). Those readers who have never experienced exile are, it would seem, his compatriots in Puerto Rico.

Ramos Otero's tracing of the cartography of the Puerto Rican diaspora acquires particular depth in "Vivir del cuento" (To live from storytelling/from a story), a narration of the Puerto Rican migration to Hawai'i based on the research of Norma Carr.[56] This story is interesting as a recuperation (and fictionalization) of a mostly forgotten episode of national history and for its comments on the migrant experience, particularly the importance of the memory of Puerto Rico for an individual who left as a small child and whose most direct links are his family relations: geography is transmitted in this case as memory, through actual human beings. The Hawaiian–Puerto Ricans' quick integration with other native and immigrant ethnic groups is also significant.

Finally, the framework for the narration and origin of the Hawai'i story, which appears in an interpolated manner as a parallel narration, tells of how storytelling can be employed as a way to maintain links between Puerto Ricans in New York (the storyteller) and those in Puerto Rico (as illustrated by "Magali," a clear reference to the writer Magali García Ramis); storytelling bridges the gaps of spatial and temporal distance. The story is really two interwoven and interrelated tales: one, the tale of Monserrate Alvarez, a Puerto Rican who immigrated to Hawai'i at the turn of the twentieth century; and another, a memoristic narration of a more recent writers' conference in Newark, New Jersey, based on a real event held at Rutgers University in 1983.[57] The two tales are connected by links of nationality, and by the mutual storytelling of all of the individuals involved. All of the characters are marked by migration: Magali wants to leave Puerto Rico; the narrator lives in New York; Monserrate, in Hawai'i.

It is not until the last two stories of *Página en blanco y staccato,* however, that the theme of homosexuality and its interconnection to migration is really developed. Just as the above-mentioned stories revealed a dramatically new approach and relation to the Puerto Rican diaspora, "Página en blanco y staccato" and "Descuento" (Discount/untelling) will significantly differ from Ramos Otero's earlier narrations. Among the most noticeable aspects of these stories, besides the frank treatment of AIDS, which devastated the Latina/o and gay communities in the 1980s, will be the autobiographical gay Puerto Rican writer/protagonist's relationship with two fellow diasporic men: one, a second-generation black Chinese Puerto Rican called Sam Fat; the other, a nameless fellow first-generation Puerto Rican artist, a character clearly based on Ramos Otero's former partner, the painter Angel Rodríguez-Díaz.[58] These relationships will be further complemented by the sequence of poems in "De polvo enamorado" (Of dust in love, in *Invitación al polvo*), which describe the poet's relationship with an exiled Cuban house painter named José.

The eponymous story which gives this collection its title, "Blank Page and Staccato," presents the encounter between an island-born Puerto Rican writer called "Manuel Ramos" (the on-and-off narrator of the story, or more correctly, the *cuentero,* or storyteller) and the U.S.-born, Chinese-Puerto Rican private detective Samuel Fat Candelas (shortened to Sam Fat) at the Aguas Buenas Social Club, a Puerto Rican hangout on Avenue A in Loisaida (the Lower East Side of Manhattan), on December 31, 1983. The general narrative frame of the story is a clear referent to the detective genre, on the one hand, and to the work of the Argentine writers Jorge Luis Borges and Julio Cortázar, to such stories as Cortázar's "La noche boca arriba," for example, and to the tradition of doppelgänger writing.

Here the generally nameless writer (referred to once as "Manuel" and at another time as "Ramos," and whose name, just like Ramos Otero's, is said to contain sixteen letters) believes that he has a double, which he has seen at different moments of his life. This double is most likely Ramos Otero's generational peer, the heterosexual Puerto Rican author Juan Antonio Ramos (1948–), whose name also has sixteen letters, and is most famous for his writings on drug addicts and other marginal figures, specifically in his *Papo Impala está quitao* (Papo Impala is clean, 1983).[59] The detective Sam Fat has had an early teenage contact with the writer/narrator Manuel Ramos and believes it is his destiny to meet him again and murder him. As such, what we have is a twist on a classic narrative genre — the detective story — where the detective is in fact the "criminal" or aggressor, but one whose "crime" is justified as it is in fact an act of vengeance, of rectifying a previous wrong committed against his family, people, or race. The narration is also untypical as it tells the story from a double perspective: that of the detective/criminal/heir of the aggrieved as well as from that of the writer/victim/heir of aggressors.

Samuel Fat Candelas is the son of Chinese and Puerto Rican immigrants and the descendant of a black woman burned at the stake for witchcraft in sixteenth-century Puerto Rico by Bishop Nicolás Ramos de los Santos; he is also the son of the deity Orunla, and as such has the potential to become a Santería *babalao,* or priest. His mother, Milagros Candelas, has always desired that he avenge the crime against their ancestor, and this can be achieved by killing one of the writers, since both share the bishop's last name. The repetition of the integer 16 in various iterations highlights Ramos Otero's narrative game, as this number is rife with cultural and symbolic meanings, including the arrival of adulthood.[60] In a rather ambiguous ending, we learn that the writer has AIDS; Sam Fat believes that the writer has made him into a murderer, as he is scripted to kill him, or perhaps (and more problematically) has already provoked this death or perhaps that of others by serving — given his identity as a sexually active, black Nuyorican hustler or *bugarrón* — as a sexual vector for HIV infection. This counterintuitive reading, which I will expand upon later in this chapter, would unfortunately seem to negate the more progressive aspects of the short story, unless its purpose was *precisely* to serve as a comment on how dominant discourses blame blacks/Africans/people of color, prostitutes/hustlers, bisexuals/homosexuals, drug users and diasporic peoples for the spread of HIV/AIDS. In fact, Ramos Otero explicitly criticized the prejudices and stereotypes associated with AIDS (initially referred to as the "gay cancer") in his poems "Metáfora contagiosa" (Infectious metaphor, 50–51) and especially "Nobleza de sangre" (Blood nobility, 62–63), both in *Invitación al polvo*.[61] Yet since Sam Fat's HIV status is never discussed in the story, this reading remains a possibility but not a given.

The general framework sketched above is enriched by a series of additional details. These include the location of the story in Loisaida, a neighborhood that is mythically associated in the story with the Río Grande de Loíza and with the predominantly black settlement of Loíza Aldea; the diasporic history of Sam Fat Candelas's family, with origins in China, Africa, and Puerto Rico; and the homosexual relationship between the writer and the detective, two diasporic Puerto Ricans, one born in Puerto Rico and the other in New York.

Throughout my analysis, I have emphasized the importance of location. As I have observed, the early stories were situated in ambiguous sites; "Hollywood Memorabilia," for example, centers on midtown Manhattan in a largely unmapped space that is probably Hell's Kitchen but is never identified as such. This is significantly different from what occurs in "The Story of the Woman of the Sea," where the city's gay neighborhood of Greenwich Village, centered around Christopher Street, becomes the main locus. In the third collection of short stories, specific sites are crucial for the construction of the narration; historically Puerto Rican neighborhoods in New York City such as Loisaida suddenly appear and become central to the events described. This is the case of "Blank Page and Staccato."

The Lower East Side has for several centuries been a neighborhood characterized by serving as the residence of poor immigrants.[62] Different ethnic groups have lived there, many moving out as their general socioeconomic status improved. In its most recent reincarnations, it has served as home to a mainly Eastern European, Jewish, and Puerto Rican (and now, Latina/o) community, in close proximity to the now rapidly expanding Asian population of Chinatown, the contracting community of Little Italy, and the massive gentrification of the area led by Realtors and institutions such as New York University. Along with El Barrio (East

Harlem), Loisaida (as it is referred to by Puerto Ricans) is the most significant Puerto Rican neighborhood in Manhattan, the site of many of its cultural institutions and political representatives.[63]

It is no coincidence, then, that Sam Fat was born near and raised in Loisaida and that this is where he meets Ramos, the writer. By setting the action in this neighborhood and its vicinity (Chinatown, Little Italy) and in fact making the neighborhood the protagonist of the story, Ramos Otero attempts to integrate the question of homosexuality to the traditional Puerto Rican enclave in a different way than that of bisexual writers such as Miguel Algarín and Miguel Piñero. While other Nuyorican writers, as Arnaldo Cruz-Malavé has shown, have traditionally presented the question of homosexuality in these communities as intrinsically abject (or at least did so in the 1970s), Ramos Otero disrupts the equation, and shows homosexuality as an integral, constitutive, and profoundly meaningful category.[64] This, of course, does not free it from stigma — that is precisely the importance of the representation of AIDS in the story. Ramos Otero is not interested in "sanitizing" homosexuality, which still remains associated with the abject; rather, he strives to exploit its subversive potential. In many ways, Ramos Otero can be seen as a crucial — albeit perhaps ignored — antecedent to Miguel Algarín's more recent, extremely moving poetic meditation on AIDS, *Love Is Hard Work: Memorias de Loisaida* (1997).

The migration of Ramos Otero's writer/protagonist and of Sam Fat's family instills "Blank Page and Staccato" with narrations of travel and with the sense of New York as a site where disparate communities come together; where many come thinking that it is a temporary stop but where they end up spending their entire lives. The way in which this holds true in the case of the Caribbean is reflected in the following passage:

> ...there is also New York, an essential point of the continent, heart of an empire that does not look like it, where the common space of uprootedness dominates, amidst men and women transplanted in flight, from faraway countries that the local newspapers do not mention, men and women who still believe that they live in New York on borrowed time (a pact with the devil) to later return to the port of origin of a collective memory: Puerto Rico, Jamaica, Guyana, Grenada, Dominican Republic, Colombia, Panama, St. Thomas, Haiti, the South. (*Página en blanco* 74)

It is interesting to observe the African commonality of this mostly Caribbean diaspora, be it English-, Spanish-, or French- and Creole-speaking, one that retraces the contours of what Paul Gilroy has analyzed in his influential *The Black Atlantic.* In "Blank Page," the narrator traces a map characterized by a common slave experience, emphasized in the story by the survival of the Yoruba religious traditions in the Americas in the often syncretic form of Santería, one that Sam Fat will be hesitant to embrace.[65]

But let us return to the Aguas Buenas Social Club. As Virginia Sánchez Korrol has documented, social clubs were one of the types of organizations — along with mutual aid societies, churches, labor unions, and political groups — that helped to cement and consolidate the displaced masses of immigrants from Puerto Rico who arrived to what often was a rather hostile environment in New York City. Social organizations were often constituted on the basis of common geographic provenance; thus, people from Aguas Buenas, a rural municipality in Puerto Rico, could gather during their leisure time at a specific location. Interactions in these spaces closely followed the models set back home.

The narrator's description of the Avenue A bar could easily have fit a similar locale in the tropics, except for the pang of nostalgia provoked by the music and its mention of the sea:

> Two men drank by the bar and a third, hovering by the jukebox, had just selected a song by Carmen Delia Dipiní — "my heart is...a ship in the stormy sea...challenging the strong gusts...of that which they call love..." — and I asked for rum with anisette on the rocks, as if to forget the bolero and neutralize the bad habit that Puerto Rico has of accosting those Puerto Ricans who left every time the word sea is mentioned. (*Página en blanco* 70)

This passage is dense in its construction of exile and nostalgia for a certain Puerto Rico, brought about through the musical form of the bolero, a favorite genre that facilitates homoerotic socialization among heterosexually identified men as well as homosexual "camp" adoration, as explored at length by Luis Rafael Sánchez in his essayistic novel *La importancia de llamarse Daniel Santos* (The importance of being Daniel Santos, 1989) and by critics such as José Quiroga and Iris Zavala.[66] Music, as Ruth Glasser, Juan Flores, and Frances Aparicio remind us, is one of the most common and recurrent cultural signifiers that serve to keep Puerto Rican immigrants in touch with the traditions and reality of their country of origin.[67] It serves to rekindle memory and to foster a sense of cultural community. In this sense, it serves a function similar to the role of music for Chicanas/os (think of corridos, for example) and for other Latinas/os.[68]

The personification of the island of Puerto Rico as a presence that exerts allegiance from its emigrant (exiled) subjects by tying its memory to the word "sea" brings together the poetic project of Julia de Burgos and Ramos Otero's continuation in "The Story of the Woman of the Sea" to this story. According to the narrator, Puerto Rico has the bad habit of accosting its wayward national subjects who are distanced from the native soil. Finally, the specific alcoholic beverage that the writer drinks (rum with anisette) is a rather idiosyncratic mention of traditional Puerto Rican culture; that he requests it "on the rocks" signals the prevalence of Spanglish as a means of communication and of Americanization (ice as a sign of modernity). This drink, popularly referred to as *chichaíto* (little fucked one), brings together Caribbean and Peninsular (Spanish) alcoholic spirits and sometimes even includes a coffee bean, extending even further the culinary/economic metaphor.

The Aguas Buenas Social Club provides the setting for the narration of the story, and for the only encounter and verbal exchange between the writer and Sam Fat that the writer is aware of. (While a teenager, Sam Fat had previously met the writer in Chinatown, by whom he was "initiated" into man-with-man sex, an experience that would lead him to become a male hustler, or *bugarrón*, in Times Square, but the writer apparently fails to recognize him the second time around.) Sam Fat's apparition is rather startling: he surges forth from the bathroom and approaches the writer in a manner more reminiscent of gay cruising than of a professional interaction between a detective and his client. Of course, the fact that they are meeting at a bar (and that the detective's "office" is really an Italian pizzeria, whose public phone doubles as his "business" phone) and that the detective moonlights as a male hustler also serves to "lighten up" the professional connotations of the encounter. It is evident that Ramos Otero has taken his cues from Hollywood film-noir, and that he is attempting to present a gay, camp, creole version.

Sam Fat's approach is easily read under codes of urban gay male aesthetics as representing a specific type of posturing or style, even if in this case he is a racialized figure. Fat's engagement with these aesthetics is clear, among other reasons, because of his clothes and physical appearance: as the narrator indicates, "The worn jeans accentuated the firmness of his thighs; the Scottish wool plaid shirt duplicated his torso" (*Página en blanco* 71), hardly what one would expect a private eye to be wearing, at least not in a film-noir genre. These garments, especially when worn by muscular, mustachioed, fit men, are iconic of a certain type of 1970s gay fashion, of men referred to as "clones" for all dressing alike, who attempted to portray a rugged, masculine, "outdoorsy" look: the complete opposite of the dominant "effeminate" paradigm. It is no coincidence that Sam Fat will later be described as a *bugarrón,* a term employed in the Caribbean to indicate men of masculine appearance who engage in sex with other men, often for money, and who ostensibly always play the "active," "dominant," or insertive role.

At the social club, Sam Fat goes up to the writer, offers him a Marlboro cigarette, requests that the writer buy him a drink, all of this while breathing down his neck, placing his arm on his back and resting his leg on the writer's leg. As this kind of intimacy seems rather unusual for a putatively "straight" Puerto Rican bar, we can say that Fat is in fact "queering" that location and behaving in a transgressive way, or perhaps simply pushing to its extreme the kind of physical intimacy that heterosexual Puerto Rican men in fact do display in such locations. As such, the gesture can be read as a critique of dominant social practices effected through parody or exaggeration.

"Manuel" is writing a story of his encounter with Sam Fat, of his becoming the persecuted one, as it is suggested that Sam Fat will kill him. As is so often the case with Ramos Otero, the story is a meditation on death. The narrator remembers two occasions in which he had near-death experiences: a failed suicide attempt in New York in 1969,[69] and an accident in Old San Juan in a crumbling building.[70] He also remembers his arrival to New York City: "it had been exactly fifteen years and four days ago that he had arrived in New York, not knowing a soul, in the midst of a huge snowstorm" (*Página en blanco* 74). A simple calculation shows that this would be December 27, 1968, which coincides with Ramos Otero's arrival.[71] The narrator also mentions that he worked in the Bronx with poor Puerto Ricans and African Americans, becoming familiarized with their plight.

As part of the series of inversions that characterize this story, the writer will be dressed in clothes typically associated with Hollywood film-noir detectives, including a felt hat and raincoat, while the detective will wear clothes more suitable for a struggling gay Puerto Rican author who dresses like other urban gay men. Manuel's raincoat will resemble a kimono (a sign of exoticizing Orientalism or Latin American modernist — and queer — affectation), and he will also carry with him an umbrella; this image will appear on the cover of the book, a painting by Angel Rodríguez-Díaz that is unfortunately not identified as such and that (according to the artist) was used without his consent.[72]

Cover of *Página en blanco y staccato*, by Manuel Ramos Otero, 1987. Painting on cover by Angel Rodríguez-Díaz.

The presentation of the history of Sam Fat's parents is interesting in terms of how it shows the links established between disparate ethnic immigrant groups, even while these maintain fierce attachments to their land of origin. In other words, there is no contradiction for them to be proud of their heritage while simultaneously intermarrying with other groups, even while this might provoke some identity problems for their children. The presentation of these cultural amalgamations was already part of earlier stories by Ramos Otero (Puerto Ricans and Italian Americans in "The Story of the Woman of the Sea," for example) but to a much more limited extent; the intermingling is a fundamental element of "Vivir del cuento," of the Puerto Rican experience in Hawai'i, where Puerto Ricans come in close contact with Hawaiians and other groups such as Japanese, Portuguese, Filipinos, Spaniards, and Italians. Yet just as in the case of Monserrate Alvarez, there is often something that leads the Puerto Rican immigrant to search for his or her own, to look for a partner who shares the same ethnic background or memory of "back home."

It is interesting that, already in "Vivir del cuento," there is a discussion of what is considered a perhaps unfortunate but at times necessary assimilation into a new culture (Hawaiian in that case). This is certainly the case of Sam Fat, who is not culturally Chinese, has had only limited contact with Puerto Rican culture, and is nothing if not a true New Yorker: born and raised in the city, the product or result of a variety of ethnic and racial experiences, and an English speaker. The Lower East Side is to Sam Fat what Manatí was to Ramos Otero: the site of origin. This is especially the case, as Sam Fat is described as also being an artist (a poet, in fact), which brings him closer to the experience of other Nuyorican writers, although with an interesting twist: *chino latino* and gay.[73]

Sam Fat's father, Ting Yao Fat, is depicted as having come to the United States from Shanghai in 1948 as an opium smuggler, the same year as Ramos Otero's (and Juan Antonio Ramos's) birth. He wanted to go to Cuba, where he had relatives in the sizeable Chinese community of Havana.[74] Before embarking, however, he married Milagros Candelas, a Puerto Rican garment worker, mainly to gain American citizenship, although there seem to have been some genuine feelings of love between the two. The similarities between their two disparate migratory experiences and backgrounds are explained as follows:

> It is known that neither of the two had relatives in the city and that the need of a family is fundamental for Chinese culture as much as it is for Puerto Ricans.

> They moved to a small apartment on Suffolk Street, specifically to a block
> dominated by Chinese and Puerto Rican immigrants. (*Página en blanco* 75)

It is only on rare occasions that Chinese and Puerto Rican cultures are
compared; here we see how spatial contiguity has a great deal to do with
the contact between disparate groups.[75]

The death of both of Sam Fat's parents also reveals their links to their
homeland. In the case of the father, after he is murdered (most likely for
his criminal activities), the mother can recognize him only by the tattoo
of China on his chest: "por un tatuaje de la China que el cadáver tenía
en el mismo centro de su pecho" (*Página en blanco* 76). This is a rather
extreme metaphor for the way in which geography marks the body in
visible ways; it is especially valid, however, considering how racialization
works in the United States to mark and distinguish so-called minorities.
This is precisely the case of Sam Fat, who has black and Chinese features,
as racial prejudice in the Chinese, Puerto Rican, Anglo-American, and
African American communities will single him out as an oddity. There
is also the question of how, even though he is racially marked as being
Chinese and Puerto Rican (or rather, Afro-Diasporic), and thus singled
out as a person of color, he has no contact (in the case of the former) or
only very limited contact (in the case of the latter) with his cultures of
origin, and as such is most authentically American.

The characterization of Sam Fat is marked in the narration by the
paucity of his lines, which are all in a rather uncolloquial, standard,
yet also poetic English, as opposed to the Spanish of the short story;
they are mostly aphorisms, almost like fortune-cookie messages. This
only changes at the very end, when the focus of the narrator shifts from
Ramos to Fat; there is also a poem in English attributed to him. This
awkwardness (the lack of a convincing vernacular) is indicative of Ramos
Otero's general weakness at a practical — as opposed to critical or theoretical — level for the representation of Nuyorican subjects. While his
intentions may be the best, there is still something that Ramos Otero did
not quite master, even if only at the linguistic level, of Nuyorican experience; or perhaps we can see this as a purposeful resistance or refusal
to mimic and thus unduly appropriate Nuyorican language.[76]

Another element that is not clear is what it means for Sam Fat to
be Puerto Rican. We know that he is hesitant to embrace Santería, although he does go on to receive his *collares* (bead necklaces), the first
step in that religion's initiation. We also know that it was hard for him
while growing up in the context of the dramatic poverty of Loisaida

to believe his mother's recollections of Puerto Rico as an "earthly paradise," a common idealization and mythification of the homeland among first-generation immigrants. We do not know how Fat has processed experiences like his childhood and his trip to the island with his mother; very little of his interiority is offered in the story, quite contrary to the case of Monserrate Alvarez. In *Caribe Two Ways,* the literary critic Yolanda Martínez–San Miguel will suggest that Sam Fat presents a "postnational" subject position, in which his Puerto Ricanness is not the central referent, but rather only one among many sources of identity (366–70).

I would like to propose several possible readings or interpretations of the homosexual relationship portrayed in this story and how it serves to mediate the distance between first- and second-generation individuals. Just as in "The Story of the Woman of the Sea," where the immigrant experience is bridged at an individual rather than community level, "Blank Page and Staccato" offers a personal relationship between two gay Puerto Rican men as an approximation to surpass or negotiate a historical distance that, to this day, still causes enormous tensions. It is a similar gesture or strategy to that which another first-generation migrant cultural producer, Frances Negrón-Muntaner, will offer in her fiction/documentary film *Brincando el charco: Portrait of a Puerto Rican*: the relationship between Claudia Marín and her girlfriend Ana Hernández, which I will explore in chapter 4. It is also similar to that of Arturella and the *princeso* in Arthur Avilés's dance-play *Arturella,* which I will discuss in chapter 5. All of these are reminiscent of how romance stories between individuals from disparate communities have been used in Latin America as grounding metaphors for projects of national consolidation, as Doris Sommer has argued in her volume *Foundational Fictions.* Yet it is also profoundly different, as the second-generation man in Ramos Otero's story is charged by his family to effect a murder.

As I have commented, Sam Fat is initiated into sexuality through his teenage encounter with the idiosyncratic figure of the (much younger at the time) kimono-clad, umbrella-carrying writer, that is to say, the narrator/storyteller. After they have sex, the narrator comments: "For the first time, Sam Fat tasted the sea and knew what it was like to be an island" (*Página en blanco* 82–83). This is an important pronouncement, considering the enormous emphasis placed in Ramos Otero's work on the sea as a signifier of Puerto Rico and of displacement, a trait shared with the Cuban Reinaldo Arenas, who will also stress the links of his island of origin to the sea. The comment alludes metonymically to the salty taste of body fluids such as semen, sweat, and blood, which are possibly exchanged during sexual intercourse and also (metaphorically) to the fact that the writer was from the island of Puerto Rico. "Being an island," most likely an allusion to Víctor Fragoso's book of poems *Ser islas/Being Islands,*[77] could be read as a reference to a moment of simultaneous individuation and loss of boundaries experienced in orgasmic bliss, akin to what the French have referred to as *la petite mort,* or, conversely, to a moment of supreme dependence and a feeling of being exposed and vulnerable to the elements. It would seem, thus, that Sam Fat's search for a meaningful identity as Puerto Rican leads him (or his destiny fates him) to his sexual encounter with another Puerto Rican male, one who is actually from the island but whom he will kill. Fat's loss of virginity will open the door to his becoming a hustler or male prostitute as well as to the risks of sexually transmitted HIV infection. And although Sam Fat is portrayed as a masculine *bugarrón,* there is no mention in the story of his having sexual relations with women.

The discussion of Sam Fat's hustling in the Times Square area is relevant in terms of what it means for men to be involved with one another while simultaneously maintaining elements of Latin codes of masculinity; what it means to have sex for money; and perceptions of hustlers and "bisexual" men-who-have-sex-with-men as vectors for the transmission of HIV.[78] That scene will in fact emphasize a distinction of positionalities, in which a *bugarrón* does not "open" himself (make himself vulnerable) physically or emotionally to his partner, while being a *maricón* entails precisely that. Evidently, the exchange with the writer is characterized as one of *mariconería,* where meaningful interaction occurs. And it is this "openness" that has possibly left the writer with AIDS, visible through the lesions of Kaposi's sarcoma on his face. This is the significance of the play with Juan Antonio Ramos as the other writer, specifically given the associations of drug use and HIV transmission as a counterpoint to Ramos Otero's homosexual (and drug) HIV links; Ramos Otero already knew of his HIV-positive status when he wrote this story.

As I mentioned earlier, "Blank Page and Staccato" is structured around the fulfillment of vengeance for a previous act of violence, the sixteenth-century burning of a diasporic African woman for her religious beliefs. This originating violence can be seen as that of institutionalized, dominant authorities against popular, minoritarian practices. The denouement of the story places the body of the homosexual Manuel Ramos as the sacrificial lamb that will pay for this aggression. What is ironic, of course, is that the individual who suffers this violence is also a victim of societal oppression and persecution. This explains Sam Fat's apprehension in carrying out his preordained role, one that he has been thrust into by his destiny.[79] It also makes his murder (which is never described in the story) potentially redundant (or was the "murder" the simple act of having potentially unprotected sex?), and at the very least quite complex: to kill a man who is about to die of an at-the-time (and still today) incurable illness can be seen as an act of euthanasia, with all of the mixed messages that this entails.

The punishment in this story, rather than fulfilling the "eye for an eye" paradigm it was initially presented as, draws a parallel between the oppression of Africans in the Americas and the suffering caused both by AIDS as an illness and even more, by the social stigma attached to the disease and by the severe lack of compassion and support for individuals who are struggling with it, such as homosexuals and intravenous drug users. Of course, as Cindy Patton and Paul Farmer have made evidently clear, 1980s U.S. discourses about the "origins" of AIDS frequently tied the epidemic to Haiti and Africa; as such, blackness, homosexuality, and drug use all share a stigmatized and pathologized status that is undermined or negotiated in the story. Ultimately, the unintended or willing "sacrifice" of the island-born, first-generation white migrant serves as a form of redemption for the complicity of island elites epitomized in the figure of the ultimate patriarch, Governor Luis Muñoz Marín, who promoted massive migration as a "solution" to the island's problems with poverty and so-called "overpopulation" and the U.S. need for cheap labor in the post–World War II period. Ramos Otero's narrator becomes the sacrificial lamb to appease, perhaps, in part, the anger expressed by Nuyorican poets such as Tato Laviera in his poem "against muñoz pamphleteering":

> and i looked into the dawn
> inside the bread of land and liberty
> to find a hollow sepulchre of words...
>
> your sense of
> stars landed me in a
> north temperate uprooted zone.
> (*La Carreta Made a U-Turn* 29)

As such, we could see this story as a case of what Juan Flores has called "The Diaspora Strikes Back," of the black, racially mixed,

English-speaking diaspora literally "killing" — in a parricidal gesture — Spanish-language island whiteness: a gesture that the literary critic Lisa Sánchez González will reproduce in her own *Boricua Literature* (against Juan Flores, of all people) in her effort to establish the autonomy of Nuyorican letters and culture in the United States.

Coda: Mirrorings of Caribbean Exilic Love in "Descuento" and *Invitación al polvo*

As I mentioned earlier, "Descuento" (the last story of *Blank Page and Staccato*) and *Invitation to the Dust* present gay relationships that are relevant to our discussion because they present first-generation, gay Puerto Rican migrant subject narrator/protagonists or poetic voices involved with another Spanish-speaking gay Puerto Rican migrant (in the first) and with a bisexual Cuban exiled man (in the second); both relationships are located in New York City, but have important links to the imaginary (symbolic) and real space of the Caribbean. "Descuento" engages in a forthright depiction of the physical and emotional violence that can occur in relationships, particularly during their demise; it is a metacritical text that attempts to "untell" rather than tell, in a literary game inspired by the Argentine Jorge Luis Borges. The poems in *Invitation to the Dust,* specifically in its first part "De polvo enamorado" (Of Dust in Love), also present a "narrative" of sorts, and are illustrative of the diverse feelings that mark a relationship; the poet portrays both the happiness and intimacy that made it relevant and the painful separation produced by the loved one's unwillingness to accept the reality of his "deviant" homosexual attraction. Both of these works are marked by strong autobiographical referents to previous lovers, specifically to Angel Rodríguez-Díaz (in "Descuento") and to a Cuban man identified as "José" (in "De polvo enamorado"). This autobiographical project extends the practice noticed in "The Story of the Woman of the Sea," based on a real relationship with a man called Angelo.

"Descuento" is a first-person narration that explores the translocal dimensions of the storyteller's life (his physical and emotional split between Puerto Rico and New York) in the early 1980s, specifically, the period between 1982 and 1984. In this story, Puerto Rico is portrayed as the place of origins and family, where friends live, where one gets source material and goes for holidays: the place of memory and childhood. New York, on the other hand, is the space of adult life, of work, of lovers, of present reality, and of the travails of a relatively poor writer struggling to make ends meet. Both are profoundly interlinked and occupy equal weight in the artist's experience and worldview, even if most of his time is spent in New York. Puerto Rico is a living presence through constant phone calls and letters he receives from friends, in addition to repeated visits.

One of the interesting aspects of "Descuento" is the particularity of the protagonist's relationship with a fellow Puerto Rican artist, a situation that allows for a symbiotic creative exchange or collaboration, a sort of feeding off each other's talents and inspiration. Also noticeable is the intimacy brought about by their common shared background, as both characters are island-born, gay Puerto Rican artists in New York, although there is still a noticeable age difference of seven years between the two. Furthermore, the story is about the dissolution or failure of the relationship, its coming apart (similar to "The Story of the Woman of the Sea"). There is much more emphasis on the pain and problems than on the joyful moments they spent together, or at the very least the pleasure is always mediated by the suffering of loss. The tone is not quite of resentment or anger, but rather of a later moment of reflection. The relationship spanned the period in which the storyteller wrote the first four stories of the book, and also included the painting of the image on the cover (a stylized portrait of the writer wearing a kimono), which the narrator deconstructs ekphrastically.[80]

This story is important for the metacritical comment it makes about Ramos Otero's written production, and his slippage between narrator/character and author is useful to understand the argument posited earlier in this chapter regarding a similar phenomenon in the essay on Luis Cernuda. There is also a fascinating discussion in "Descuento" of other authors such as Jorge Luis Borges and Truman Capote, on the nature of writing, on fiction, and on the relationship of different literary genres to each other. In fact, this story builds upon a poem by Víctor Fragoso — "El regreso de las tortugas" (The Return of the turtles), quoted in part — on the precarious nature of the reproduction of sea turtles and all of the deadly threats the newly hatched face in their journey from the beach to the sea; it also incorporates a poem: "Apartamiento vasto" (Vast apartment, or distancing).

"Descuento" is a meditation on death, dissolution, and change. The narrator provocatively names his story an "untelling" rather than a "telling," as he is going to focus on loss and endings: the death of several of his cats, of the sea turtles mentioned in Fragoso's poem, of several of his favorite authors including Julio Cortázar or friends who are authors

(John Anthes, Fragoso himself), and the end of his relationship with his lover, referred to as *el amante* in the story and "the Angel" in a poem included in the text. The story in fact reconstructs the relationship from a position of its inevitable demise, a somewhat overdetermined telling in which the end of the story has already been told, and as such we are simply learning its prehistory. This backward telling allows for a profound deepening of our knowledge primarily of the storyteller and of the book we have just read, since the narrator metacritically comments on the four preceding stories, but also on the relationship. That is to say, we learn about it from the perspective of its end, disrupting the more traditional narrative structure where suspense is based on learning the conclusion, especially the "happy ending." In a sense, this would seem more like a detective story in which we already know the crime and the culprit but are learning about the process that led to a specific denouement. And of course, there is always a suggestion of possible rapprochement, of the reconciliation or the reestablishing of ties between the storyteller and his ex-lover. Here the meaning of friendship as part of and as opposed to boyfriends is also fundamental. There is also a fascinating discussion of his numerous female friends, including Margarita and Malvaloca in Puerto Rico and La Corsa and Cucumber Annie in New York.

Invitation to the Dust, Ramos Otero's second book of poems, appeared posthumously; it offers us a different view on Caribbean same-sex male love. The book's cover has a photograph of the author standing behind and embracing a statue of an angel in a cemetery in Manatí, while a young, slightly chubby boy stands behind him to his left, his crotch pressed sideways into a cross. The title of the book and the photo suggest that the word *polvo* (dust) is a reference to death, yet the provocative pose of the poet (as if "fornicating" with the statue — *dándole chino*) refers to the second meaning of the word *polvo* (sperm) and to the sexual possibilities of reading the title as a double entendre.[81]

"Dust in Love," the first section of *Invitación al polvo* (also a reference to the Spanish Golden Age poet Francisco de Quevedo, as indicated in an epigraph), is a set of twenty-nine interlinked, untitled poems identified by numbers. These focus on the complexities of a relationship between the poet (a gay-identified, exiled Puerto Rican poetic voice) and an exiled Cuban house painter called José, who does not self-identify as gay, drinks excessively, is either married or in a relationship with a woman, and has several children. The poetic suite explores the rise and fall of the relationship; the early notice of separation in poem #2 serves to indicate

 Biblioteca de Autores de Puerto Rico

INVITACION AL POLVO

Manuel Ramos Otero

Plaza Mayor

Cover of *Invitación al polvo*, by Manuel Ramos Otero, 1992. Cover photograph by Doel Vázquez.

the similarity of this sequence to "Descuento," although there are also poems that celebrate the intensity of the relationship, specifically in its sexual/corporeal dimensions. Poem #10 ("Tus manos José") is especially moving in its incantatory enumeration of the loved one's body parts (hands, fingers, arms, shoulders, eyes, and hair), which then lead the poetic speaker to offer his own body (and fragmented or deconstructed body parts) back in return (*Invitación al polvo* 19).

Two elements stand out in "Dust in Love": one, the particularities of the Hispanic Caribbean (Cuban/Puerto Rican) bond; the other, the poetic subject's struggle to challenge and transform the loved one, to instill in him a sense of the validity of same-sex love, of transgressing dominant social norms regarding love.[82] The poet becomes quite frustrated at his lack of success, combined with his pain at the dissolution of the relationship. By the end of the poetic sequence (poem #29), the speaker shows a less passionate (less angry) and more moderated or calm poetic tone, and reflects on the experience as a whole.

These poems are notable in their development or expansion of the topic of shared Caribbeanness, especially in relation to Cuba and Puerto Rico; as the poetic voice states, "Cuba and Puerto Rico are / the two ephemeral wings of the angel of love" (*Invitación al polvo* 9). This comparison points to a similarity in the experience of exile, of being from a tropical island country with an indigenous past and Afro-European (creole, *mulato*) present, with a tradition of romantic bolero music and the linguistic commonality of the Spanish language and a shared love for poetry. In fact, José will memorize and recite the compositions that his poet lover writes. These similarities, which unite the men and would seem to make them a perfect match, are nevertheless insufficient; or rather, it is precisely the legacy of sexist, homophobic prejudice from those islands — maintained in exile by José — that limits the relationship, although one could argue that José's "traditional" masculinity is precisely one of the attractions, and as such, the relationship is a negotiation of contradictions. The poetic speaker will paint a pathetic portrait of José as an alcoholic and will address his working-class status in different ways. Several of the most notable poems will stress the commonalities between different forms of oppression: that experienced due to class, race (blackness), gender (women), and sexuality (see especially #5 and #8); poem #18 will celebrate the strength of female friends of the poet whom he calls "witches" (Australia Marte, Lesbia López, and Carmen Sánchez), similar to the invocation of female friends in "Descuento." In the depiction of José, we can also see interesting parallels, highlighted by the poetic speaker himself, with Angelo, the working-class Italian-American from New Jersey who appeared in "The Story of the Woman of the Sea"; in fact, in poem #29 there will be a listing of the poet's four main relationships: John [Anthes], Angelo, Angel [Rodríguez-Díaz], and José.

The poems in this sequence include some of the most direct, straightforward defenses of same-sex love in all of Ramos Otero's work. In poem #25 ("Habrá quien diga, corazón, que nuestro amor") the poet systematically goes over diverse forms or sources of oppression (family, the psychiatric establishment, the church) and outlines options for response: martyrdom, silence, hiding, death, or liberty. The poetic speaker will ultimately claim liberty in his defense of men's right to same-sex relationships. The words "gay" or "homosexual" never appear in these poems, but rather vernacular, highly specific terms such as *pato, pájaro,* and *bugarrón,* which serve to insist on the cultural specificity of the discussion and also present this type of liberation as an intrinsically Caribbean possibility, not one "imposed" from above by the dominant Anglo society. Interestingly, there is no mention of AIDS in these poems. This is in great contrast to the short stories discussed previously and to the poems in the next section of *Invitation to the Dust,* "La víspera del polvo" (The eve of dust), which are to a great extent mostly focused on the poet's HIV diagnosis and his poetic engagement with this news.

A sweeping, panoramic analysis of the short stories and poems of Ramos Otero in the context of his own critical writing about another gay exiled poet (Luis Cernuda) and of his fictional reflections on other authors, especially the poet Julia de Burgos, allows us to see the evolution or transformations of Ramos Otero's thoughts and the multiple ways he sought to articulate his vision. By highlighting a self-referential, autobiographical "mask" or "persona" in his fiction, nonfiction, and poetry, Ramos Otero constructs a highly stylized, particular, yet striking image of a displaced, exiled gay Puerto Rican man in New York. Much as in Gloria Anzaldúa's *Borderlands/La frontera,* Ramos Otero uses a variety of genres to convey his readings of Puerto Rican, Hispanic and world literature: to comment on or pay homage to those authors he admires, and to criticize those from whom he wishes to disassociate himself.

By reading Ramos Otero's production in chronological sequence, as a temporal progression, following the model proposed by Juan G. Gelpí and Arnaldo Cruz-Malavé, we are able to see a distinct development and change in perceptions and relationship to Puerto Rico and the United

States. Ramos Otero is a fundamental Puerto Rican and Nuyorican/DiaspoRican writer, in spite or because of himself — what Juan Flores has called a "bridge." And much like the contributors and editors of Gloria Anzaldúa and Cherríe Moraga's *This Bridge Called My Back* or those of Ruth Behar's *Bridges to Cuba,* Ramos Otero physically places his body (of writing, of flesh and bone) as a space of encounter.

Chapter 3

Women's Bodies, Lesbian Passions

> Like the majority of Puerto Rican gay
> and lesbian writers in the U.S.A., I left
> because of persecutions — even from the
> police — for my sexual preference.
> — Luzma Umpierre,
> interview with Marie José Fortis

AT TIMES lesbian women have found Puerto Rico to be a place of intolerance or of limited opportunities and have migrated elsewhere as a form of liberation or escape. This is very much the case of Luz María Umpierre, a groundbreaking poet, scholar, and human rights activist, who left the island in 1974 and has lived in the United States ever since.[1] The analysis of her life and work, especially of her production from the 1970s and 1980s, can offer us valuable insights as to what might be some of the particularities of queer Puerto Rican women's migratory experience, and how these experiences change according to historical moment and general social trends. Umpierre's production is in many ways a reflection of the times she wrote in and of the dominant strands of feminist and nationalist Puerto Rican politics that were articulated in the 1970s and 1980s and that she helped to define but also challenged and rewrote. The author forms part of a strong and very vocal feminist movement, one that had very diverse ideas about the best solutions to women's problems, including empowerment, recognition, validation, willful scandal, transgression, the violation of taboos, or even (for some women) lesbian separatism; this movement was also profoundly divided along racial, ethnic, and class lines. One of the main arguments I will advance is that Umpierre's poetry and scholarship were fundamental to the growth and consolidation of U.S. Latina feminism, even if her role has not been fully recognized in current accounts of this field.

Like other diasporic Puerto Rican lesbian poets and writers of her generation, such as Nemir Matos-Cintrón and to a more limited extent Carmen de Monteflores and Luisita López Torregrosa, Umpierre brings together feminist literary and political affirmation and a celebration and profound exploration of women's bodies and relationships.[2] In her work we are made aware of the particularities and symbolic meanings of women's corporeal experiences and body processes such as menstruation and lactation, as well as of the complexities of women's spiritual and carnal love for each other. For Umpierre, the body is central as a source of meaning and power; as she has stated, "We have to be bold, daring with our ideas; writing from our ovaries, from our intestines, from our fallopian tubes, from our pubic hair, from our clitoris, from our vulva. If Freud said we had 'penis envy,' we have to show *him* that he had vulva envy" (interview with Fortis, 58). As this quote indicates, the poet is quite willing to be graphic, but also maintains a sense of humor. Umpierre's work is an acknowledgement but also a lament of the situation of women generally conceived and especially of lesbian experience; it is a rallying call, for women to come together, but it is also a profoundly personal, intimate description of one woman's life. Her writings also give us privileged access to the particularities of Puerto Rican women's diasporic experience, which have to do with the specificities of their bodies, language and identity, and with the fact that in addition to racism and homophobia, they have to deal with misogyny and patriarchal, antifemale prejudice.

Some of the most striking features of Umpierre's work are the strength of her poetic voice, the great struggles she has overcome, the pain of her solitude, her commitment to social justice, and the intensity of her passions and desires. She has been marginalized and is at the same time a Puerto Rican/Latina everywoman: a subject searching for physical, emotional, spiritual, intellectual, and political plenitude through love and intellectual pursuits; through nationalist affirmation in the face of heterosexist colonial oppression; through poetry and words. Umpierre reminds all of us of the power of literature as a tool to effect social change and achieve personal growth; she believes in the magic and potentiality of poetry and encourages her readers (who are generally envisioned as women) to join her and partake of that aesthetic revolution.

On the Difficulties of Being
a Diasporic Puerto Rican Lesbian

Like other diasporic Puerto Rican lesbian women in the 1970s and 1980s, Umpierre did not initially disclose her sexuality; instead, she chose to focus on issues of community poverty, discrimination, and the condition of women and did not fully "come out" in print until 1987. This reticence can be seen as directly tied to the homophobic views of the diasporic Puerto Rican community, which do not differ much from island views, as well as to generalized homophobia in mainstream American society. Umpierre's experience is very similar to that of the Nuyorican community leader and educator Antonia Pantoja, the founder of the youth enrichment and advocacy program ASPIRA and cofounder of the National Puerto Rican Forum and the Puerto Rican Association for Community Affairs (PRACA), who was also born in Puerto Rico, came to the United States as a twenty-two-year-old in 1944, received the Presidential Medal of Freedom from President Bill Clinton in 1996, and came out only in 2002, shortly before her death at age eighty.[3] Pantoja's 2002 autobiography, published under the title *Memoirs of a Visionary* by Arte Público Press, refers to her nearly three-decades long relationship with the African American educator Wilhelmina (Mina) Perry, mostly in relation to their professional collaborations and not to their romantic life. Even near the end of her life, Pantoja felt the tension that full disclosure of her personal affairs would have of people's reception of her legacy.

An opposite example is that of the sociologist and university professor Juanita Díaz-Cotto, a well-known, and highly respected scholar, writer, and activist, who has used the pseudonym of Juanita Ramos when engaged with issues of lesbian visibility, specifically with the publication of her groundbreaking anthology *Compañeras: Latina Lesbians* (1987), which is now in its third expanded edition (2004).[4] In this case, Díaz-Cotto (or, as she is known by many, Ramos) has led a strikingly public life as a visible Puerto Rican lesbian leader and intellectual, but using a name that would not compromise her family. The community activist Carmen Vázquez, the politician Margarita López, the scholars Hilda Hidalgo and Iris M. Zavala, the research scientist Angela Pattatucci-Aragón, and the musicians Avotja, María Cora, and Lourdes Pérez are some additional examples of highly visible, openly lesbian diasporic Puerto Rican women.[5] The processes by which these women came out and became well-known and recognized varies greatly and often reveals the complexities of contemporary American culture.

It is clear, however, that the strategic silencing and reticence that marked Umpierre's and Pantoja's lives have actually been quite common among the lesbians who came of age during this period, not to mention those who came before. They correspond in interesting ways to a pattern Hilda Hidalgo and Elia Hidalgo Christensen noted in their pioneering study on diasporic Puerto Rican lesbians published in 1977, that is to say, a lesbian generational divide in which older women did not disclose their sexuality as a means to insure that they could be fully involved in Puerto Rican community issues, while younger women were more willing to come out but maintained a more strained, distant relationship with their ethno-national community.[6] According to Hidalgo and Hidalgo Christensen, many lesbians in positions of leadership within the Puerto Rican community stayed in the closet for fear of jeopardizing their community ties and careers. The opposite happened for younger women:

> Although lesbians [18–25 years of age] make periodic attempts to keep in touch with the Puerto Rican community through participation in political and cultural activities, the Puerto Rican community is not the center of their social life. They said that the reason they do not become more involved with the larger Puerto Rican community is their fear of rejection and/or censure. Puerto Rican lesbians over thirty are more closely tied to the community — often having a position of leadership; however, they carefully guard their identity as lesbians, and many are married and live a double life. ("The Puerto Rican Lesbian" 116)

These types of negotiations occur in the polarized context also described by Oliva Espín in her research, where she shows how immigrant communities often prefer to believe that homosexuality and lesbianism are foreign concepts and not part of their culture.

More recent scholarship on the 1970s and the 1980s and activist-generated oral histories and anthology projects such as Ramos's *Compañeras* and Ana Irma Rivera Lassén and Elizabeth Crespo Kebler's *Documentos del feminismo en Puerto Rico: Facsímiles de la historia* (2001) have highlighted general social transformations as well as Puerto Rican lesbians' involvement in LGBT activism and in the feminist and women's movement on the island and in the diaspora;[7] the situation described by Hidalgo and Hidalgo Christensen and by Espín changed for the better in the 1990s and 2000s but has still not been totally resolved.

Luz María Umpierre's biography and poetic corpus are marked by constant movement and physical displacement similar to that of Antonia Pantoja and Juanita Ramos, by a general sense of being unmoored, of "carrying home on her back," to loosely paraphrase Gloria Anzaldúa, while also violating many social taboos, preestablished orders, and conventions.[8] Umpierre's work is riddled with images of dislocation, moving across the Atlantic (from Puerto Rico to the United States, from the United States to France) and within North and Central America (Pennsylvania, New Jersey, Kansas, Ohio, New York, Costa Rica); the poet has also lived in Kentucky and presently resides in Maine. The nomadological quality of her work becomes especially acute as we read her fifth book of poetry, *For Christine* (1995), in which she talks about being institutionalized for Post Traumatic Stress Disorder as well as becoming homeless and living in her car. Poems such as "Cruising" (in *Y otras desgracias*) further highlight the sexual implications of these displacements.

1970s Arrival and 1980s Disclosure: Shifts in Umpierre's Poetics

In her groundbreaking volume *Lesbian Voices from Latin America* (1996), Elena M. Martínez discusses how Luz María Umpierre's coming to consciousness as a lesbian woman and her public disclosure of this through her poetry correspond to very specific developments in lesbian-of-color feminism, especially during the 1980s, defined by the work of women such as Gloria Anzaldúa, Cherríe Moraga, Audre Lorde, and Cheryl Clarke. Umpierre's immigrant experience was fraught with many of the difficulties that other Puerto Ricans (especially women) have also experienced, which she vividly portrays and denounces.[9] A comparison of Umpierre's work to that of other Puerto Rican lesbian/feminist women, for example the oral histories and personal essays collected by Ramos, can also be profoundly revealing, as *Compañeras* is a book that shares much with Umpierre's positioning in terms of what we can identify as second-wave feminism.[10] In general, most criticism on Umpierre partakes of some form of gynocritical or female-centered analysis, locating her work with Latin American, Latina, or U.S. women-of-color feminist women's writing and activist traditions, and/or studying her linguistic dexterity; the poet has received a considerable amount of critical attention, mostly from Latina, feminist, and queer scholars, and the bibliography on her work is quite extensive. In spite of this U.S. academic recognition, most experts on Puerto Rican literature neglect her work; she is often not included in leading anthologies; and most Puerto Ricans (and many Latinas/os) are unaware of her existence. I would like to propose an expansion of the rich feminist critical project that has validated her poetry and work toward integrating this analysis into general discussions of Puerto Rican (and Latina/o) literature and culture.

Umpierre shares important commonalities with other first-generation 1970s and 1980s queer diasporic writers such as Manuel Ramos Otero (the focus of the previous chapter), starting with the closeness of their dates of birth (Umpierre, 1947; Ramos Otero, 1948) and the fact that they both migrated in their twenties (he was twenty; she, twenty-seven), after completing undergraduate university studies in Puerto Rico (and an M.A., in Umpierre's case), although Ramos Otero's migration to New York (1968) preceded Umpierre's move to Philadelphia (1974) by more than five years. In their work, albeit in very different ways, both explore the experiences of migrants who confront traditional Puerto Rican values and foreign realities in the United States; as Betsy A. Sandlin has carefully explored, both identify themselves profoundly with the life and work of Julia de Burgos, another Puerto Rican migrant writer, who died destitute on the streets on New York in 1953 but whose poetic corpus is considered one of the most important contributions to Puerto Rican letters.[11] Ramos Otero and Umpierre were (and Umpierre continues to be) poets and scholars, and their literary scholarship can be seen as a parallel endeavor to their creative work; just as Ramos Otero honors the Spanish poet Luis Cernuda, Umpierre analyzes and explores the production of Puerto Rican women poets in the Diaspora, most notably Julia de Burgos, Lorraine Sutton, and the Nuyorican/Dominican poet Sandra María Esteves, who are her ideological peers, as well as other authors, such as Pedro Juan Soto, Rosario Ferré, Iris Zavala, Myrna Casas, Marjorie Agosín, Manuel Puig, and Isabel Allende.[12] She also elaborates poetic dialogues with or pays homage to deceased, subversive Puerto Rican writers such as the gay poet Víctor Fragoso (who died of AIDS) and to a rather extensive number of U.S. and Latin American women such as Sor Juana Inés de la Cruz, Julia Alvarez, Marge Piercy, and Ana Castillo, in addition to interviewing writers such as Cherríe Moraga. Umpierre has also engaged in well-known polemics with Esteves (another poet who closely identifies with Julia de Burgos), most notably in the celebrated "María Christina" poetic exchange. Perhaps the biggest difference between Ramos Otero and Umpierre is their initial geographic location in the United States (New York as opposed to Philadelphia); their relationship to the English language and to the Puerto Rican diasporic community, a situation most likely linked to the fact that Umpierre's mother was a return migrant to Puerto Rico, having spent a considerable amount of time in New York (from the ages of five to twenty-three); and the fact that Ramos Otero died of AIDS-related causes before completing his Ph.D.

Umpierre's exploration of immigrant experience occurs through her poetry, in which she freely switches from Spanish to English; in her work, we see a progression from initial engagement with the diasporic Puerto Rican community in Philadelphia and with general feminist issues to a later explicit acknowledgement of her lesbianism. Her work engages with the experience of the Puerto Rican community in the United States but also addresses gender-specific issues, arguing forcefully for female emancipation and empowerment. It is also a ferocious denunciation of the prejudice and stigma attached to lesbianism and to mental illness.

Umpierre's arrival in Philadelphia, where she came to pursue graduate studies in Hispanic literature at Bryn Mawr College, is significant given that, as Carmen Whalen reminds us in *From Puerto Rico to Philadelphia,* by the 1970s there was already a large, historically significant Puerto Rican population with severe social problems in this city.[13] Other scholars, such as Marc Stein in his *City of Sisterly and Brotherly Love: Lesbian and Gay Philadelphia, 1945–1972,* have emphasized the particularities of this city as a site of an active (albeit predominantly white, but also African American) lesbian and gay community in the years previous to Umpierre's arrival; in fact, Umpierre will pitilessly mock the city's moniker of "Brotherly Love" for its hypocrisy. Nevertheless, Philadelphia is a fascinating and important location to observe the intersection of Umpierre's ethno-national and sexual identities, especially as this city will also be of great importance to other queer Puerto Rican women such as Frances Negrón-Muntaner and Erika López, whom I will discuss in the next chapter.

A reading of Umpierre's work in chronological order reveals significant shifts in her thematic concerns, style, and language use, although her interest and defense of women's autonomy and of feminist values and her identification as a Puerto Rican and Latina writer is constant. She has, to date, five books of poetry, in addition to numerous critical and autobiographical essays, some published in book form. Her literary production includes *Una puertorriqueña en Penna* (A Puerto Rican in Penna, 1979), whose title plays with the traditional abbreviation for Pennsylvania (Penna.) and the Spanish word for suffering or pain (*pena*); *En el país de las maravillas (Kempis puertorriqueño)* (In wonderland [Puerto Rican Kempis], 1982); *... Y otras desgracias/And Other Misfortunes...*

(1985), a book that signals a transitional period in terms of language use and sexuality; her dramatic coming out volume *The Margarita Poems* (1987); and *For Christine* (1995). The first three books have names that indicate pain or disgrace/misfortune or that allude to it in an ironic manner, while the fourth and fifth books are dedicated to specific women, either objects of her affection or good friends/professionals who have helped her in different ways.

How is migratory experience articulated in Umpierre's work? It can be argued that her poetic corpus reflects at least three stages of migratory/lesbian experience. At first, the shock of migration is initially felt and articulated through issues of language prestige (as Puerto Rican Spanish is frowned upon by Americans who favor Castilian), culture shock (Puerto Rican versus American culture), and an acute awareness of class difference and the differential treatment that results from elitist, anti-working-class prejudice, specifically in the context of her situation as a graduate student at Bryn Mawr; this poetry is predominantly in Spanish. Umpierre expresses immediate solidarity with the Puerto Rican working-class immigrant community of Philadelphia and her work enacts a denunciation of social oppression, as well as a phonetic reproduction and exploration of linguistic practices, including code-switching, and an articulation of a feminist positionality. Umpierre's verbal dexterity has been noted by critics such as Frances Aparicio, who locates the poet's work in relation to the broader project of Nuyorican aesthetics, as well as by Alma Simounet, who offers a nuanced political and linguistic analysis of Umpierre's poetics from the perspective of discourse analysis.[14]

The experience of migration provokes self-awareness and knowledge; as Umpierre describes in her prologue to *Una puertorriqueña en Penna*:

> When I stumbled into Philadelphia and Bryn Mawr College in 1974, as a graduate student who was leaving her homeland for the first time, I knew that something would change in my life. What I didn't know then and do now is that my stay in the city of "Brotherly Love," in the State of Liberty and the cradle of elitism would lead me to feel more Puerto Rican today than ever before. The situations I saw and those in which I was involved led me to believe, from a certain moment on, that I was going crazy. I decided to write what I was feeling with the double purpose of venting in that insensible microcosm and of desacralizing that environment. (3)[15]

As we can see, this is quite a dramatic contrast to the first reactions of Manuel Ramos Otero, who in fact did not address issues of the Puerto

Rican immigrant community until much later, and who had already started writing and publishing before he left the island. At the same time, and unlike Ramos Otero, there is no overt mention of issues of queer sexuality.

Several things are suggested by this prologue. First of all, for Umpierre, literature becomes a form of therapy, a way to survive, and also a way to transform or desacralize space around her and, thus, a weapon of resistance. Second, exile or migration produces acute awareness of nationality. Finally, oppressive conditions make the author feel a proximity to madness, a theme she will explore and develop throughout her entire poetic oeuvre. This link between poverty, oppression, and madness among Puerto Ricans in Philadelphia has been extensively explored by Patricia Gherovici in her volume *The Puerto Rican Syndrome,* where the Argentine Lacanian psychoanalyst discusses her therapeutic social work and clinical interventions in North Philadelphia and critiques colonialist medical models that pathologize colonized populations, something that Vilma Santiago-Ortiz and Caridad Souza have also done.[16] What this suggests is that Umpierre's observations and life experiences are hardly marginal or unusual, but rather a very unfortunate reality faced by many women in similar situations.

Umpierre's third book of poetry, ... *Y otras desgracias/And Other Misfortunes...,* marks a different stage of her production, a second moment signaled by a move toward more writing in English, although she will never stop writing in Spanish. ... *Y otras desgracias/And Other Misfortunes...* is evenly split in terms of language, as is indicated by the very title of the work. In this second stage of Umpierre's production we observe a continuation of her thematic concerns but still no open disclosure of lesbianism, except perhaps the somewhat veiled suggestion in poems such as "Transference," "Climax," and "Cruising," as Elena Martínez has observed,[17] or in others such as "Neoteny." For Martínez, the strategy followed by Umpierre seems closer to what Lillian Faderman has called "lesbian encoding," in other words, the practices through which lesbian writers veil their intent so as to make it decipherable only by a knowledgeable few. This strategy is perhaps akin to what Umpierre herself has called "lesbian tantalizing" in her analysis of Carmen Lugo Filippi's short story "Milagros, calle Mercurio" (Milagros, Mercury Street), although in that case it is not about covering up but rather about playing (consciously or unconsciously) with the ambiguity and polymorphous perversity of desire.[18] Nancy Mandlove's introduction to *Y otras desgracias* can also be seen as a coded declaration, in her description of Umpierre's work as a double-headed labrys (battle axe), a well-known lesbian symbol (ix). Reread after the publication of *The Margarita Poems,* several of these poems seem quite clearly Sapphic in their intent.

In broad terms, the thematic concerns of *Y otras desgracias* can be described as follows: a rejection of dominant models of femininity ("In Response," "Cuento sin hadas"); the conjuring of a community of female writers ("License Renewal," "Creation") as well as a homage to a deceased gay male poet ("Poema para Víctor"); madness and the destruction provoked or caused by poetry, or in the process of writing poetry ("Creation," "Miscelánea"); disillusionment with the United States, the struggle against racism, and the limitations of poetry to address or overcome these issues ("To a Beetle," "Y otras desgracias," "Poema para Víctor"); metapoetical writing; female sexuality and religion ("¿Sacrilegio?"); international politics ("A Rizos de Oro," "Justicia poética," "Monumento"); and lesbianism or female homosocial bonding.

Of all the poems in this volume, "In Response" is by far the best known. As its title indicates, it is a poem written as a reaction to another poem, "A la Mujer Borrinqueña" (To the Puerto Rican woman) by Sandra María Esteves, the best-known woman member of the 1970s Nuyorican Poets Café.[19] In Esteves's poem, the first-person poetic voice identifies herself as "Maria Christina," "a Puerto Rican woman born in el barrio," who goes on to pledge allegiance to her family and peers and to traditional female values such as motherhood, cooking, and caretaking, all on behalf of the well-being of her community. While Esteves's Maria Christina seems to accept dominant patriarchal impositions, she does see her role as revolutionary: as she says, "I am the mother of a new age of warriors"; she acknowledges being the product of racist and imperialist politics that have affected Africa and the Americas, and offers her resistance to these forms of abuse.

Umpierre's response to this poem takes "Maria Christina" and Esteves to task for what is perceived as acquiescing to patriarchal exploitation and abuse. In "In Response," the poetic voice proclaims:

> My name is not María Cristina.
> I am a Puerto Rican woman born in another barrio.
> Our men . . . they call me pushie
> for I speak without a forked tongue
> and I do fix the leaks in all faucets.
>
> (*Y otras desgracias,* 1)

The poetic voice goes on to openly challenge the legacy of men ("their ways / shed down from macho-men ancestors"); defends women's right to a free and unregimented sexuality outside of the control of men ("I sleep around whenever it is possible; / no permission needed from dearest *marido* / or kissing-loving papa"); and refuses traditional roles such as cooking ("I need not poison anyone's belly but my own; / no cooking mama here").

This nameless speaking subject identified as "not María Cristina," the poetic "I" that seems an authorial self-projection of Umpierre, affirms her independence and the difficult consequences her choices have implied, as a subject embroiled in a struggle against dominant norms. She refuses a specific kind of destructive or violent maternity ("I am not the mother of rapist warriors"), affirms being the survivor of childhood sexual abuse ("I am the child that was molested"), and also identifies herself as a teacher aged by life and experience, "who at 35 is 70." Challenging labels against her ("they call me bitchie"), she claims truth-telling ("I speak without a twisted tongue") as well as autonomy and manual dexterity ("I do fix all leaks in my faucets"). This last phrase can be seen as an oblique allusion to masturbation, yet Umpierre has stated that it is not a sexual metaphor but rather a reference to women's technical mastery and skills.[20]

Esteves and Umpierre's poetic debate has received considerable critical attention, and in fact entails an additional two poems: Esteves's "So Your Name Isn't María Cristina," part of *Bluestown Mockingbird Mambo* (1990) and Umpierre's "Musée D'Orsay," published in *For Christine* (1995). Yamila Azize Vargas, Asunción Horno Delgado, Elena M. Martínez, and Carmen S. Rivera are some of the women critics who have commented on the dynamics of this exchange, specifically on the first two poems.[21] There have also been attempts by male critics to interpret this exchange, at times with quite infelicitous results. In his notable misreading, William Luis focuses on the first three installments.[22] While attempting to understand the particularities of Puerto Rican women's experience in the United States, Luis makes significant factual errors (he ignores Umpierre's lesbianism, the fact of her upbringing in a marginal *barrio* in San Juan — *la veintiuna* — and Umpierre's mother's life experience in the United States) and carelessly dismisses the history of feminism in Puerto Rico, claiming that Umpierre's embrace of women's liberation is an American phenomenon that distances her from Hispanic culture.[23] Umpierre herself has criticized this misreading, also commenting on how people have insisted on her "animosity" against Esteves, when in fact the two women maintain a cordial relationship.[24]

The Margarita Poems (1987)

Umpierre's third stage, her radical, open disclosure of her lesbianism, occurs in her book *The Margarita Poems,* which has been described as a lesbian manifesto.[25] This collection is characterized by the free mixing of languages and by a desire, similar to that of Monique Wittig and U.S. Latina authors such as Gloria Anzaldúa and Cherríe Moraga, to find a language of her own, true to lesbian experience and to her political concerns (at least at that time): the independence of Puerto Rico.

This slim volume, widely heralded as Umpierre's most important book, begins with a dedication: "For Margaret and Julia," followed on a subsequent page by three epigraphs, which all allude in one way or another to *margaritas,* or daisies, be they flowers, alcoholic beverages, specific women, or works of art inspired by them, as in the case of Manuel Tavárez's classic nineteenth-century Puerto Rican *danza.*[26] Significantly, the last epigraph is by Julia de Burgos, from "Ruta de sangre al viento" (Blood route to the wind), a poem in her posthumous book *El mar y tú* (1954):

> Cuando ya no te acunen margaritas
> porque me van siguiendo,...
> ¿Con qué amor, amor mío, cuidarás de mis versos?
>
> When daisies no longer cradle you
> because they are following me...
> With what love, my love, will you care for my verses?

These lines suggest the links between romantic loss and flowers, portraying botanicals as the personified representation of comforting natural forces.

In her introductory essay "In Cycles," Umpierre will explain the conditions of production of this book and the multiple Julias and Margarets and Margaritas that inspire her verses (*Margarita Poems* 1–3). She clearly positions herself as part of a broader women-of-color and lesbian literary movement incorporating such figures as Audre Lorde and Cherríe Moraga — in fact, she states that the book is a response to Moraga's *Loving in the War Years: lo que nunca pasó por mis labios* (1983) — and also credits progressive female writers and poets such as Margaret Randall, Julia Alvarez, Julia de Burgos, and the Nuyorican Lorraine Sutton as sources of inspiration.[27] Umpierre emphasizes the physical and psychic spatial dimensions of the poems, their link to place and displacement: "Most of these poems were written in movement.... All the others were written in a different state of the mind" (2). Most importantly, she openly affirms that these are love poems dedicated to a woman or to women, and that she is willing to disclose "that which I had not uttered, and which was being used as a tool in my oppression" (1). As she says, "What I needed to verbalize is the fact that I am, among many other things, a Lesbian. Second, I wanted to communicate in some viable form with some One who came to represent all women in me" (1).

The author's essay is followed by three short critical essays by Julia Alvarez, Carlos Rodríguez-Matos, and Roger Platizky, which strategically serve to validate and locate Umpierre's work in the context of U.S. Latina women's writing, Puerto Rican and Hispanic literature, and the English-language poetic tradition. If we also consider Cheryl Clarke's and Marjorie Agosín's blurbs on the back cover and the imprimatur of Third Woman Press (a small, independent publishing house established and run by Chicana scholar Norma Alarcón), it becomes clear that this book's paratextual or framing apparatus seeks to establish its importance and validity and guard it against attacks in a quite hostile environment. This is not surprising for a number of complex and interrelated reasons having to do with controversial language use (Umpierre's mixing of Spanish and English poems and her code-switching), the location of poetry within the larger literary and scholarly market (one dominated by an emphasis on narrative and the essay), and the overwhelming discrimination against lesbians and diasporic Puerto Rican women. It can also be seen in the context of the delicate (some would say precarious) state of U.S. Puerto Rican and Latina/o Studies at that moment — 1987 — not to mention the incipient status of the field of Latina/o lesbian and gay studies and the personal attacks, harassment, and discrimination that Umpierre felt she was experiencing at her place of employment, Rutgers University, which led her to file an EEOC (Equal Employment Opportunity Commission) complaint against her employer.[28] Then again, the coincidence of the publication of Anzaldúa's *Borderlands/La frontera: The New Mestiza* and Ramos's *Compañeras: Latina Lesbians* all in the same year as *The Margarita Poems* (albeit all published by small, independent, feminist presses) signal the novelty and vitality of this literary and theoretical moment, one that closely followed from Anzaldúa and

Moraga's 1981 anthology *This Bridge Called My Back* and Moraga's *Loving in the War Years*. As I previously mentioned, Umpierre should be seen as a key (if often unacknowledged) participant and member of this historical moment in the development of Latina feminism.

The Margarita Poems consists of nine interrelated poems, although, as the poet clearly states in her introduction, "there are Margarita poems in my collection ... *Y otras desgracias / And Other Misfortunes...* which could be brought out here also" (2). For the sake of expediency, I will focus on six (all from *The Margarita Poems*): "Immanence," "Transcendence," "No Hatchet Job," "Madre," "Ceremonia Secreta," and "The Mar/Garita Poem." As is evident from their titles, some of these poems are in English while others are in Spanish; some, in fact, will mix both languages or are in the opposite language than the title would suggest. These poems will construct a very elaborate female poetic speaker and pose her in relation to the absent figure of the loved one, to a hostile, vicious, and violent world, and to a select number of allies who understand her and can participate in this poetic invocation, a ritual or process of mourning and of utopian dreaming. As Alvarez and Platizky indicate, these are quest poems centering on the poetic speaker's search for her loved one; yet, as I will contend, the poems ultimately transcend or displace the centrality of this relationship in a double movement, both inward (reconciliation with the self, masturbation, self-gratification) and outward (social transformation, the creation of a new society, of a sisterhood of empowered subjects who embrace political and social liberation).

This poetic journey begins in "Immanence" as the poetic speaker describes her physical displacement:

> I am crossing
> the MAD river in Ohio
> looking for Julia
> who is carrying me away
> in this desire. (16)

The next four stanzas will repeat this and other similar verses at their opening ("I am traversing," "I am transferring"), semianaphoras that locate the poetic speaker as a subject in transit and transformation. In the second stanza, we learn how the Mad River's name (an actual river located between Springfield and Dayton, Ohio) also serves to express the poetic speaker's inner feelings, specifically, her reaction to outward oppression, to the names and adjectives placed on her: "sinful, insane and senseless, / a prostitute, a whore, / a lesbian, a dyke" (16), all because of her love of another woman, and more specifically, for the "frantic / excitement for your / SEX," a sex that becomes "my Margarita, / my yellow margarita, / my glorious daisy," a set of verses that reappear throughout the poem as a refrain (16). In her enumeration of epithets, Umpierre follows Nemir Matos-Cintrón's earlier gesture in "Me robaron el cuerpo" (They stole my body, from the 1981 collection *Las mujeres no hablan así*), with the difference that in Matos-Cintrón's poem, it is the poetic speaker who rhetorically calls herself these terms:

> Yo Puta Sanjuanera
> Yo Monja Lesbiana
> Yo mujer estéril
> Yo Mujer Cero Población
> mujer de veinte hijos
> obrera mal pagada
> Me robaron el cuerpo
>
> I Whore of San Juan
> I Lesbian Nun
> I sterile woman
> Zero Population Woman
> woman of twenty children
> poorly paid worker
> They stole my body (4).

The first two stanzas of Umpierre's "Immanence" introduce some of the most important topics and poetic structures and devices that the writer will employ in her poetic suite. The poetic speaker struggles in her search for the loved one against a hostile environment, and the intensity of her passion defines her state of mind. There is a counterpoint as the invoked figure of Julia leads her desire for Margarita. The author's language play makes full use of the double bilingual valence of *margarita* / daisy as proper name and flower and extends the metaphor to the female body, specifically to the erotogenic zones (the vagina, the clitoris), partaking in a dominant trope engaged in by other queer artists such as Georgia O'Keeffe and Robert Mapplethorpe in their visual work and by 1970s lesbian feminists and poets. Julia, in turn, is the poetic entity brought forth in the third stanza by a wild, unrepressed Amazon-like female spirit that allows her this "transubstantiation / or arousal" (*The Margarita Poems* 16); the name Julia can also be seen as a homophonic stand-in for "jewels" as a reference to the sexual organs.[29]

It is fascinating to note that "immanence" in fact means "the state or quality of being indwelling or inward or of not going beyond a particular domain: inherence as the condition of being in the mind or experientially given; in Kantianism: the condition of being within the limits of possible experience — contrasted with *transcendence*" (Webster's). Umpierre's poem, in fact, suggests a double movement: one, that of the poetic speaker's physical displacement across a specific geography (Ohio); the other, an inward journey, an act of conjuring spirits in the mind, a type of magic or witchcraft that will bring Julia forth. The magic-ritual dimensions become apparent as the poetic speaker casts a spell or invocation referred to as an enchantment: "Come, Julia, come, / come unrestrained, / wild woman, / hilarious Julia, / come Julia come forth" (17).

Crossing the river (similar to Charon's crossing the river Styx) augurs a profound transformation. This "[bringing] my Julia forth" entails assuming or proclaiming a spiritual and poetical possession, as Julia is the embodiment of the "lesbian woman, / who'll masturbate and rule / over my body, Earth, / parting the waters / of my clitoral Queendom, / woman in lust, / who'll lose her mind / and gain her Self" (18). And once the poetic speaker crosses the river, she fully engages the double valence of Margarita as loved object/woman and as her own sex: "my margarita, / my carnal daisy / that buds between / my spread out legs" (18). The poem concludes with an appropriation of a lover's game: plucking petals to learn whether the loved one loves in return. In this case, it is a game of auto-eroticism in which the poetic speaker proclaims: "I touch my petals" and ultimately concludes: "I love me!" This loving of oneself entails the physical act of masturbation but also the spiritual/psychic coming to terms with a marginalized identity.[30]

The highly explicit character of this poetry and its celebration and open depiction of female sexuality, and specifically lesbian sexuality, is a landmark in U.S. Puerto Rican literature, comparable only to the verses of Nemir Matos-Cintrón, who in 1981 broke all dominant taboos in Puerto Rico with her own "scandalous" lesbian erotic verses, ones that also employ water and floral metaphors:

> Vuelo en las aletas de tu crica en pleamar
> al mar abatido en los acantilados de tu cuerpo
> Vuelo al origen del agua
> Vuelo en los pétalos de tu crica
>   a la flor de la caléndula.

I fly on the fins of your cunt at high tide
to the depressed sea in the cliffs of your body
I fly to the origin of water
I fly on the petals of your cunt
   to the flower of the calendula. (7)

This poem, illustrated by the Cuban/Puerto Rican artist Yolanda Fundora (who was Matos-Cintrón's lover at the time), forms part of their collaborative portfolio *Las mujeres no hablan así* (Women don't speak that way), and describes a similar voyage or journey, in this case "a la semilla / al ciclo secreto de la vida y la muerte" (to the seed / to the secret cycle of life and death), and eventually to all of the parts of the flower in a circular or cyclical process that seeks to engage with that which is eternal. In Matos-Cintrón's lyrical poem, the act of cunnilingus (or at the very least, of female same-sex eroticism) leads to an understanding of the most profound mysteries of nature. Fundora's monochrome illustration (a detail of a linoleum print entitled "El Sol y el Mar," 1979), is circular in nature, suggesting the folds of the vulva engulfed in the waves of the sea, which could also be the petals of a rose or some other flower. In this poem (a description of this vital sexual process), the communion of two women serves to achieve fullness, much in the way the poet's own collaboration with the visual artist whose image shares the same page allows for the joining of different registers and languages. And although Matos-Cintrón published this poem while living in Puerto Rico, it was after spending some time in the United States completing a master's degree at Syracuse University, which would suggest that her overseas experience was empowering; she soon after migrated and has been in the United States for more than twenty years, first in New York and now in Florida.

Umpierre's next poem, "Transcendence," is in Spanish in spite of its title. In fact, these two poems ("Immanence" and "Transcendence") serve as a portico to the collection, one in English and the other in Spanish. Both trace a route from Julia to Margarita. While the first described a journey through Ohio (what we could call a rural interstate crossing, that of Umpierre's displacement from Kansas to New Jersey), the second focuses on the urban sphere, most likely New York City, where the poetic speaker has gone (or rather, returned to) to undergo a profound ritual of transformation through abjection, a poetic simulation of Julia de Burgos's life, to be accomplished by walking. In contrast to the first poem's concluding physical gratification (masturbation), in this poem

El Sol y el Mar (detail), by Yolanda Fundora. www.yolandafundora.com. From Nemir Matos-Cintrón and Yolanda Fundora, *Las mujeres no hablan así*, 1981.

there is mortification of the body, as the female poetic speaker reenacts a Via Crucis of penance, allowing hostile natural and social forces to wreak havoc against her. This sacrifice is readily done as a means to ensure access to Margarita's sexuality.

"No Hatchet Job," the third poem in the collection, is once again in English, and in fact contains translated verses from the previous poem. Unlike the first two, however, this poem is in the third person and describes society's desire to domesticate and control or break down rebellious women's subjectivities:

> They would like
> to put the tick and flea collar
> around her neck and
> take her for walks on sunny afternoons
> in order to say to the neighbors:
> "We have domesticated this unruly woman." (21)

Other stanzas portray society's desire to step in and "cure" the frail (destroyed) remains of such a woman, to see her unkempt and dirty as a sign of society's victory over her, or to have her suffer from drug overdoses and eating disorders that can ultimately bring about her death. Once she is dead (and neutralized), society gladly celebrates her legacy and contribution.

In the last stanza of the poem, this oppressed woman is described as resisting her tormentor's oppression and engaging in an act of liberation:

> Eternally she breathes
> one line after next,
> unrestrained, unshielded
> willfully
> WRITER
> WOMAN. (22)

In this, as in other poems by Umpierre, we see the poet's use of capitalization as a means to emphasize her statements in a written (graphic) way, alluding to the resources a poet has in oral declamation to increase volume or tone while speaking. In fact, to witness Umpierre reciting these poems is an incredibly transformative experience, and reading them on the page barely offers a weak approximation to the strength and modulated rage expressed in her performance. In this sense, Umpierre's work is similar to that of her generational peer, the now deceased feminist Puerto Rican poet Angela María Dávila, author of *Animal fiero y tierno* (Fierce and tender animal, 1977), who also possessed a magnificent stage presence that complemented the raw force of her verses; Ramos Otero's dramatic readings of his poetry, with stage props, lights, and costumes, were also quite stunning, according to those who witnessed them.

"Madre" (Mother) is another poem in Spanish, an apostrophe to the poetic speaker's mother. This poem presents lesbian love as a recuperation of the mother's love and of female bonding, a theme that will reappear in Umpierre's "A Letter to Moira" in *For Christine* (32–38).[31] The poetic speaker did not drink from her mother's milk as a child and feels that this was the root of her later anorexia. Maturity leads her to seek contact with this lost substance through other women's bodies. The poem is full of sensory images and metaphors, as the poetic speaker describes voyages across human and geographic landscapes, engaging bodies that become flowers and topographic features. The speaker is led in an almost mad pursuit to satisfy this profound craving, which leads her to the most diverse of experiences. She finally finds satisfaction and completion (a return to the mother) in her union with Margarita:

> Y heme aquí hoy, madre
> intoxicada en jugos de Margarita,
> feliz, al fin, de conocerte
> y saborearte en este líquido rojo
> que escapa por mi piel.

> And here you have me today, mother
> intoxicated in the juices of Margarita,
> happy, at last, to meet you
> and taste you in this red liquid
> that escapes through my skin. (28–29)

This enigmatic ending suggests links between blood, milk, and vaginal secretions (a variation on the links between medieval humors), but also reminds us of the sweet nectar of flowers drunk by hummingbirds and butterflies; in fact, sucking this liquid (for example, from red *cruz de malta* and hibiscus) is a favorite pastime of children in Puerto Rico.

"Ceremonia secreta" (Secret ceremony), the next-to-last poem, is also in Spanish. This poem is an apostrophe to Margarita, who has fled; the poem describes the pain of separation and serves to set up the context for the last poem in the book, "The Mar/Garita Poem." In "Ceremonia secreta," the poetic speaker describes how she can't find Margarita and looks for her desperately in the kitchen (through cooking) and even by having sex with men, suggesting that Margarita, in addition to being an individual woman, can be imagined as a particular feeling of spiritual/physical plenitude. The poet goes on to describe the scene of her own death and the police inventory of her remaining possessions, similar to an earlier poem, "Miscelánea" (in *Y otras desgracias*), which mentioned a list of belongings of a dead woman in Kansas.

This search for Margarita leads the poetic speaker in the second stanza to look for her in her own body, through masturbation, screaming out Margarita's name at the moment of orgasm: "lo que llaman placer / y yo nombro soledad entre mis piernas" (what they call pleasure / and I call loneliness between my legs, 30). The speaker also looks for her outside and describes how she called her by masculine names to fool or confuse those around her, and so be the sole possessor of her real identity.

In the fifth stanza, the poetic speaker describes how she receives the help of other women who have known Margarita and who seek to intoxicate her (the poetic speaker) and make her forget, which she refuses to do. The poem then has a pause indicated by a single-word verse/stanza, indented and marked by parentheses:

(Pausa) (31),

a common strategy in many of the compositions; these serve as an extension of the notion of caesura, almost as if they were stage notes, with a more pronounced effect. The second part of the poem describes the "secret ceremony" indicated by the poem's title, as a witch shows up at the poetic speaker's door and tells her that she can recuperate Margarita through a spell (*un conjuro de palabras*). This entails *acertijos* (riddles) involving the letters *m* and *j* (most likely references to Margarita and Julia) and the eyes (that is to say, the participation or sympathy) of the reader, as well as the moon. The riddle entails a castle in Mexico as well as the figure of the renowned seventeenth-century Mexican nun and poet Sor Juana Inés de la Cruz. Widely admired for her baroque, highly philosophical poetic ruminations, her scientific inquiry, and her critique of dominant patriarchy (especially in her couplet "Hombres necios que acusáis... "), Sor Juana is described by some as a lesbian, as she wrote same-sex love poetry.[32] The nun poet is, in fact, an important Latin American precedent, and Umpierre will once again invoke her name in the last poem in the series. Umpierre's allusion to the castle and the moon can be seen as a reterritorialized, New World play on the Spanish mystic Santa Teresa de Jesús's *Las moradas del castillo interior* (*The Interior Castle*), or perhaps a reference to Sor Juana's most famous and complex poem, the *Primero Sueño*.[33] It can also be seen in relation to the Castillo de Chapultepec in Mexico City, invaded by the U.S. military during the 1846–48 Mexican American War, as well as a play on the name of the bisexual Chicana writer Ana Castillo, who in fact is mentioned in another poem in this collection, written as a brief memo to her from Sor Juana.[34] The final verses of "Ceremonia secreta" suggest that the secret ceremony begins as the reader proceeds to the next poem.

"The Mar/Garita Poem" concludes this collection and attempts to bring together and transcend the poetic motifs developed so far. There is an interesting shift in this poem, which is predominantly about language, female solidarity, and anticolonial politics: while up to now, "Margarita" has been a symbol of sexuality, genitals, and the loved one, in this poem, "Mar/Garita" becomes the symbol of an internal conflict as the world itself is deconstructed, and the poet proposes the alternate union of *mar* (sea) and *isla* (island), as well as *mar* and *luz* (light, but also a proper name in Spanish; in fact, the author's name; "mar," of course, being the first three letters of "María"; Luz Mar thus becomes a shortened version of her own name). The linguistic play of "Margarita" as a proper name and a flower (daisy) leads to a different type of gesture, one that operates within the realm of the *untranslatable,* as Yolanda Martínez–San Miguel has shown in reference to other Latina/o literary productions.[35] In fact, in this poem, female poetic language is explored as a form of liberty. There is a curious turn away from sexual emphasis toward one of national liberation, perhaps emulating the poetic turn from love to patriotism in Julia de Burgos's signature poem, "Río Grande de Loíza," as well as toward feminist sisterhood, notably among women writers. The poem is conceived as the "liberation of the muse," a process that entails an anticolonial mental process engaged during the diaspora, specifically in Edison, New Jersey.[36] The verses are also rich in allusions to classical Greek and Christian myths and stories, particularly the centrality of the Muse for artistic creation; the poet overcomes the pain of romantic separation by embracing poetry and anticolonial liberation struggles in a feminist context. In this sense, Umpierre embraces and exemplifies many of the dominant trends of post-1960 American women's poetry that Alicia Ostriker has identified in her critical volume *Stealing the Language* (1986), including experimentation and reclamation of language, the articulation of rage, declaration of affinity with the figure of the mother and of other women, erotic disclosure, and an engagement in myth-making. Here it is perhaps worthwhile to mention or reassert the influence and debt of Umpierre to white Anglo-American women writers such as Virginia Woolf, Adrienne Rich, Sylvia Plath, and Marge Piercy, as well as and especially to women-of-color poets such as Audre Lorde, Cheryl Clarke, and Cherríe Moraga.

Umpierre's "The Mar/garita Poem" begins with water onomatopoeia ("Glu, glu, glu, glu, glu"), a poetic device or verbal effect that can also be associated to the link between water and female sexuality, something extensively explored in the previous poems. The image is that of drowning, much as in Luis Rafael Sánchez's short story "¡Jum!" (see chapter 1), but is also reminiscent of birth, as in a fetus in the amniotic sac, which it has to break in order for birth to occur. The very next stanza ("Buried, cemented in, / 20 feet down / under the sea") describes female (or a woman's) language, imprisoned underwater; we soon learn it is that of the poetic speaker's Muse, held hostage by means associated in the popular imagination to the criminal underworld: "Two cinder blocks, / metal, cement, concrete, / 50 feet down / buried alive, / disconnected from Self the Muse/The Sea" (34–35). This imagery, as Elena Martínez has observed, serves to establish a dialogue with or allude to Adrienne Rich's well-known poem "Diving into the Wreck" (1973), as both portray women submerging themselves in the water in search of language and vision.[37]

In Umpierre's poem, the poetic speaker identifies herself as a poet distanced from her Muse, a Muse enslaved, destroyed by patriarchal and colonial oppression. As such, the poetic speaker seeks to resurrect her as if Lazarus conjured by an atheist: "How does one bring Lazarus forth / without being the funky Jesus Christ / without believing in / religious myths?" (34). As Lázaro Lima has also observed, this reference to Lazarus can be seen as a point of contact with Sylvia Plath and her poem "Lady Lazarus" (1962), where Plath's thirty-year-old female poetic voice describes surviving yet another physically grueling suicide attempt in a Nazi-like world of rigid gender expectations marked by "Herr Doktor" and "Herr Enemy."[38] Umpierre's poetic speaker struggles with how to achieve the liberation of the enslaved Muse, also undergoing physical pain or strong feelings as she embarks on the creative process:

> Explosions in my chest.
> This is the day in which
> I must invent a language
> to heroinely save hers or
> we will perish.
> But how does one invent a language?
> Jerigonza would do! (34)

According to the Spanish lexicologist María Moliner, *jerigonza* is "incomprehensible and complicated language or discourse; informal language used by a certain type of person";[39] in Puerto Rico, it simply means breaking words into syllables, inserting the syllable *chi* before each syllabic utterance, and pronouncing the new word with the tonic stress on the last syllable.[40] This language game, which has different variations in diverse geographic locations, is commonly engaged in by children, and is perhaps akin in spirit to pig Latin.[41] In Umpierre's case, the poetic speaker uses jerigonza to send a message in not-so-secret code, which will be understood only by those who can decode the message. It is this game that brings about the language shift in the poem from English to Spanish, to the language that is ultimately portrayed as able to liberate the poet. The coded message reads as follows (albeit missing the written accent marks that would more accurately convey actual pronunciation):

Chiyo chitu chinos
chine chice chisi
chita chimos
chilen chiguas;
chisi chilas chilen chiguas
chino chise chiu chinen
chino chiha chibrá
chila chu chinión chisal chiva chidora
chidel chimun chido
chiy chide chila chigue chirra.

I you we / need tongues / if the tongues / do not unite / there will be no/ saving union / of the world / and of war. (34)

This message, somewhat cryptic even in Spanish and paradoxical in nature, suggests a messianic strand in Umpierre's work, a desire for a language (tongue) that transcends linguistic differences (like Esperanto, perhaps) and that leads to a different form of communication. At the very least, it suggests the necessary union between English and Spanish for subjects who, like Umpierre, live in a linguistic situation where the mother tongue is suppressed because of politics and prejudice. At the same time, the game-like insertion on the syllable *chi* at times has the effect of creating words that in fact do have meaning in English (chide) and Spanish (*chino* and *chinos*, Chinese), *chita* (ankle bone, also the name of a game), and *chiva* (female goat or kid), not to mention all of the possible homophonic associations in both languages (i.e., *chita* as cheetah, *chisi* as cheesy, *chilen* as chillin', etc.).

The next stanza suggests a link between language (poetry) and thread, specifically, the physical act of spinning thread (or yarn) or perhaps embroidering, like Penelope in the *Odyssey* or Arachne, classical references that have now become well-established metaphors linking women's labor with storytelling. In fact, the poetic speaker will suggest that metaphors will allow for the spinning (union) of the world, portrayed as the brocade of a redemptive tapestry that can save the Muses. The next stanza will propose such a union through jerigonza: "ChiMar / chy / chigarita" (35).

The rest of the poem explores the linguistic disintegration of the word Margarita into two constitutive morphemes: *mar* (sea) and *garita*, a sentry box, post, or turret, as in a military fortification, specifically those of the Spanish colonial forts or "castles" at the entrance of the City of San Juan, including El Morro, San Cristóbal, and San Gerónimo, or around the walled city; these forts were later used by the U.S. army for many years, especially during World War II.[42] This fragmentation of the name "Margarita" allows for a juxtaposition of water (which, as we have seen, is employed as a metaphor for women) against a symbol of masculine, patriarchal colonization (Spanish military architecture, then taken over by Americans), which appears as the mental oppressor that keeps the poetic subject at a distance from the sea. Specific reference is made to *las garitas del Diablo en el Morro* (the devil's sentry posts at El Morro Castle, 35), referencing a popular historical legend or tale of love and superstition from 1790 recorded by Cayetano Coll y Toste about a lonely young male soldier who mysteriously "disappears" or, more likely, runs away with his female lover, during the period of Spanish colonial rule.[43] Umpierre's poem thus proposes a historical and political analysis through the deconstruction of this metaphor of Puerto Rico's political situation; yet the name of Puerto Rico (which appears in the introductory essays to the volume) is never mentioned in any of the poems in the entire book, a quite noticeable omission.

This divided subjectivity (Mar/Garita) entails a desire to rescue the sea (woman, nature, island); what in many ways can be seen as a reactionary or at least very traditional (masculinist) opposition linking the feminine to the earth and sea and the masculine to society and architecture. *Isla* (island) and *mar* (sea) are presented as divided entities, kept from one another by the effect of the military walls surrounding the old capital city; men (masculinity), in effect, thus divide and separate women (femininity). This rupture of the natural world (land, water) is caused, it is suggested, by a man-made fortification.

An ensuing stanza locates the speaking subject in Edison, New Jersey, and proposes the re-creation of the island and of the Caribbean outside of Puerto Rico, in physical and geographic terms in the diaspora (similar to the artist Ana Mendieta's earth mounds outside of Cuba), in what would amount to be mental maps formed by affect and memory.[44] This "pro-island," "anti-military-fort" conceptualization contrasts with other phenomena, for example vernacular architecture such as the *casitas,* or rural, wooden houses built in abandoned lots in New York City and other sites in the diaspora, where physical structures are seen as a noble or positive embodiment of cultural nostalgia, as Luis Aponte-Parés and Juan Flores have argued.[45] As such we should point out that Umpierre's critique is of a very specific type of construction, one associated with repression or protection and war, made out of masonry and stone, more like a prison than a house. In fact, El Morro Castle was used as a prison, and the U.S. government imprisoned the Puerto Rican nationalist leader Pedro Albizu Campos there.

In Umpierre's poem, given the lack of physical referents in the diaspora, emotions fill in and serve to construct an island of the mind:

> Hay una isla en Edison, New Jersey
> una isla edificada con la tierra
> de la amistad, el fuego de la pasión,
> las palmas de la nutrición, el río de la sabiduría,
> el aire del AMOR.

> There is an island in Edison, New Jersey
> an island built with the soil
> of friendship, the fire of passion,
> the palm trees of nutrition, the river of wisdom,
> the air of LOVE. (35)

Friendship, passion, nutrition, wisdom, and, quite markedly, *AMOR* (LOVE), are portrayed as the human characteristics or traits that can reconstitute social bonds. Physical displacement and nostalgia can be overcome in this way. While the recuperation of territorial definition is a common feature of many diasporic writers (Rane Arroyo's poem "Island to Island" from *Pale Ramón* comes to mind), Umpierre's stress on love seems closer to Chela Sandoval's theorization in *Methodology of the Oppressed* on that affect as a key strategy and component of U.S. Third World feminism: love as a revolutionary, healing, transformative act, an image also conjured in his speeches by the Reverend Dr. Martin Luther King Jr. and by Bob Marley in his songs.

In "The Mar/Garita Poem," the English language and prejudice are seen as enemies that attack the sea, which metaphorically stands in for woman (source or origin). Thus the poetic speaker's desire to reestablish contact between the land and the sea, which is separated by the *garita*. The poetic speaker interpellates female readers or listeners to do the necessary work, to contribute their own words, as women's speech (symbolized by a reference to Cassandra) is identified as the required tool, that which contains the power to transform, or bring about transformation. Women are thus incited by the poet to fill their mouths with the words they have stored in their entire body; the listing of these body parts, which culminates in those specifically feminine (*ovarios, tubos de falopio, vagina*) is reminiscent of Umpierre's earlier poem "El ascensor" (*En el país de las maravillas* 30), which has links to Monique Wittig's *Le corps lesbien* (1973), a gesture also taken up by the Puerto Rican writer Giannina Braschi in the first part of her experimental novel *Yo-Yo*

Boing! (1998).[46] In all of these cases, we can see an effort to recuperate these physical cartographies, organ by organ. The words become a rabid scream (*ese grito de pasión agreste*), and women are invited to deform and transform language in order to help the poetic speaker, who identifies herself as a new "JUANA DE LA CRUZ," in reference to Sor Juana, although perhaps also referring to herself as a masculine version of the Spanish mystic poet San Juan de la Cruz or to a female (Juana) crucified on the cross (Cruz), which would link this poem/image to other Christological references in the work of queer Puerto Rican writers such as Luis Rafael Sánchez, René Marqués, Angel Lozada, and the Spanish–Puerto Rican Carlos Varo.[47]

This dramatic linguistic ritual is followed in the next stanza by a turn to the abject, as the poetic speaker declares that these shared words pour forth onto the page in the form of vomit, a redemptive effluvium that serves to *hilar* (thread), *hilvanar* (mend), and *conectar* (connect) the pieces of a jigsaw puzzle (the diaspora, the fragmented body of women as individuals and as a social group). The noxious mixture of vomit and words, this unpleasant and painful process, brings truth and reconciliation:

LA FOTO VERDADERA
LA VISION DE LA ISLA CON EL MAR SIN OLAS

THE TRUE PHOTO
THE VISION OF THE ISLAND WITH THE SEA WITHOUT WAVES (37)

In the following verses, we observe a linguistic play between *amor* (love) and *mar* (sea), as the sea finally joins the island in a kiss or embrace. This ritual, in fact, frees the enslaved muse from the bottom of the sea and allows her to spring forth, liberated:

> Ya la oigo venir
> viene silvando la mar
> ha roto su lógica garita
>
> I hear her coming
> she comes whistling, the sea
> has broken her logical *garita* (38)

In fact, what this community of women have achieved (the poetic speaker and her female allies, including the female readers or listeners of the poem in the act of reading or listening to it), is to create *nuestro logos interno* (our internal logos), one characterized by *desorden* (disorder) that will free the world from solitude: "salvará / ya de la soledad al mundo" (38). This emphasis on logic (logos) is notable, if we consider how the collection started precisely with two poems ("A Immanence" and "Transcendence") named after key Kantian terms, which are subsequently deconstructed and resignified in a diasporic, Puerto Rican lesbian context. Most significantly, what these poems propose falls in line with the severe critique of Western rationalism embraced by poststructuralism and by radical, feminist postmodernism, a critique developed by other Latina feminists such as Gloria Anzaldúa in *Borderlands/La frontera.*

In Umpierre's utopian world, the revitalized waters of the sea rejoin the formerly lonely, abandoned land; the *golondrinas* (sparrows) return, chirping the names LUZ and MAR. The sea, at the same time, sings of freedom. The poem then concludes in what can be described as a classic or typical gesture of second-wave feminism: by celebrating the links of sisterhood that have joined the poet (Umpierre) to other female writers (Julia de Burgos, Marjorie Agosín, Marge Piercy). The liberation of the muse is accompanied by a different onomatopoeic utterance (*gla gla gla gla gla*), and the allegorical romantic interlinking of *la mar* (the feminine sea, taking advantage of the poetic license that allows the word *mar* in Spanish to be gendered as either masculine or feminine) and *mi isla* (my island), an island located in-land, in New Jersey. Here language is linked to the liberated female body, one that freely claims her right to an Amazonian sexuality and also demands political liberation for her country. Just like de Burgos's "Rio Grande de Loíza," the poem ends with a declaration of anticolonial politics:

> Hay un pueblo isleño
> esclavo en el Caribe
> pero una isla amazónica libre
> en el exilio:
> aquí en mi cuerpo,
> que hoy se llena de libertad y luz
> con la llegada del mar
> y la desplamación de nuestro idioma inventado.

> There is an island people
> enslaved in the Caribbean
> but a free Amazonian island
> in exile:

> here in my body,
> which fills today of liberty and light
> with the arrival of the sea
> and the unfolding of our invented language. (39)

The poem ends with a date: "Día de la libertad / Diciembre 10, 1985" (Day of liberty / December 10, 1985).

Umpierre's *The Margarita Poems* are a fundamental contribution to Puerto Rican, Latin American, and U.S. Latina literature. In her stress and insistence on water, she fully engages with the importance of this symbol not only in the Hispanic literary tradition (Jorge Manrique's medieval *coplas* or couplets, "nuestras vidas son los ríos / que van a dar en la mar..."), but more significantly, with the importance of this symbol for *queer* (sex and gender radical) diasporic Puerto Rican poets such as Julia de Burgos (*El mar y tú*), Manuel Ramos Otero ("The Story of the Woman from the Sea"), and Víctor Fragoso (*Ser islas/Being Islands*). Her radical gesture of dismemberment and reconstruction entails multiple forms of directionality toward language (in all its complexity) and the body, including a profound transcription of masturbatory longing for a missing Other, the desired love object. Umpierre manages to synthesize migratory angst with a political anticolonial gesture, all the while centering on feminist solidarity and lesbian eroticism. *The Margarita Poems* are, without a doubt, one of the most powerful expressions of poetic and vital sentiment in late twentieth-century writing.

Chapter 4

Visual Happenings, Queer Imaginings

FRANCES NEGRÓN-MUNTANER, Rose Troche, and Erika López are three diasporic Puerto Rican queer women artists who came of age in the 1980s and 1990s. They work in visual mediums that are strongly associated with popular and mass culture, but that also have important experimental, vanguard traditions: film, video, and television, in the case of Negrón-Muntaner and Troche, and cartoons, illustrated novels, and performance in the case of López. Located at different moments in places as diverse as New York, Philadelphia, Miami, Chicago, Los Angeles, and San Francisco, the three have garnered much attention and have had significant critical reception. While Negrón-Muntaner has made major inroads in alternative/independent circuits and in academia, Troche has achieved major commercial success in Hollywood, and López has had three novels published by Simon and Schuster, a major publishing house, in addition to working with smaller presses and making books by hand. The analysis of Negrón-Muntaner's scholarly, editorial, and film production (especially of her film *Brincando el charco: Portrait of a Puerto Rican*), of Troche's film *Go Fish,* and of López's cartoons, novels, and performances (especially *Lap Dancing for Mommy* and *Flaming Iguanas*), will allow us to explore lesbian and female bisexual generational similarities and differences, i.e., the ways in which their work complements but also differs from each others, and also furthers and/or diverges from that of earlier, second-wave, women-of-color feminist artists such as Luz María Umpierre and Nemir Matos-Cintrón.[1]

In spite of their similarity in age, Negrón-Muntaner (b. 1966), Troche (b. 1964), and López (b. 1968) are very different artists with very different viewpoints, life experiences, and agendas. In many ways, Negrón-Muntaner, who was born on the island and came to the United States as an adult, is the closest in spirit and ideology to Umpierre and also shares points of contact with the gay writer Manuel Ramos Otero.[2]

93

Negrón-Muntaner, Umpierre, and Ramos Otero all are (or were) first-generation, adult migrants who maintain(ed) very strong ties to their place of birth, but who also simultaneously develop(ed) new allegiances and attachments to their new homes. This, I would argue, is the dominant, albeit not the only possible model that first-generation artists tend to follow.[3] Negrón-Muntaner's work has always been very closely tied to Puerto Rican issues, be they diasporic (specifically in Philadelphia) or island-centered. Compared to Troche and López, Negrón-Muntaner is the one most invested in Puerto Rican political debates and questions of national sovereignty and identity.

Troche's and López's preference for popular or mass-media forms and themes distances them from first-generation migrants like Ramos Otero and from more traditional second-wave feminists such as Umpierre and even from Negrón-Muntaner. Second-generation migrants, Troche and López were born and raised in the United States outside of diasporic Puerto Rican communities; their work is predominantly if not almost exclusively in English and does not focus on the island of Puerto Rico. Both stress other types of identification well beyond their ethnicity, particularly sexuality and the arts. In the case of Troche, this was initially to the lesbian community of Chicago, while in López's case, this has been principally to the alternative, progressive, queer, and straight artistic communities of San Francisco, although also to New Jersey, where she grew up, and to Philadelphia, where she went to school.

These three women can all be considered part of or sympathizers with U.S. Third World feminism, a predominantly working-class, women-of-color movement that appeared in the 1970s and 1980s as a counterpart or reaction to predominantly white, middle-class second-wave feminism, although Troche and López, by virtue of their age and radical embrace of humor, eroticism, and popular culture, are closer in spirit to what is now identified as "third-wave" feminism, a new conceptualization with a younger perspective that distances itself from 1960s and 1970s views and proposes a different type of politics.[4] While second-wave and U.S. Third World or women-of-color feminists shared a focus on the destabilization of patriarchal structures of oppression, second-wave feminists tended at times toward an essentialist understanding of women as a fixed (and universal, i.e., not race-specific) identity (notwithstanding Simone de Beauvoir's important arguments about the social construction of womanhood), while the latter emphasized a marked analysis and critique of issues of race, ethnicity, class, and colonialism, particularly of the interrelated or intersectional nature of these as multiple, simultaneous, and competing axes of identification and (at times) oppression. Third wavers, a somewhat controversial group who are often dismissed and accused of being apolitical, move away from dogmatic conceptions and are more open to humor, nontraditional sexualities, and myriad gender expressions, including, at times, a celebration of traditional feminine aesthetics. Exploring the work of Negrón-Muntaner, Troche, and López in unison will give us a privileged glimpse of more recent formations of queer Puerto Rican women's diasporic culture making, and of the important differences that characterize it.

Barrio Logos: Mapping a Queer Rican and Latina/o Philadelphia

Frances Negrón-Muntaner left Puerto Rico in 1986 to obtain a Ph.D. in sociology at the University of Massachusetts, Amherst, but quickly abandoned her program of study and in a few months ended up working at a community newspaper in Philadelphia.[5] How she got there is quite interesting. The artist had initially envisioned herself living in Northampton, a lesbian enclave of great repute near Amherst. Negrón-Muntaner had already come out of the closet as an adolescent while attending the University of Puerto Rico, Río Piedras, where she obtained an undergraduate degree in sociology and was actively involved in lesbian activism on the island; she describes being by far one of the youngest women among her activist colleagues, suggesting that she was ideologically shaped by second-wave Puerto Rican lesbian feminists.[6] When Negrón-Muntaner arrived in Northampton, she was shocked by its white, middle-class homogeneity and lack of political engagement: "The town was supposed to be an American lesbian haven, but I felt the whole scene was extremely superficial, white, and privileged."[7] After a brief stint in New York City, her friend Alba Martínez invited her to Philadelphia, and she decided to stay and work as a photographer at *Community Focus,* a local newspaper. Negrón-Muntaner would go on to pursue an M.A. in Visual Anthropology and an M.F.A. in film at Temple University, also located in Philadelphia. Following in her parents' footsteps, both of whom are university professors in Puerto Rico, she went on to receive a Ph.D. in Comparative Literature at Rutgers University, New Brunswick (2000), while commuting from Pennsylvania to New Jersey. She credits her interest in film to her grandfather, an aspiring (if frustrated) filmmaker who encouraged her as a child to make movies.

Negrón-Muntaner's early work is marked by its deep connection to Philadelphia, specifically to the Puerto Rican and queer-of-color communities of that city. The artist became extremely involved after arriving in 1986; her films and videos *AIDS in the Barrio: Eso no me pasa a mí* (1989), *Brincando el charco: Portrait of a Puerto Rican* (1994), and *Homeless Diaries* (1996) and the anthology that she edited of Philadelphia Latina/o writers entitled *Shouting in a Whisper/Los límites del silencio* (1994) are testaments of this commitment.[8] In a sense, Negrón-Muntaner seems to have echoed Luz María Umpierre's earlier experiences in Philadelphia; this period was decisive for both women in their political, feminist, and artistic development, particularly as a result of their involvement with the Puerto Rican community there. Both also share a period in New Jersey, as Umpierre taught at Rutgers during the 1980s, although she had already left by the time Negrón-Muntaner became a graduate student there.

One of the strongest links between Negrón-Muntaner and Umpierre is their portrayal and critique of the social problems of Puerto Ricans in Philadelphia.[9] Their critical engagement with these impoverished sites and their attention to the cultural and political work of community building (what we could describe as a reterritorialization and revalorization of the ghetto) make their work akin to what the Chicano scholar Raúl Homero Villa has called *barriology* in his groundbreaking study *Barrio-Logos*: a conscious gesture of recuperation and acknowledgement of spaces that are stigmatized and marginalized by dominant, white society, where Latinas/os lead meaningful (if difficult) lives. It is also similar to the cultural phenomenon that the Chicana feminist scholar Mary Pat Brady analyzes in her volume *Extinct Lands, Temporal Geographies,* where she highlights the gendered particularities of women's art-making practices as an attempt to recuperate history and community and their links to space and place.

A brief revision of some of Luz María Umpierre's early production will allow me to better explain why she is an important antecedent for Negrón-Muntaner's work. Several poems in Umpierre's 1979 debut volume *Una puertorriqueña en Penna* such as "Rubbish," "Título sobreentendido," and "Dios se muda" serve to denounce the material and economic poverty in which Puerto Ricans live in Philadelphia, but also to propose alternatives. In "Rubbish," the poetic voice alternates Spanish thoughts and curses with English expressions and apologies; she ultimately declares a rebellion against this prescribed social and linguistic regime that imprisons her. "Título sobreentendido" (Implicit title)

TITULO SOBREENTENDIDO

```
    L A C L A V E          ONE TWO THREE    ONE TWO THREE   ONE TWO THREE    BONGO BONGO    CONGA CONGA    S A L S A

 N         L A             ONE TWO         ONE TWO THREE    ONE TWO          BONGO BONGO    CONGA CONGA    HAPPINESS   HAPPINESS
    A V A L C               
       A V E L C                            ONE TWO THREE   ONE TWO THREE    ONE TWO THREE    BONGO BONGO    CONGA CONGA    S A L S A
```

Luz María Umpierre, "Título Sobreentendido" (Implicit Title).
From *Una puertorriqueña en Penna*, 1979.

is a concrete poem in which the words such as the names of musical instruments, rhythms, and phrases associated with music (la clave, one two three, bongo, conga) are employed to spell out the letters of the word "GHETTO," the O being formed by the words "SALSA" and "HAPPINESS." This gesture of seeing the positive value of Puerto Rican community life even when it is marked by poverty, and of resignifying its negative valence, is very reminiscent of the Nuyorican aesthetics outlined by Miguel Algarín in 1975 that are clearly visible in works such as Miguel Piñero's "A Lower East Side Poem" and of what Juan Flores has identified as one of the key stages of Nuyorican cultural consciousness.[10] It is also important to remember that salsa music, a dominant Nuyorican cultural form with very political content in the 1970s, was also being used in this period as a tool for community empowerment and consciousness-raising; in his book of poetry *La Carreta Made a U-Turn* (1979), specifically in the third section, "El Nuevo Rumbón," Tato Laviera also portrays music as a tool that can serve to overcome oppression.[11] Yet not everyone likes these rhythms: Umpierre's critique of social conditions continues in "Dios se muda" (God is moving away), a highly ironic poem that enacts an impeachment of God for turning his back on Puerto Ricans and for quite literally moving out of their neighborhood in North Philadelphia, escaping from the urban poverty, dark skin, overly pungent aromatic cooking, and (alas) loud salsa music.

A decade later (but five years before Jonathan Demme's Hollywood blockbuster *Philadelphia*), Negrón-Muntaner and Peter Biella codirected *AIDS in the Barrio: Eso no me pasa a mí* (That does not happen to me, 1989), a thirty-minute documentary that explores many of the most pressing social issues affecting Puerto Ricans and Latinas/os in North

Philadelphia, specifically those pertaining to the AIDS crisis, drug addiction, and poverty, while also proposing community-based solutions, particularly through peer education and empowerment, especially that of women and gays. Negrón-Muntaner has discussed her experience of working on this film in her essay "Insider/Outsider: Making Films in the Puerto Rican Community," where the filmmaker explains the origins of the project as a collaboration with the young Puerto Rican Community Legal Services lawyer Alba Martínez, with whom she coproduced the film: "we decided that through the making of a film we could both channel our need to make a modest contribution regarding the AIDS crisis and develop a tool that would also address other issues — non-medical ones — which, as women, we saw as crucial" (82).[12] Since Negrón-Muntaner and Martínez did not have extensive filmmaking experience at the time and an experienced male Puerto Rican collaborator had to abandon the project, they ended up hiring the white, middle-class, male Peter Biella to codirect and assemble a professional crew.

AIDS in the Barrio is a remarkable film in many respects and prefigures many of the more distinctive traits that will characterize Negrón-Muntaner's later film production, including a multivoiced approach, aggressive Spanish/English bilingualism, a focus on women's experience, migration, and social matters, and a critique of homophobia. Negrón-Muntaner and Biella interviewed a significant number of people ranging from anonymous informants on the street to people with AIDS (George Santiago and a couple identified only by their first names, Ramón and Juana), the family members of people who are sick or have passed away (Migdalia Ramos, Nydia Rivera, Ana Santiago), and community leaders such as the Episcopal minister Floyd Naters-Gamarra, who provides insightful analysis about how the stress of migration and poverty can lead to drug abuse, illegal activities, and exposure to HIV through infected needles. The interviews are deftly intercut with images of community sites, including murals such as one with the Statue of Liberty covered by the Puerto Rican flag, a reference to a famous 1977 anticolonial activist action, and with images of people of all ages, especially children.[13] They are also linked by sound bridges, particularly of a salsa song in Spanish ("Eso no me pasa a mí"), and by images of police cars and ambulances and their sirens, making the film a fast-paced, lively, yet also somewhat intimidating (perhaps pedagogical or state disciplinarian) document. How rigorously or scientifically effective this video is as an AIDS-prevention tool is of less importance to me right now than how remarkably rich it is in capturing people's voices and experiences, making them more willing to discuss AIDS issues as well as challenging social norms concerning women and homosexuals. For example, Gregory M. Herek has criticized the film's lack of more explicit discussion of AIDS transmission mechanisms and prevention techniques, and the fact that many of the people portrayed convey incorrect health information; he does recognize the film's high production value and its emphasis on family values, or *familismo,* as a source of strength and support. Yet in "Insider/Outsider," Negrón-Muntaner discusses how the film was taken up by community members and activists, who felt they were well represented; the filmmaker also stresses the importance of generating media images of a community that had not seen itself represented visually and aurally, and that for the most part did not have or was only beginning to obtain the technical know-how to do so. While most of those interviewed are Puerto Rican, there are other individuals who also appear, for example the openly gay Colombian poet and AIDS activist Juan David Acosta, who is not identified by name in the film, and Naters-Gamarra, who is Panamanian. The somewhat well-known heterosexual Puerto Rican Hollywood film and television actor Luis Guzmán (*Boogie Nights, Traffic*) also appears, although he is not identified by name.

Negrón-Muntaner will continue her cinematographic exploration of the Philadelphia Puerto Rican experience in many of her additional works including *Brincando el charco* (which I will soon discuss at length), but also in her video *Homeless Diaries,* where she will document and analyze "the experiences of several Puerto Rican families living in Tent City, erected on a Kensington lot" in Philadelphia in 1995, whom she "follows . . . on their subsequent occupations of Independence Hall and St. Edwards Church."[14] As the *Philadelphia Weekly* journalist Sarah Miller describes, "Her inspiration for *Homeless Diaries* came from an article in the *Inquirer* about a woman who had come from Puerto Rico to Philadelphia only to find herself and her children homeless. Her interest grew as she began to feel that as a Puerto Rican living in the United States, she had no real home. It is a thread of anxiety that runs through all her work" (11). Elfrieda Abbe describes it as "a video journey" where the filmmaker "interweaves video, home movies, images of children living in Tent City and coverage of the city" and also states: "It's a multilayered exploration of how different media represent displacement and social movements" (9).

In addition to Negrón-Muntaner's film and video work, she has made important interventions in terms of documenting and giving public voice to the literary contributions of Latinas/os in Philadelphia. These include the production of a fifty-minute radio documentary called "We Are Not a New York Suburb" (1991) and the editing of *Shouting in a Whisper/Los límites del silencio* (1994). This book, published in bilingual format, was the first-ever collection of Philadelphia-based Latina/o writers, and features ten poets, including five Puerto Ricans, in addition to an afterword by the queer Puerto Rican scholar Carlos Rodríguez-Matos. Several of the contributors (including Negrón-Muntaner herself) were founding members or editors of a Philadelphia Latina/o literary journal called *Desde este lado/From This Side,* which although not officially queer, had a significant queer presence. The queer content in *Shouting in a Whisper/Los límites del silencio* is especially noticeable in the poetry of Juan David Acosta, the Puerto Rican William Manuel Mena-Santiago (who died of AIDS in 1994),[15] and Negrón-Muntaner herself; Rodríguez-Matos's participation, as well as that of the lesbian Chilean American writer and activist Mariana Romo-Carmona as translator, also contribute to make this a key queer Latina/o document.[16] In addition, there are two very important U.S. Puerto Rican participants, Zulma González-Walker (who was born in Philadelphia) and Catalina Ríos (who was born in Hartford), whose work has more direct ties to the Nuyorican or DiaspoRican poetry movement and to U.S Latina/o political concerns and aesthetics. González-Walker's poem "Purely Perfect Puerto Rican," which will be showcased in *Brincando el charco,* is included here; the poem discusses the quandary of an English-speaking, black Puerto Rican woman whose Puerto Ricanness is not acknowledged in the United States, where she is often incorrectly perceived as being a (non-Hispanic) African American.

Translocal Philadelphia: Circuits of Sexile

Negrón-Muntaner's film *Brincando el charco: Portrait of a Puerto Rican* (1994) allows us to think in a different way about the jump from the island to the mainland, to that "other island of Puerto Rico," as Ramos Otero would say.[17] Set principally in Philadelphia, *Brincando el charco* (which literally translates as "Jumping the Puddle") is a hybrid film in which the fictional, semiautobiographical story of a character called Claudia Marín (played by the filmmaker herself and inspired, at least in part, by her life) is interspersed with intra- and extra-diegetic sequences of interviews, performances, archival footage, news-like demonstration coverage, and lesbian erotic fantasies. The film loosely takes place over a period of three days (a weekend in December 1991), although there are several flashbacks and temporal leaps that make this structure somewhat more vague and harder to grasp. On the first day, Claudia receives news of her father's death and is encouraged by her family to return to Puerto Rico for the funeral; she has not been on the island for over five years. During the three days of the diegesis, we follow Claudia as she engages in numerous activities, including talking to a literary agent or publisher, developing (and overexposing) photos in a personal lab, photographing diverse people in a studio and on the street, reading, watching videos, attending and filming a party, having a nightmare, and talking with her girlfriend, the lawyer Ana Hernández, a character clearly based on Alba Martínez and played by the Honduran American actress Natalia Lazarus. On Sunday, Claudia finally boards a plane, en route back to Puerto Rico.

Although not a documentary, *Brincando el charco* is clearly in conversation with the tradition of Puerto Rican documentaries and experimental films by and about women that Yamila Azize Vargas and Negrón-Muntaner have carefully studied.[18] Negrón-Muntaner employs a series of cinematic devices that at once fragment and order the film. Intertitles appear between segments and are superimposed onto images that are frozen at times, giving the impression that they are slides. Voiceovers and narrations, such as those written and performed by the African American author Toni Cade Bambara (who talks about the arrival of Puerto Ricans to Harlem in the 1950s) and by Zulma González-Walker (who performs "Purely Perfect Puerto Rican"), contribute to the sense of the film as a multivoiced essay. *Brincando el charco* is in English and Spanish and switches back and forth from one language to the other. It is, accordingly, a *bilingual* film that attempts to reflect and sound out the experiences of a bilingual and bicultural people.

The last name of the protagonist Claudia Marín is the same as that of former Puerto Rican governor Luis Muñoz Marín, a patriarchal figure who actively encouraged migration to the United States as a strategy for economic development and as a way to alleviate poverty on the island in the 1940s and 1950s. It was under his stewardship that the "Great Migration" of Puerto Ricans took place, something that Nuyorican poets like Tato Laviera have vociferously decried. Negrón-Muntaner places herself solidly in the framework of the *gran familia puertorriqueña* (great Puerto Rican family)[19] by adopting Marín as the surname for her allegorical film persona. She also makes clear the stature and importance that she expects her ideas to receive, as the direct, if rebellious, heir of the

great patriarch, even if it is as an inheritor of his maternal, and not paternal, surname.[20] If Manuel Ramos Otero, by way of the abject, tended to
deconstruct and delegitimize the master narratives with which Negrón-
Muntaner flirts, the filmmaker herself has stated in various essays and
interviews that she too is engaging in deconstruction.[21]

   Brincando el charco begins with a slow-motion introductory sequence
of the Philadelphia Puerto Rican Day parade, full of American and
Puerto Rican flags and of faces that we assume are those of Puerto
Ricans.[22] The film's Spanish title is superimposed on the images while
a voice-over in English posits, in a manner that recalls the 1930s intellectual Antonio S. Pedreira (yet another of Puerto Rico's paternalist
cultural figures) what could be understood as the central question of the
film: What is a Puerto Rican? Or rather: How have traditional definitions of Puerto Ricanness excluded numerous types of individuals? In the
words of the narrator: "From the moment I learned how to read I have
known of Puerto Ricans asking themselves, to the point of despair: Who
are we? What is our common destiny? I am an echo of these questions,
even as I contest them. That is why I must point my lens elsewhere, to see
what escapes the us in *nosotros*." The voice that we hear is that of the
main character, the photographer and filmmaker Claudia Marín. Yet, of
course, it is also the voice of the photographer and filmmaker Negrón-
Muntaner, who plays the role of Claudia, and who is, in fact, the person
responsible for *Brincando el charco*.[23] Just as with Ramos Otero, we
see the intersection of autobiography and narrative (and of the authorial persona) in the construction of the diasporic document, something
we also see in Umpierre, in the intersection of autobiography and poetic
voice. Claudia is based on a real lesbian Puerto Rican emigrant filmmaker; hers is not, in other words, some random role that is played
by some random heterosexual actress. Negrón-Muntaner's strategy of
self-representation is not uncommon among lesbian and gay independent filmmakers, who often include themselves in their productions, as
the film scholars Richard Dyer and Judith Mayne have observed; Cheryl
Dunye, Rose Troche, Marlon Riggs, Richard Fung, and even the Brazilian Karim Aïnouz (not in his best-known *Madame Satã* but rather in
his earlier *Seams*) come to mind as some queer filmmakers of color who
have done this.[24]

   The validation of Claudia Marín's character as a "real" subject who
goes through a series of events, some of which are akin to the ones in
which the filmmaker participates in daily life, operates in tandem with
the notion that the individuals interviewed in the film are not fictitious

subjects. I am referring not only to the aforementioned performances by Bambara and González-Walker, but also to five "portraits," specifically those of Ramón ["Ray"] González, who is shown "vogueing" at the beginning of the film; Sandra Andino, an island-born black Puerto Rican woman who at the time was a student at Temple University and is currently the director of education at Taller Puertorriqueño (Philadelphia); Agnes Lugo-Ortiz, currently a professor of Latin American literature at the University of Chicago, who speaks about lesbian invisibility; Moisés Agosto, a gay, HIV-positive poet, short-story author, and AIDS activist, who at the time lived in New York City and now lives in Puerto Rico; and Chloé S. Georas, an at-the-time exiled poet and scholar who currently resides in Puerto Rico and who explains her notion of "travel" as a way to redefine her relationship to the island at the end of the film. (Georas lived in the United States and France when portrayed, and states on camera that she found it nearly impossible to live on the island, as she found it boring. Her bourgeois sense of entitlement and mobility, i.e., her notion of tourism as a remedy for diasporic longing, is very alienating to many viewers.)

While González, Andino, Lugo-Ortiz, Agosto, and Georas are not identified when they first appear, the credits at the end of the film reveal who they are; as the writer Mayra Santos-Febres observed in her 1995 review of the film ("La memoria como viaje"), most of them (all except Ray González) were close cohorts of Negrón-Muntaner and of Santos-Febres herself as undergraduates at the flagship campus of the University of Puerto Rico in Río Piedras, which gives them a distinct island-born, university educated, migratory generational feel. Since several of the people portrayed have relatively public profiles, such as Lugo-Ortiz and Agosto, the film "speaks" with a certain documentary authority.

It is not surprising that Negrón-Muntaner would want to take advantage of the audience's tendency to grant documentary a higher truth-value than fiction. It is also no coincidence that groundbreaking women-of-color feminist and lesbian anthologies such as *This Bridge Called My Back* (1981), *Compañeras: Latina Lesbians* (1987), *Chicana Lesbians: The Girls Our Mothers Warned Us About* (1991), and *Telling to Live: Latina Feminist* Testimonios (2001) include many testimonial and oral history pieces in which speaking subjects attempt to validate their assertions by drawing on personal experiences.[25] *Brincando el charco* flirts with testimonial narratives while refusing to be a documentary; and yet it is nonetheless caught up in documentary discourse all the same.

The problem with flirting with testimony and documentary is, of course, that people tend to believe everything they see.[26] This is rather notoriously the case with the representation of the expulsion from Puerto Rico: a "typically," or "stereotypically," dominant father, who is called Claudio, kicks his daughter Claudia out of their home after he finds out that she is a lesbian by seeing photos of her with a woman.[27] While the situation is plausible, the scene itself, according to the director, was inspired by, and styled in the manner of, melodrama — specifically, Latin American *telenovelas,* or soap operas — albeit as parody.[28] Furthermore, it does not exactly correspond to the filmmaker's actual experiences in Puerto Rico: as previously mentioned, Negrón-Muntaner left the island only after finishing college in order to pursue graduate studies in the United States; she was asked to move out of her parents' house when she came out of the closet as an undergraduate, but it was not by her father but by her mother, who quickly reconciled with her.[29]

Critics of *Brincando el charco* such as Licia Fiol-Matta and Rubén Ríos Avila have argued that the representation of the family, particularly with its prominent religious iconography, relies on stereotypes of working-class intolerance that are misleading and incongruous with the characterization of the protagonist.[30] Dorian Lugo Bertrán has also found the scene rife with stereotypes: "patriarca duro, mater dolorosa, la santa familia puertorriqueña como espacio cerrado y religioso" (hard patriarch, sorrowful mother, the sacred Puerto Rican family as a closed and religious space, 138). People nevertheless come up to Negrón-Muntaner all the time and thank her "for showing it the way it really is." The attractiveness of this type of representation as a foundational expulsion narrative is further verified by the fact that a rather similar scene appears in Rose Troche's *Go Fish,* except that in that case, it is the mother who is depicted as the intolerant aggressor.

Both Negrón-Muntaner and Ramos Otero avail themselves of romantic relationships between island-born and U.S.-born queer individuals to explore different experiences and perceptions of Puerto Ricanness, such as those of Manuel Ramos and Sam Fat in "Blank Page and Staccato" and of the Nuyorican lawyer Ana Hernández and Claudia Marín in *Brincando el charco.* (In Umpierre's poetry, the loved one is usually portrayed as not being Puerto Rican, at least in *The Margarita Poems.*) As Negrón-Muntaner has observed, these pairings constitute "foundational fictions" in the sense advanced by the literary critic Doris Sommer, yet with an important difference.[31] In traditional nineteenth-century Latin American novels centered on family romances, the pairings of opposites tended to

Natalia Lazarus and Frances Negrón-Muntaner in *Brincando el Charco: Portrait of a Puerto Rican* (Frances Negrón-Muntaner, 1994).

resolve differences through procreation: the protagonists' children represented the hope for a new society over and against regional, economic, and social distinctions that threatened to pull apart the national whole. Of course, sexual reproduction is by no means a given in queer narratives and, in fact, does not occur in the Puerto Rican texts analyzed so far, except perhaps in Umpierre's discussion of "lesbian motherhood" in relation to her association or friendship with Moira ("A Letter to Moira," *For Christine*). What we do see in Negrón-Muntaner is a gesture toward the construction of a new community based on better understandings of human differences and, quite differently, in the case of Ramos Otero, on revenge and murder.

Negrón-Muntaner's film, unlike Ramos Otero's and Umpierre's writing, funnels the process of migration to the United States into two moments: expulsion from Puerto Rico and incorporation into a multicultural community composed of different migrant generations. Tellingly, the film ends with the protagonist boarding a plane to return to the island for her father's funeral. It is quite possible that the compression or ellipsis of a longer migratory process corresponds to the chronological difference between Negrón-Muntaner's film (produced between 1989 and 1994), Ramos Otero's work (written, roughly, between 1967 and 1990), and Umpierre's poetry (particularly that published between 1979 and 1995). The gay and lesbian authors are important precedents for the lesbian filmmaker. But what exactly does this heritage entail? Claudia Marín has a Nuyorican girlfriend (Ana Hernández) and queer and straight Latin American, Spanish, African American, Korean, and Latina/o friends who debate questions of race, ethnicity, and nationality, and more pointedly, of racism, ethnocentrism, and ultra-nationalism in the United States. Claudia has affirmed bonds with the African American community *and* with the LGBT community, including African American gay men. She has friends of many ethnicities; she has a grasp of the history of Puerto Rican migration, both its causal socio-economic factors and its impoverished, ghettoized results; and she also has friends in Puerto Rico who keep her abreast of the state of queer politics and activism on the island. As mentioned, it is suggested that she eventually returns to Puerto Rico to reconcile with her estranged family, after the death of her "evil" father. In a sense, it appears that she comes to have her cake and to eat it too. But does she really?

Negrón-Muntaner has claimed that the film is a provocation, a means to bring about discussion and generate controversy.[32] She has certainly succeeded in doing just that. I, for one, believe that perhaps the greatest merit of Negrón-Muntaner's project is, quite simply, that it is a film and, as such, that it partakes of what is arguably the most important medium of the twentieth century. As I have discussed elsewhere,[33] the film problematically portrays Americanization in Puerto Rico as a positive step to gay emancipation, a controversial position that coincides with Negrón-Muntaner's later defense of "Radical Statehood," which sees annexation as an opportunity for progressive, leftist politics.[34] She also inadvertently misrepresents the predominantly English-speaking Puerto Rican trans activist Cristina Hayworth,[35] who originated the Gay Pride Parade on the island, as "una travesti americana" (an American transvestite), a common confusion on the island where language is frequently seen as synonymous with nationality and where distinctions of transgender status are often imprecise.[36]

But perhaps the film's greatest pitfall and limitation, if you will, is its heavy-handed, serious, even dour tone — an overintellectualization that makes the film feel didactic at times and that drains the humor that does manage to surface on occasion. That, and the lack of clear, visible acknowledgment of the people who participated in it (the lack of intertitles identifying the documentary subjects) have meant that most people who see the film walk away with the impression that it is (at best) a directorial machine (i.e., a vehicle for Negrón-Muntaner and a large additional cadre of anonymous people), assuming viewers even realize that the director is also the lead actress of her own film.[37] Given the long period it took to make the film (five years), we even notice physical changes in the actress herself, who goes from looking like a very young, somewhat innocent woman (in a random, somewhat unnecessary and very distracting New York City flashback sequence near the end) to the much tougher, hardened, leather-jacket, jeans-and-combat-boots-wearing protagonist, who dons a skirt and high heels only as she prepares to return to Puerto Rico. *Brincando el charco* is eminently a pedagogical device that is extremely useful in American college classrooms, where it allows for the discussion of the interconnection of myriad topics. But it is a film devoid of much pleasure, even if it does have a seminude lesbian erotic sequence, a landmark along with Rose Troche's *Go Fish* in the history of Puerto Rican filmmaking.

More recently, Negrón-Muntaner has collaborated with the writing and the production of a short film on youth sexuality called *Just Like You Imagined?* (2000), directed by David Frankel (*Sex and the City, The Devil Wears Prada*) and cowritten by the young Cuban American Verena Faden.[38] This remarkable fifteen-minute film, which in some ways can be seen as an updated, youth-oriented, fictional remake of *AIDS in the Barrio,* interweaves three parallel narratives involving a multiracial, multiethnic group of teenagers in Hialeah, a working-class suburb of Miami with a large Latina/o (mostly Cuban) immigrant population. The film discusses issues of loss of virginity, teenage pregnancy, intravenous drug-user HIV transmission, and gay dating. It has extremely high production values, is shot in a visually exciting style, and was produced and is distributed by Scenarios, USA, a "nonprofit organization that aims to inspire teens to make healthier and safer decisions by offering them a creative approach to thinking through and discussing their lives, their choices and their future" (website).

As of this date (2009), Negrón-Muntaner is currently involved in the postproduction of two made-for-television documentaries that do not focus on issues of sexuality: *Regarding Vieques* and *War in Guam,* this last one coproduced by the Nuyorican filmmaker Bienvenida (Beni) Matías. In addition to her film work, Negrón-Muntaner has continued her scholarly and anthological pursuits in her book *Boricua Pop* (2004), largely based on her 2000 Ph.D. dissertation, as well as in two anthologies, *Puerto Rican Jam* (coedited with Ramón Grosfoguel, 1997) and *None of the Above* (2007). *Boricua Pop* is particularly interesting in that she explores the work of many Puerto Rican gay male artists and drag queens, although there are no mentions of Puerto Rican lesbians. Negrón-Muntaner is a prolific essayist and has also published articles in numerous journals and volumes, in addition to organizing several academic conferences.

Chicago Dykes: Troche's *Go Fish* (1994)

To go from Frances Negrón-Muntaner to Rose Troche is a rather dramatic jump, but a nevertheless fascinating one, especially considering that the two women have publicly stated their disagreement with each other's projects and views.[39] While Negrón-Muntaner's films have achieved great exposure in the academic and alternative distribution system, Troche has achieved much more mainstream commercial success, having her first feature-length narrative film *Go Fish* picked up for distribution by the Samuel Goldwyn Company at the Sundance Film Festival in 1994, then directing a high-budget English gay comedy (*Bedrooms and Hallways,* 1998), a major Hollywood film (*The Safety of Objects,* 2001, starring Glenn Close and Patricia Clarkson), and some of the most talked-about cable television programs in the United States, including numerous episodes of Showtime's *The L Word* (a lesbian-focused series that she also cowrites, although one marked by its poor representation of Latinas) and one episode of HBO's *Six Feet Under.*[40] Whereas Negrón-Muntaner has centered her work insistently on things Puerto Rican (or having to do with Latinas/os and U.S. colonialism), Troche has barely or only tangentially touched on them.[41] And while Negrón-Muntaner has to a certain degree distanced herself from issues of lesbianism in her more recent academic and film projects, Troche has fairly consistently worked on queer topics, or managed to infuse straight productions with a rather queer sensibility. In many ways, the two make strange bedfellows: the island-born, first-generation migrant, now Ivy League–scholar and filmmaker activist vis-à-vis the Chicago-born, second-generation migrant, experimentally trained, now commercially successful, Hollywood film and television director. In this section, I will expand on Troche's work, focusing in particular on her feature-length directorial debut *Go Fish,* a narrative (fictional) black-and-white film that appeared the same year as *Brincando el charco.*[42] The great differences that we will observe between these two films will have to do with location (Philadelphia vs. Chicago), place of birth of the directors (Puerto Rico vs. the United States), migratory life experience (first generation vs. second), film tradition (documentary vs. experimental, albeit both of these subservient to narrative), production (marginal vs. integrated), and authorship (solo vs. collaboration). Troche's work will illustrate one variant of second-generation experience, namely, that of distancing or alienation from source culture.

Go Fish was cowritten and coproduced by Troche and her then-girlfriend Guinevere Turner, a white woman who is not of Puerto Rican or Latino descent; the film was initially conceptualized in August of 1991 and made with an extremely limited budget and with nonprofessional volunteer actors over a period of several years. In its original inception, it was envisioned as being a mix of documentary and fiction, although the documentary sequences filmed in 1991 were later dropped.[43] The movie was completed with the help of queer executive producers Christine Vachon and Tom Kalin, responsible for many of the most important 1990s American lesbian and gay films, who connected the filmmakers with John Pierson, a major funder of independent productions.[44] *Go Fish* went on to become a box-office success, achieving major national and international distribution, and has been frequently identified as a key component of the 1990s American "New Queer Cinema." It is often compared to Spike Lee's debut film *She's Gotta Have It* (1986) and described as doing for lesbian film what Lee did for African American cinema, a comparison that unfortunately is often read as devoid of racial/ethnic specificity and that by extension suggests it refers to "white" lesbian film.[45] In spite (or perhaps because) of this, the film is very rarely considered to be a "Puerto Rican movie."[46] Rather, people tend to see it as centered on the romantic experiences of two non-Latina white women — a young, trendy, somewhat angst-ridden writer/college student called Max (played by Guinevere Turner herself) and a dowdy, hippyish, slightly older veterinarian's assistant called Ely (V. S. Brodie) — in the context of a group of multiracial and multiethnic lesbian friends — a butch African American college teacher named Kia (T. Wendy McMillan); her girlfriend, a femme, semicloseted, divorced Puerto Rican nurse named Evy (Migdalia Meléndez); and a sex-radical, "happily promiscuous," lesbian-identified, slightly butch young white bartender named Daria (Anastasia Sharp) — who conspire to bring Max and Ely together in early 1990s Chicago, specifically in Wicker Park, a neighborhood that before gentrification was a part of West Town and

Migdalia Meléndez, Guinevere Turner, and T. Wendy McMillan in *Go Fish* (Rose Troche, 1994).

that for a brief moment in the late 1980s and early 1990s had an important multicultural lesbian community.[47] It is fair to say that there is a tension in the film as to whether it is predominantly an ensemble piece in which these five characters are all central, or whether the romantic comedy film narrative really privileges the characters portrayed by V. S. Brodie and especially by Guin Turner; in fact, the film's original name was *Ely and Max,* and Turner is the only protagonist who has gone on to have a significant Hollywood acting career.

Audiences' and (most) critics' lack of awareness about the Puerto Rican specificity of *Go Fish* has to do with widespread lack of knowledge about the history of Puerto Ricans in Chicago and also (and especially) with the subtle, almost incidental, and oblique treatment of this issue in the film: Wicker Park is not portrayed as a neighborhood with a Latino population (which it was, or had historically been, as Gina Pérez and Félix Padilla have noted), but rather as an artsy, bohemian, and lesbian one (i.e., the one it was becoming as a result of white artist and gay and lesbian migration and yuppy gentrification that started in the 1970s). The words "Puerto Rico" or "Puerto Rican" are never mentioned in the film, and while Evy and her mother speak Spanish and code-switch between Spanish and English, the only way to know that they are Puerto Rican is by recognizing distinctive linguistic markers (accent and vocabulary, particularly the use of the word *pata* to mean lesbian, but also her ex-husband's nickname, "Junior," a very common Spanglish appellative), by being familiar with the history of Latino populations in the Near Northwest side of Chicago (including Wicker Park but also the nearby West Town, Humboldt Park, and Logan Square), or by simply making an interpretive assumption and speculating that the character is a stand-in for the director herself.[48] There are specific filmic elements that make Evy's Puerto Ricanness difficult to grasp, and as a result, it is much easier to perceive Evy as a generic *Latina* than as a Puerto Rican, suggesting Troche's possible (perhaps unconscious) critical move away from nation-specific identities toward more panethnic, collective ones, or a belief that Puerto Ricanness can be determined by simply looking at someone and hearing that person speak Spanish, a tricky and imperfect test. Complicating this even further is the fact that Troche's own comments on her Puerto Rican heritage, frequently articulated in interviews, and her discussion of the importance of Migdalia Meléndez's Puerto Ricanness are often implicitly dismissed and/or not perceived as (or just simply unknown) by most people familiar with the film.

Of the five main characters, Evy was the last to be cast, and she is by far the least developed, although Troche has expressed that she had a significant number of prerequisites for the person who would play this part. According to Troche, "It was important for me to cast a woman who was Puerto Rican in the role and one who could also speak Spanish and one who also was a lesbian and one who also would give an open ended commitment to the project, through thick and thin. No big thing, right?" (Turner and Troche 18). While articulated with humor, Troche's high expectations reveal a number of things, specifically the importance that she attributed to the actor's identity and linguistic competency as a means to ensure representational authenticity, a position that resonates with Negrón-Muntaner's casting of herself as the lead in *Brincando el charco*. In fact, Troche has stated that she considered playing the part herself, but later changed her mind:

> "I saw her at a bar," says Troche of Migdalia Meléndez, who plays the closeted Evy in the movie. "I was looking for a Puerto Rican character, and it's kind of funny — what do you make a Puerto Rican lesbian look like? I was originally

going to play the character myself, but I'm a little too whitewashed for my own good — but when I saw Migdalia, I could see that we had a certain amount in common." Meléndez agreed to the role, on one condition: She had to bring the child she baby-sat with her. (Willis, also cited in Anderson-Minshall)

What these quotes suggest is that Troche is relying on a certain visual legibility (Puerto Ricanness as something that can be seen) even when, at the same time, she acknowledges that this is impossible: Troche herself does not fit the bill (or stereotype) of what a Puerto Rican should "look like," as she considers herself to be "too white," a characterization that I would argue has less to do with her skin tone or phenotype than with her sense of being too assimilated as a result of her life experiences, particularly of living in the suburbs with her family and having gone to college and graduate school (Troche has a B.A. and an M.F.A. in film from the University of Illinois, Chicago).[49] This personal sense of alienation and distance is negotiated through humor: "She jokes that, being Puerto Rican, she ought to have rhythm," the lesbian film critic B. Ruby Rich writes, then quoting Troche: "But I'm so whitewashed, it's like: excuse me, could I have some of my culture back now?" (16).[50]

What is strange, of course, is that Troche (who in fact, does appear in several nonspeaking cameos in the film, as a bookstore cashier and in the experimental antiwedding montage) would go on to make a film in which visual and aural (sound) clues are all we have; where a simple linguistic (performative) utterance ("I am Puerto Rican") would have solved or solidified the character's background. Furthermore, Troche's desire for the actor to not only be Puerto Rican but *also* speak Spanish implicitly suggests the director's awareness that not all Puerto Ricans know that language; in fact, that speaking Spanish is not a definitive trait of Puerto Ricanness; and thus, that Puerto Rican identity has to do with something else. At the same time, it suggests her belief that one is perceived as "more" Puerto Rican (or "more authentically" or "more legibly" Puerto Rican) if in fact one does speak this language.

Puerto Ricanness holds complex meanings for Troche. Obviously, it is something with which she identifies, thus her desire to have a Puerto Rican character in her debut film. Yet, at the same time, in *Go Fish,* the director presents Puerto Ricanness as repressive, conservative, and traditional, for example the portrayal of Evy's mom as intolerant of lesbianism. Troche's ambivalence regarding Puerto Rican culture also comes across in disidentificatory autobiographical statements such as the ones expressed in the 1997 documentary *Lavender Limelight,* which really seem to hint at class location (and immigrant mobility) as much as ethnic background:

> I would love to say that since I was six years old I wanted to be a filmmaker, but you have to understand how unrealistic that would have been for me. I think it has a lot to do with being Puerto Rican because women aren't artists, OK? Women aren't...women are, like, you can be a caretaker, you can be an educator, you can be something. My parents' whole thrust for me, their dream for me was for me to become a nurse and have twenty kids, you know? My dad still asks me what I do. Last time I saw him, like several years ago, he asked me what I did. I'm like, "I make films." I was right in the middle of *Go Fish* at the time. "I make films." And he goes, "What? Why don't you just find yourself a nice man?" (Mauceri)

Troche portrays her childhood experiences as a lower-middle class, diasporic Puerto Rican in the United States as marked by no exposure to Puerto Rican women artists (at least none that she can remember), thus her belief that there were none, a similar situation to that described in relation to the Bronx by Abraham Rodríguez Jr. in his novel *Spidertown,* where the protagonist believes that there are no Puerto Rican writers.[51] Family dynamics are also framed by Troche's father's highly gendered expectations for middle-class, heteronormative adulthood, which imply not acknowledging his daughter's lesbianism or career choice; it is thus not surprising (albeit still painful) to hear Troche say that she hasn't seen her father in several years.

Go Fish is, in general, a light-hearted, very entertaining, and at times very cute romantic comedy, although it has several moments of disciplining and violence that serve to contextualize this and maintain a more realist tone, at least insofar as sex-radical women and women of color are concerned. The film also highlights young women's anxieties about lesbian identity and same-sex relationships (Max is scared she will never find a girlfriend and end up marrying a man), as well as generational differences and shifts in lesbian values and aesthetics, particularly issues about butch/femme, hippy vs. trendy, monogamous vs. multiple partners, and about having sex with men while being lesbian-identified. As such, *Go Fish* proposes an in-group conversation that can account for disagreements and changes within the lesbian community itself. The film also highlights or parodies many elements of 1970s–1990s American lesbian culture: the need or advantages of having short fingernails in order to have sex; the tendency of some couples to forego sex altogether, referred to as "lesbian bed death"; the tendency to have many different kinds of herbal tea.

Go Fish has been celebrated by critics and audiences alike because of its low-key, fairly realistic, positive representations of what seem to be predominantly happy lesbian-of-color and white lesbian characters, at times engaging in sensuous lovemaking, in a film with catchy music including Cuban mambo as well as acoustic folk rock by Mila Drumke, particularly the theme song "Something"; fascinating lighting; unusual camera shots; and masterful experimental editing done by Troche herself. The scholar Lisa Henderson, who has written the most nuanced analysis of this film available to date, argues that "in moving back and forth between its lesbian characters' and audiences' senses of longing, humor, and self-recognition, *Go Fish* produces a communal ethos" (38), by which she means to highlight the film's function as a cultural production that helps to create a sense of community; she has also written, "*Go Fish* offers a modest lesbian utopia" (40), a sentiment also echoed by other viewers.[52]

Unfortunately (and here again, Henderson's analysis is quite insightful), the film (its basic plotline) can also be read, perhaps in a more cynical or uncelebratory way, as the process by which three semimarginalized lesbians facilitate the meeting and development of a relationship between two femme, somewhat virginal (or not that experienced) white women (Ely and Max) who are differentiated by age and style and playfully described by Daria as "a couple of geeks." By "semimarginalized," I am referring to specific ways in which Kia, Evy, and Daria are stigmatized in the film: Kia is harassed on the street (she is called a "fuckin' dyke," to which she responds, "Hey, fuck you!"), an incident that can be read in reference not only to her butch gender performance but also to her race; Evy (whose name is reminiscent of Eve and thus, of the biblical fall of man from grace) is spied on by her ex-husband, Junior (a character played by Troche's brother, Alfredo D. Troche) and shaken up and thrown out of her house by her Spanish-speaking mother (played by the Native American actress Betty Jeannie Pejko); and Daria is referred to as a "slut" by Max (albeit defended by Kia), suffers a guilt-induced paranoid delusion after having sex with a man (she imagines a trial in which eight lesbians criticize and judge her for her actions), and is also questioned by her peers for her frequent, nonmonogamous sexual liaisons with numerous women of diverse ethnic and national backgrounds, including Evy (a fact that nearly provokes Kia into a jealous rage). As such, the film oscillates between a truly radical social vision of multiracial, multiethnic integration (the idea of an incredibly diverse lesbian community in Chicago, engaging in complex living experiences), and a more typical or problematic Hollywood-style narrative in which interracial sexual relations (of whites with others) are not encouraged and in which the hegemonic white subjects (albeit awkward lesbian ones, in this case) benefit from the labor and efforts of marginalized and racialized characters, who are used as supplements or props in order to achieve the white women's own narrative closure: a satisfying, monogamous (and to follow Manolo Guzmán) *homoracial* love relationship.[53] It is precisely this "happy ending" that most "mainstream" film viewers, myself included, have typically reacted to in an endearing, uncritical way.

This rather pessimistic critical or deconstructive accounting of *Go Fish* is attenuated to a certain degree in the film by somewhat parallel or incidental minor storylines, nondiegetic, experimental scenes, voice-overs, image and sound edits, and montage sequences that propose a different worldview and destabilize the simple plot, a fact that other critics such as Jonathan Romney and Lizzie Francke have also noticed. *Go Fish* is, quite fortunately, a multilayered film that offers a complex (and perhaps contradictory) set of meanings and cinematic experiences. Unlike mainstream, realist-style Hollywood films, *Go Fish* breaks up its narrative with frequent metacritical scenes in which the characters comment on the plot developments (perhaps closer to Woody Allen's deconstructions in films such as *Zelig* and *The Purple Rose of Cairo*); it also includes dream-like montage sequences (including the all-female, antiwedding scene), the paranoid persecution scene, and copious use of abstract, diary-like reflections. The film is, in many ways, a community portrait that shows friends frequently talking, getting together, and partaking of spaces such as bars, bookstores, and coffeehouses, in addition to meeting in each other's homes. It is also balanced by the perception that it is the racially and sexually marginalized characters themselves (specifically Kia and Daria) who facilitate or orchestrate the actions of the "hegemonic" white lesbians, although this also has its problems (i.e., the idea that their altruistic matchmaking can serve as an ennobling, destigmatizing, or legitimating strategy).[54]

Go Fish's multiracial/multiethnic integration is limited to white, African American, and Latina (or Puerto Rican) lesbians, as there are no clearly visible or explicit incorporations of Asian American, Arab American, or Native American women. None of the characters ever discuss cultural or ethnic elements upfront; Kia never talks about being black, and Evy never mentions being Latina, nor does anyone talk about it either; for Evy, language (Spanish) and culture serve as the key identifiers of difference, although we could argue that she is also racially or phenotypically marked (and certainly racialized by the other characters), albeit in a different way than Kia. There is also absolutely no discussion of lesbian women's religious beliefs, and religion surfaces only in relation to Evy's mother's belief that God opposes lesbianism and will punish lesbians. Critics have assumed this is a Catholic portrayal, ignoring how widespread Protestant and Evangelical beliefs are among island and diasporic Puerto Ricans.[55]

As the film does not register any kind of explicit tension among women due to race, ethnicity, or religion, it can be said to present a utopian or idealized vision of integration among young (twenty to thirty-something) lesbians in Chicago; there are no older lesbians portrayed. This film does not register the significant struggles and difficulties that lesbians of color made manifest in the 1970s and 1980s that led to key affirmations of lesbian of color subjectivity in the work of such authors as Audre Lorde, Gloria Anzaldúa, Cherríe Moraga, Luz María Umpierre, and Cheryl Clarke. It would seem as though the film advocated or presented a post–racial tensions moment, as it naturalizes these tensions by elision. There is always a risk in this, in having spectators not notice or pay attention, or at the very least, not be aware of the complexity and enormous achievement that this actually represents. One could also argue that there is a racial and ethnic "silencing" insofar as these differences are never explicitly acknowledged or even brought up in the most cursory way, at least not in the dialogue, except perhaps in one scene between Evy and Max that I discuss below.

The most significant rupture to the film's ethno-racial utopian harmony occurs in relation to Evy, the only character who is shown having significant interaction with her family, which is portrayed as living in the Puerto Rican neighborhood of Humboldt Park. In this case, language plays a major role in the construction of her as different or Other. All of Evy's key scenes of family interaction (first, when she speaks to her mom on the phone while at Kia's house, and then when she is thrown out of her house after her mom learns about her lesbianism) are predominantly in Hispanic English marked by significant Puerto Rican Spanish code-switching and lexical borrowing. The serious nature of Evy's face-to-face conversation with her mother in the fight scene is indicated linguistically by a shift into Spanish, by her mother's refusal to be kissed by her daughter, by her command to sit down, her use of her daughter's formal given name ("Evelisa"), and by her accusation that her daughter is a *mentirosa* (a liar):

> MAMI: No me beses. Siéntate, yo quiero hablar contigo. [Don't kiss me. Sit down, I want to talk with you.] Evelisa, where were you last night?
>
> EVY: I . . . I was with Marta.
>
> MAMI: ¡Mentirosa! [Liar!] [*Mother slaps Evy.*] Junior told me where you was at last night. He said he saw you at one of those gay bars. Is it true? Oh my god. Is that how I brought you up? Is that what I taught you, to become a *pata* [dyke]? Ay, no me digas. No wonder Junior left you. (Troche 1994)

The mother's act of addressing her daughter by her full given name and in Spanish signal the gravity and seriousness she intends the conversation to have. These acts reaffirm family bonds but also infantilize Evy and frame her exchange with her mother within specific norms of conduct and appropriate rearing. The performance signals a reestablishment of typical immigrant parent/child power relations, in which the use of the parent's dominant or native language and of the highly stigmatized term *pata* also alludes to a code of beliefs and practices from the place of provenance, that being Puerto Rico. The mother's lack of understanding of Evy's sexuality (the mother's conception that lesbianism is gender inversion) is further displayed in her mother's questions — "So what you are? You sleep with women? You think you're a man?" — and Evy's response: "Mami, you don't understand" (Troche 1994).

This communal tension or disagreement regarding contemporary U.S. queer formations, what could also be referred to as a different formulation of sexuality, also comes across in Ana Yolanda Ramos-Zayas's research on Latinas/os in Chicago. Ramos-Zayas's Latina ethnographic informants, specifically the women identified as "Hilda Ayala" and "Brenda Ramírez," simultaneously criticize and socialize with the "white artists" of Wicker Park, describing them as people who "desire to have all sexualities" (what we could describe as being, among other things, bisexual, and/or polyamorous).[56] Ramos-Zayas, who is a Puerto Rico–born anthropologist, conducted her core fieldwork in Chicago from April 1994 to September 1995, shortly after the release of *Go Fish,* but was not familiar with the film at the time. She does not document or discuss having had any contact with queer people of color who lived in or

moved to Wicker Park; they seem to be invisible to her and to her informants, as queerness is perceived as being the equivalent of whiteness, or
perhaps by the moment she arrived, the multicultural lesbian phenomenon of Wicker Park had significantly diminished, as the Chicago-based
Cuban American lesbian writer Achy Obejas has suggested.[57] Ramos-
Zayas also states having felt "confused by consistent referents to 'the
artists' to designate a population of white twenty-somethings living in
the Wicker Park area," signaling that rather complex social negotiations
were in fact taking place and not being linguistically or conceptually accounted for — as Ramos-Zayas states, "At times I felt that 'the artists'
and 'the yuppies' were confused and represented ambiguous categories
that did not designate anybody in particular."[58]

It is very telling that neither Ramos-Zayas's informants nor the ethno-
grapher herself distinguished queer individuals as a subset distinct from
the "artists" and "yuppies," signaling a lack of legibility as a specific
identity formation (if one is to subscribe to such a notion), especially of
queers of color, on the one hand, and also an ability to pass and be incorporated into an ambiguous social mix that allowed some Latinas/os
and African Americans a different type of sociability. It also belies the
myth of the gay ghetto as an exclusively queer space, or perhaps speaks
to the ephemeral nature of some queer neighborhoods, which can sprout
up and disappear in a short matter of time.

The slap that Evy's mother proffers and her aggressive grasping of
her daughter is significant, for it is one of few moments in which violence is used in *Go Fish* to penalize characters' behavior, outside of the
trial and street harassment scenes. The mother/daughter interrogation
parallels the questioning that Daria experienced at the hands of militant lesbians in her nightmare delusion/trial. Yet, unlike that scene, this
parental ostracism or rebuff is not portrayed as unusual and corresponds
to dominant views that stigmatize lesbian behavior and that stereotype
Latinos as violent, anger-prone, religious, family-oriented people. And,
as previously mentioned, it closely parallels a similar scene in Negrón-
Muntaner's film that has remarkably similar results, although in *Go Fish*
the character does not cross the ocean to get away from her family.

Critics have had mixed reactions to this scene. Jonathan Romney,
for example, describes it as one of the principal points of rupture in the
narrative, "a too-familiar scene of family conflict, which comes across as
a cursory nod to genre conventions" in a film that he otherwise classifies
as "an almost Utopian picture of a republic of gay women . . . very much

set in a free-floating, multiracial woman-world" (34). Lisa Henderson has an even more pointed critique:

> The relegation of race representation and interracial antagonism to the mise-en-scène perhaps spares *Go Fish*'s many white lesbian fans the discomfort of complicity, the sense that we too participate in a social world that consistently imposes white dominance while denying or underrating its historical and everyday effects. Evy's fight with her mother, moreover, relocates the most pointed and visible moment of antagonism away from the film's interracial lesbian community, depositing it instead in the *intra*racial milieu of an "ethnic" and working-class family. Like many typifications, the scene is plausible and may even resemble some viewers' experiences — but that does not wholly transform its stereotypical meanings. (56)

This key scene of expulsion is immediately followed by a scene of Evy waiting on the street and taking the bus (albeit in the wrong direction) in front of Roberto Clemente High School, a local landmark named after an important Puerto Rican baseball player and civic figure, and then walking to Kia and Max's apartment. Her actions are juxtaposed with rapid cuts to Max doing dishes while listening to her walkman. These images are accompanied by a voiceover in Spanish of a conversation between an unseen small girl and her mother. This voiceover, which competes not only with the visual montage sequence but also with a distorted electronic jazz music soundtrack, is presented with no subtitles, suggesting—to follow Yolanda Martínez-San Miguel—a certain "untranslatability" (that is to say, a deliberate aesthetic choice to privilege bilingual audiences and exclude or limit the comprehension of non-Spanish speakers).[59] The film's translated voiceover, which differs slightly from the dialogue in the film, appears in the published script as follows:

GIRL: I want to be a teacher.
MOTHER: What kind of teacher?
GIRL: A music teacher.
MOTHER: And why do you want to be a teacher?
GIRL: Because I like my music teacher the best and I want to be like her.
MOTHER: And will you have a house?
GIRL: I don't know, maybe.
MOTHER: And what will your husband be like? Tall, like Papa?
GIRL: No, because ... because ... I don't want him to be like Papa because Papa doesn't yell, but he doesn't talk much either.

MOTHER: And where will you live?
GIRL: I want to live in a house with my best friend.
MOTHER: Do you love me?
GIRL: Yes, I love you very much. (Turner and Troche 113–14)

This voiceover seems to suggest a type of flashback that reveals Evy's interiority: a different type of mother/daughter bond or relationship, marked by innocence but also by rejection of the paternal figure, who is described as being too quiet (*no habla mucho*), perhaps a sign of being cold or distant. The young girl is clearly expressing an antiheteronormative standpoint in which she wishes to emulate female adult role models (the music teacher she so admires) and does not necessarily wish to marry a man (in the film, the mother asks "¿Y te vas a casar?" (Are you going to get married?) as opposed to "And will you have a house?" as indicated in the published script, to which the girl responds in the negative). The girl also states that she wants to live with her best girlfriend ("la amiga que me gusta más"), a gender subtlety lost in the translation, and affirms her love for her mother. I would argue that the girl is expressing a proto-lesbian identity or dream scenario.[60] This voiceover proposes a counternarrative to the Latino scene of violence we have just witnessed; it is a strictly female world, where men are mentioned or referred to but do not participate in the conversation.[61] The deliberate lack of subtitles for the Spanish-language voiceover and the relatively low volume of the conversation make it rather difficult to hear: an apt metaphor for the marginalization and silencing of Spanish as a language and of Latinas/os and Puerto Ricans as a culture in Chicago and the United States as a whole, but also perhaps an indication that Evy is abandoning her childhood ties and associations to this language and culture as she moves toward the English-only lesbian world portrayed, a type of forced or auto-imposed assimilation provoked by family rejection and violence. Spanish represents a site of origin that cannot be appropriated or even understood by most mainstream American film viewers, but it also stands for the character's past, one that does not become seamlessly integrated into her lesbian present experience.

Evy's expulsion scene culminates in a sequence showing her arrival to Kia's apartment. First we see Evy ringing the buzzer and knocking at the door of the building where Kia and Max live, but Kia is not in. A sound bridge ties this scene to the previous two, as we hear faint Spanish conversations in the background, on the street, an aural clue referencing the Latino continuity between her mom's neighborhood and Wicker Park, where the lesbian characters live. These background sounds also serve to remind viewers (even if only subconsciously, given their relative low volume) that Latina/o culture and the Spanish language are not an isolated, "foreign" element that can be easily delimited or closeted. It is actually a principal language of the geographic site where the film was made.

As the final act of the film's "Puerto Rican drama," this scene focuses on Evy as she is processing her trauma and assessing her personal situation. As Evy sits quietly on the stairs of the building, Max comes up with a variety of revenge plots against Junior that greatly annoy Evy, leading her to tell Max, "You don't know when to be quiet." The revenge scenario that Max conjures is eerily similar to the trial scene that Daria imagined, except that it culminates by murdering Junior; it is the fantasy of an antiheterosexual Latino/Puerto Rican lynching, if we are to understand a lynching as a racially motivated execution of a man, often predicated on his presumed sexual transgression against a woman, in this case to be conducted by lesbians.[62] Max is so caught up with her anti-Junior tirade that she is not really able to commiserate or give comfort to Evy. At the same time, Evy comes across as very practical, as she is concerned with what has happened ("I've just gotten kicked out of the house"), with her relationship with her mother ("My mom thinks I'm going to hell"), with where she is going to live, and not with revenge (as she states, "I really don't give a fuck about Junior"). All this, not to mention the possibly profoundly traumatizing implications of having a white woman (Max) suggest to a Puerto Rican woman (Evy) that she should partake in a lynching against a person of her same background (Junior)! As such, Evy's repeated requests that Max "be quiet" can be seen as an antiracist gesture of defense against a well-meaning but ultimately ignorant young white woman. Max proceeds to invite Evy to move in with her and Kia: "You can live with us, we can be your new family." Evy responds with a somewhat resigned or even sarcastic "Fine!" suggesting it is more a sign of exhaustion than a genuine acceptance of Max's idealistic but also naïve pronouncement.

I am interested in this sarcastic response as it suggests that real life is hardly as simple as Max believes; this scene is a critique of white lesbian aloofness. Evy does seem to move in with the other two women, and their relationship is "family-like" in the sense that they spend lots of time together and share many experiences. In fact, alternative, new family configurations are a major component of queer world-making. Yet what this scene also suggests is that, for Latinas/os, the abandonment of families of origin is not as simple as it is for white lesbians and gay men; family bonds tend to be stronger, and perhaps this is why Evy is the only character in the film whose family is directly portrayed.[63]

In spite of all of its shortcomings, *Go Fish* is a landmark film that has been seen as an important precedent for lesbian-of-color filmmaking. This is most evident in the African American director Cheryl Dunye's 1996 feature-length narrative debut, *The Watermelon Woman,* a film set in Philadelphia that pays homage to and riffs off the topics presented in *Go Fish* in several different ways, even if leading critics have consistently ignored or preferred not to discuss this link.[64] This homage or riffing off occurs explicitly in *The Watermelon Woman*'s diegesis — at a certain moment, the protagonist talks about "what Rose and Guin did in *Go Fish*" — and also happens through casting. Dunye's film centers on the efforts of the protagonist (a character called "Cheryl" and played by Cheryl Dunye herself, much in the style of *Brincando el charco*) to recuperate black lesbian film history, specifically the history of a fictitious black lesbian Hollywood actress called Fae Richards, a.k.a. "The Watermelon Woman." This can be seen as akin to Kia's introductory classroom scene in *Go Fish,* where the students are asked to come up with a list of famous lesbians in history. *The Watermelon Woman* also portrays Cheryl's (the protagonist's) relationship with a white woman ("Diana") played by none other than Guinevere Turner, whose character is described as having just moved to Philadelphia from Chicago, a clear allusion to the setting of *Go Fish*. V. S. Brodie also appears in this film, making a cameo as a bad white lesbian karaoke singer who is then humorously followed by an even worse black lesbian one, played by Kat Robertson. Philadelphia's black lesbian community is portrayed as more racially segregated than the community depicted in *Go Fish,* and interracial dating is decidedly looked down upon. To the film's great credit, Dunye attempts to validate positions both for and against interracial relationships. Unfortunately, there is no visible Latina lesbian representation in *The Watermelon Woman,* something that would have linked this film more directly to Negrón-Muntaner's and Erika López's Philadelphia works. The only mention of Latinas occurs in a hilarious (albeit mean) faux-documentary sequence, when three gay black men who are standing on the street are asked if they know who the Watermelon Woman was, and they confuse her with "the lady with the fruit on her head" (the Brazilian Carmen Miranda), who one of them insists is really the Puerto Rican actress Rosie Pérez (the female lead of Spike Lee's major crossover hit *Do the Right Thing,* 1989).[65]

Erika López's Trans-American Road Trip: From Philadelphia to San Francisco

Matters of Puerto Ricanness assume a significantly different spin in the work of writer, cartoonist, and performance artist Erika López, who in many ways is closer to Troche than to Negrón-Muntaner.[66] López's production is characterized by her innovative approach to gender and sexuality (defending bisexuality, for example), her engagement with third-wave feminism, and her reassessment of ethnic and racial identities in the United States. López's genius resides in her ability to use drawings, visual images, words, humor, and her own body to discuss sexuality openly. Drawing on high and low cultural forms (novels, cartoons, and performance art inspired by stand-up comedy routines), López moves between learned and mass media in a manner reminiscent of Nuyorican dancers and performers like Arthur Avilés and, especially, Elizabeth Marrero (the focus of chapter 5), but quite unlike such a second-generation artist like the writer Rane Arroyo, who establishes a poetic dialogue with the high Modernist canon even while addressing working-class, gay Puerto Rican issues in the Midwest. López shares the militant social aspirations of poets such as Miguel Piñero, Pedro Pietri, Umpierre, and Sandra María Esteves, but she completely reorients their worldview into one that reflects her queer, hip, eccentric, and contemporary San Francisco–based Latina perspective.[67]

If lesbian and feminist discourse in the 1970s and 1980s was marked by a passionate and militant stance vis-à-vis women's liberation, the advances and failures of those struggles led younger Latina women writers in the 1990s to adopt a more humorous and less rigid and dogmatic approach, particularly in comparison to authors and artists such as Anzaldúa, Moraga, Umpierre, Juanita Ramos, and even Negrón-Muntaner.[68] Such is the case with Erika López, who began her career as a visual artist and who has published, to date, a book of cartoons and stories titled *Lap Dancing for Mommy: Tender Stories of Disgust, Blame, and Inspiration* (1997); three illustrated and loosely autobiographical novels that have at their center the exploits of a half–Puerto Rican bisexual Quaker motorcyclist from Philadelphia named Tomato "Mad Dog" Rodríguez; and an artist's book with the text of her 2002 performance piece *Nothing Left but the Smell*. Her "Trilogy of Tomatoes," as her three novels are known, is comprised of *Flaming Iguanas: An Illustrated All Girl Road Novel Thing* (1997), *They Call Me Mad Dog! A Story for Bitter, Lonely People* (1998), and *Hoochie Mama:*

The Other White Meat/La otra carne blanca (2001). The first novel recounts how Tomato crossed the United States on a motorcycle from New Jersey to San Francisco in a journey of self-examination and discovery that culminates with her first fulfilling lesbian sexual relationship with a woman named Hodie, renamed Hooter Mujer.[69] The second describes how Tomato's plans for revenge against the unfaithful Hodie lead Tomato to jail, unfairly accused of murder, where she is raped by a male janitor, helped by a nun, and also engages in lesbian intercourse and in comical phone sex. The third describes Tomato's return to civil society and, more specifically, to a gentrified, over-commercialized, unrecognizable Bay Area overrun by *Latte people* and other Silicon Valley yuppies. The centrality of California in these texts is key in as much as it addresses the dispersion of Puerto Rican culture across the United States, from sea to shining sea — complementing Ramos Otero's discussion of Puerto Ricans in Hawai'i in his story "Vivir del cuento" and Horacio Roque Ramírez, Isabel E. Vélez, and María Cora's research on queer Cali Ricans.[70]

As Laura Laffrado has also observed, López's *Lap Dancing for Mommy* includes two pieces on the character Pia Sweden that can be seen as an important antecedent to Tomato Rodríguez: "Pia Sweden: Idle Chatter" and "Pia Sweden Falls in Love with Hooter." Pia's mixed ethnic background is presented as the somewhat funny source of identity problems, specifically in relation to her body and linguistic skills: "Being ½ Puerto Rican + ½ Regular-White-Girl has left Pia Sweden a very hairy woman who doesn't know how to speak Spanish" (3). She also idolizes Farrah Fawcett as well as "that little blonde girl w/ bangs on 'No More Tears' spray-on conditioner (made by Johnson + Johnson)," in other words, "the queens of THE HAIRLESS BLOND PEOPLE" (3). The graphic illustrated story concludes by describing how Pia, in her "lesbian student mode," attends a talk by Susie Bright, the radical sexual thinker, and goes home and demands that her heretofore sensitive boyfriend have rough sex with her — a feat which he finds almost impossible to perform.

This humorous approach incorporates a challenge to the ways in which mass media and advertising contribute to dominant modes of racialization in the United States and the ways in which nonwhite children internalize racism and white phenotype models as ideal images of beauty. This alternative exploration of race is continued in *Flaming Iguanas* where the pages of the book itself (at least its hardcover edition) are not white but rather brown, as if a paper bag or kraft paper: perhaps a comment on or critique of the African American "paper bag test" used

Erika López, "Pia Sweden." From *Lap Dancing for Mommy*, 1997.

to discriminate against blacks who were deemed "too dark," or as a comment on the shame or ostracism implied in the use of a paper bag over the head.

Humor also posits a different conception of female sexuality, what the critic Melissa Solomon has termed "the lesbian bardo," in reference to the queer scholar Eve Sedgwick's theorization of the Buddhist concept for "the space in-between." Solomon brilliantly elucidates the radical nature of López's conception of sexuality, but she misses the ethnic and racial dimensions of the Puerto Rican novelist's work. Solomon also does not mention third-wave feminism or broader social movements as significant to an explanation of the author's approach to sexuality. In this sense, I clearly side more with Laffrado's critical approach and her close attention to ethnicity and artistic form.

The shift from Pia Sweden to Tomato Rodríguez in these works indicates a conscious choice on the part of the writer to go from a name that indicates whiteness — "Pia," a likely reference to the actress, singer, and scandal-mongering sex symbol Pia Zadora, and "Sweden," a Scandinavian country that stands (or historically stood) for white homogeneity, modern design, and cold weather — to one that indicates difference: the equally strange, cartoonish nickname "Tomato" (a fruit often associated with comedy or contempt, as in to throw "rotten tomatoes," frequently considered to be a vegetable, the key ingredient in Mexican salsa, from the pre-Hispanic Nahuatl *tomatl*) and "Rodríguez," a Spanish surname. In fact, midway through the first novel we learn that Tomato's real name is Jolene Gertrude Rodríguez, names and a surname consistent with the character's mixed ethnic background, which is tellingly disguised by her comical nickname.

López's semiautobiographical character Tomato Rodríguez is presented as the daughter of a distant and abusive Afro–Puerto Rican father and a German American lesbian mother. The early parental separation and subsequent retreat into mostly white suburbia results in a somewhat artificial link to Puerto Ricanness for the protagonist. While there is never a disavowal of Puerto Rican identity, there is a recognition that it is constructed on the vaguest of referents, mostly acquired from dominant stereotypes. Scholars of migration have scarcely considered such identity fashioning except in negative terms. But it also represents a departure from the central, first-generation characters portrayed by Ramos Otero and Negrón-Muntaner and comes closer to their depiction of second-generation individuals (Sam Fat and Ana Hernández), as well (perhaps) to Troche's Evy. López's work reverses the typical sources of identity models; she and her characters grow up in white (European American) lesbian households and glean an ethnic identity from random sources.

Profusely illustrated with rubber stamp art and cartoons, López's narratives are further distinguished from more conservative Latina texts by their explicit sexual descriptions, their presentation of bisexuality as a valid sexual orientation, and their emphasis on humor, which recalls stand-up Latina lesbian comedians and performers such as Marga Gómez, Mónica Palacios, Reno, and Carmelita Tropicana. There is a significant difference between López's approach and that of such previous, earlier generation Latina lesbians as Anzaldúa, Moraga, and Umpierre. Even as humorous a play as the Cuban-American Dolores Prida's 1977 musical *Beautiful Señoritas* (which does not focus on lesbianism) seems overtly militant if oddly dated in its denunciation of women's oppression in comparison to the riotous excess of Tomato Rodríguez's adventures and travails.

This is not to say that López's work eschews social criticism, quite the contrary. Its fundamental difference is one of tone. While the political exigencies of the 1980s under Reagan and Bush might have demanded a particular insistence and seriousness, the transformed panorama of the 1990s under Clinton allowed for a different type of expression. Humor, however, did not constitute the only means of transcending rigid boundaries. For example, if it was once inconceivable for a feminist lesbian to interact sexually with men and to maintain her dignity (a view that tended to invalidate bisexuality as either "noncommitted" or "intermediate"), nowadays bisexuality has come to be more openly discussed,[71] something that Troche and Turner also address in *Go Fish* and that Negrón-Muntaner has argued is also part of Claudia Marín's erotic universe, notably when she photographs the voguer Ray González.[72] As Tomato puts it in *Flaming Iguanas,* "I wanted a Bisexual Female Ejaculating Quaker role model" (251). This is also made manifest in the drawing of the hyper-eroticized Carmen Miranda/Vargas pin-up-girl biker chick on the cover of the book, an image that reappears at different moments in the text and in other sources. Tomato has, in short, varied relationships and struggles to reconceptualize categories in order to find something suitable to her own desires and idiosyncrasies.

Some other outstanding characteristics of López's writing are her link to popular culture, especially camp and Latino kitsch; her interest in lesbian genealogies (lesbian daughters and mothers); and her consideration of what it means to be Puerto Rican or Latina, especially when not raised in a Latino environment. Carmen Miranda, the guardian angel Chiquita (a direct allusion to the United Fruit Company's trademark logo mascot of Chiquita Bananas),[73] and the "Puerto Rican eyebrow" (a reference to cosmetic practices and specific notions of style), in addition to a meditation on "passing" as African American, are some of the main referents of Latinidad in López's work.

López broke into performance art in 2002 with a piece first entitled "Grandma López's Country-Mad Medicine Show (A Food Stamp Diatribe-in-Progress)" that then became "NOTHING LEFT BUT THE SMELL: A Republican on Welfare" in 2003 under the direction of

Mary Guzmán (see www.thewelfarequeen.com). This piece centered on López's critique of classism and racism in American society and on her indictment of the corporate world, particularly of her former publisher, Simon and Schuster, whom she accused of poor treatment and inefficiency.[74] The artist incorporates humor into her harangue and into her exploration of life on the welfare line, where she has become "the Welfare Queen" as she waits for unemployment checks and food coupons. López confronts dominant stereotypes about racialized Latina women like herself, portrayed as oversexed individuals dependent on government support, vis-à-vis the reality of artists who refuse to feed blindly into a capitalist cultural industry.

The publicity materials for this performance featured an image of a highly stylized, voluptuous Carmen Miranda-like figure with a flaming headdress, showing her naked buttocks and breast covered only by paste-on stars. The figure also wears large gold hoop earrings, red opera gloves, and provocative red thigh-high high-heel boots, while her body is enveloped by what appears to be a gigantic gray feather or fur boa. The Welfare Queen's buttocks mark the very center of the postcard. This brazen, explicit image clearly alludes to the history of representation of black and Latina women, well exemplified by controversies regarding the performer Jennifer López's body (as Negrón-Muntaner has discussed), but also a much longer tradition, discussed in chapter 1, of figures like Luis Palés Matos's Tembandumba (in his poem "Majestad Negra"), the performer Iris Chacón (discussed by Edgardo Rodríguez Juliá), and to the analysis of black men and women's butts in the work of Luis Rafael Sánchez ("¡Jum!") and Isabelo Zenón Cruz (*Narciso descubre su trasero*). Erika López comes closest to her generational peer, the Bronx-born, second-generation performer Jennifer López, who has strategically embraced her body as a tool for professional, artistic, and economic advancement, but pushes her analysis in a more conscious, critically feminist direction.

In a gesture of self-reliance and independence, López opted to put the text of this performance on the Internet and to release a limited edition in the form of an artist's book made by hand, titled *Grandma Lopez's Country-Mad Fried Chicken Book* (2003), in the belief that this anti–mass market project would enable her to revive a sort of "direct touch" with her craft, responding — indirectly, perhaps — to views such as those expressed by Laffrado, who has questioned López's "marginality." This book, in fact, has a (tongue-in-cheek) "Xeroxed interior on cool paper, country-mad red or brown." According to the last page, it is a:

Erika López, "A Postcard from the Welfare Line." Promotional material for *Nothing Left but the Smell: A Republican on Welfare*, 2002.

Varied/mystery limited edition unmarred with silly "artist signatures" — please simply enjoy this for what it is and chill out on the "collecting crap" thing! / Cover (some, none, or all): hand-drilled masonite; baked Fimo breasts, painted with acrylic wash and nail polish; bottle cap — xerox cameos on thread; balsa wood titles . . . (?) Spiral binding: old wire hangers or copper. . . . May be in a drawstring muslin bag with hand-carved block print. Who knows?

López also maintains an informative website, www.erikalopez.com, and a subscription e-mail list, regularly bringing her fans up to date about current developments in her life, and has also developed a line of merchandise (Crack-Ho cosmetics), which she sells through the Internet and at her presentations and performances. She has also embarked on a filmmaking project under the name Monster Girl Movies, www.monstergirlmovies.com.

A sustained look at the work of Luz María Umpierre, Frances Negrón-Muntaner, Rose Troche, and Erika López allows us to see different ways in which queer Puerto Rican artists have addressed their experience as racially or ethnically marked women who diverge from dominant norms in many respects and seek to build community and survive. These women's engagement with Philadelphia, New Jersey, Chicago, and California serves to decenter New York as the exclusive locus of diasporic Puerto Rican culture. Furthermore, given their generational, ideological, and artistic differences (second-wavers/Third World feminists like Umpierre and Negrón-Muntaner vs. third-wavers à la Troche and López; first-generation immigrants vs. U.S. born; East Coast vs. West Coast vs. Midwest; poets and filmmakers vs. cartoonists, performers, novelists, or scholars), we can see the great heterogeneity and the historic shifts and transformations that queer diasporic female artists and writers have embraced and participated in.

Chapter 5

Nuyorico and the Utopias of the Everyday

THE LIVES of racialized, frequently poor or working-class Puerto Rican migrants in the United States, especially those who are queer, are often marked by social exclusion, discrimination, and stigma. Grassroots queer Puerto Rican cultural workers such as the dancer and choreographer Arthur Avilés and his first cousin, the performer and stand-up comedian Elizabeth Marrero have systematically attempted to transform and change this situation and empower people in their communities.[1] New York–born and Bronx-based, Avilés and Marrero offer potent counterarguments to the recent uninspired disenchantment expressed by Frances Negrón-Muntaner in her book *Boricua Pop* (2004) and to other negative assessments, such as José Quiroga's critique of Latina/o gay community activism and of the politics of outing and his call for an embrace or recognition of tactics of mediated silence or secrecy (specifically the use of masks), as articulated in his *Tropics of Desire* (2000). The radical potential of Avilés and Marrero's work, which is very much "in your face" or explicit and geared for wide audiences, comes much closer to the community bent of Negrón-Muntaner's earlier Philadelphia-based, cinematic production — films such as *AIDS in the Barrio* (1989) and *Brincando el charco: Portrait of a Puerto Rican* (1994) — although it does so with a lighter, less dogmatic, and less dour approach. It is also closer to the community-based artistic projects of the San Francisco–based AIDS-prevention group Proyecto ContraSIDA por Vida that Juana María Rodríguez has carefully discussed in her book *Queer Latinidad* (2003), to the HIV-education interventions of Luis Alfaro and Teatro Viva in Los Angeles, as analyzed by David Román in *Acts of Intervention* (1998), and to the film and performance work of Carmelita Tropicana and her sister Ela Troyano, which has been well-documented by José Esteban Muñoz.[2] It is the kind of artistic and community work that most appeals to me, and as such it makes a fitting conclusion to this book.

131

Many exciting things are happening in the South Bronx.[3] Out of the devastation of 1970s urban poverty and decay, phoenix-like, many cultural activists and artists have engaged in creating intrinsically dynamic queer spaces that embrace lesbian, gay, bisexual, transgender, and transsexual people of color. Arts community groups and spaces such as Pregones Theater (led by Rosalba Rolón, Alvan Colón-Lespier, and the queer actor and director Jorge Merced), the Arthur Avilés Typical Theatre (AATT), the Bronx Academy of Arts and Dance (BAAD!), led by Avilés and his partner, the playwright Charles Rice-González, and The Point Community Development Corporation, initially led by Mildred Ruiz, Steven Sapp, María Torres, and Paul Lipson, made the 1990s and the first decade of the 2000s a period of queer effervescence in the northernmost borough of New York City.[4] This occurred even while many of these groups had to overcome numerous obstacles, did not always have the support they deserve, and in some cases still face formidable hurdles and financial instability. By drawing on their own backgrounds and life experiences, many of these artists account for different immigrant experiences (particularly those of U.S.-born, second-generation migrants), and try to reconcile and overcome the violence of assimilation and of diverse forms of prejudice.

Imagining Nuyorico as Utopia

Avilés and Marrero have chosen to make the South Bronx not only their home and worksite, but also one of the central topics of their artistic production. Their neighborhood-based, transgressive performances and local interventions offer new social visions and spaces for Puerto Ricans and other queer people of color: pragmatic yet at times also profoundly utopian glimpses of a world often referred to as Nuyorico, a concept that riffs off the tradition of Nuyorican cultural resistance that has been a hallmark of diasporic Puerto Rican life since the late 1960s but also points toward more recent cultural developments. The term itself, an apocope or contraction of New-York-Rico, is defined as "the land of the rich at heart" in their dance-play *Maéva de Oz*, alluding to the meaning of the word *rico* (rich or wealthy or delightful) in Spanish and to the affect of love (referenced through the heart) to make an explicit counterpoint or negation of the poverty often associated not only to Caribbean island colonies, but also to Northern, metropolitan ghettos. Nuyorico stands for a space of liberation, tolerance, and social justice, or at the very least, one marked by queer visibility and fulfillment; a ghetto utopia most visibly inhabited by progressive Puerto Ricans, Latinas/os, and African Americans, and to a lesser extent, by Asian and Arab Americans, yet unfortunately at times also marked by tensions between some of these groups.[5] A concept, in other words, that still has room and a pressing need for political growth, but that offers a vision of possibility.

In constructing Nuyorico as an intrinsically queer space, Avilés, Marrero, and other Bronx-located, queer Puerto Ricans such as Charles Rice-González, Jorge Merced, and Janis Astor del Valle reformulate the most basic tenets of island and diasporic Puerto Rican culture and society. Here the South Bronx is conceived of not simply as a part of the broader geography of the Puerto Rican diaspora, but as its very center, an integral space, and one marked by the recognition of queer experience. This intrinsic queerness makes the formulation "queer Nuyorico" redundant, something that is clearly not the case for the Chicana/o formulation of Aztlán, as Cherríe Moraga's "Queer Aztlán" has amply shown. The term "Nuyorico" itself suggests, in some senses, a vast yet also very localized geography, perhaps the land of the Nuyoricans, or imaginary mind/landscape of all Ricans in the diaspora, including queers.

Nuyorico can best be described as a space of cultural contestation, of community building, and of friendships; it manifests itself at a variety of older and newly gained institutional spaces in the South Bronx such as Eugenio María de Hostos Community College, the Hostos Center for the Arts and Culture, the Bronx Museum of the Arts, and the previously mentioned The Point/CDC, BAAD! and Pregones Theater, but also wherever artists and cultural activists take it, be it to the streets and parks of the city (Central Park in Manhattan or Prospect Park in Brooklyn), or to other places such as Lincoln Center's Out-of-Doors Festival, the Dance Theater Workshop in Manhattan, or the Nuyorican Poets Café. Nuyorico is an *embodied mindscape* as it is portable, constructed, and mutable. As a malleable or flexible concept, it can change and accommodate difference. While much less widespread than the concept of Aztlán, it functions in similar ways, yet it does not stem from historical discourses of lands lost in wars or to activist movement struggles, and it does not refer to an imagined past or spiritual/geographic location or mythic homeland, but rather to a spatiotemporal potentiality of the future, as suggested by its etymological origins in the word "new": something to be built, as in a city on the hill, or Oz. And, while I am especially interested in analyzing the ways Avilés and Marrero conceptualize Nuyorico, it is important to point out that it is necessarily not *bound* to them, even if they might have originated the term; it is a collective community process, aspiration, dream, or imaginary utopia that takes life in other places, such as in La Bruja (Caridad de la Luz)'s performances and her compact disk *Brujalicious* (2005), where she raps about what Nuyorico ("that place somewhere between the Empire State and El Morro") means for her. What is most striking about Avilés and Marrero's project is how developed it is, especially in terms of their aesthetic vision, cultural work, and community-building, even when they still face notable financial and institutional challenges.

Avilés/Marrero Counterpoint

Arthur Avilés was born in Queens in 1963, the fourth of eight children of working-class Puerto Rican parents who emigrated from the island's countryside as adolescents during the 1950s. He grew up in the Bronx, Queens, and Long Island, in a household often marked by poverty and financial privation, and participated in social programs such as those sponsored by the Fresh Air Fund.[6] At eighteen, he went to Bard College, where he majored in theater and dance. Having excelled at sports such as wrestling, diving, and gymnastics in high school, and being very graceful, agile, and strong have contributed to make him one of the most outstanding Latino modern dancers currently performing in the United States; Anna Kisselgoff of the *New York Times* went so far as to describe him in 2003 as "one of the great modern dancers of the last 15 years."[7] This is a remarkable achievement given his socioeconomic background and that he has what is widely considered to be a short, muscular, "non-dancer's" body.[8]

Avilés gained great notoriety during his eight years as one of the main dancers of the world-renowned Bill T. Jones/Arnie Zane Dance Company, a group characterized by its radical racial and body-type inclusivity and for the fact that many of its former dancers have gone on to become successful choreographers themselves. Avilés was in this troupe from 1987 to 1995, receiving rave reviews for his performances and winning a Bessie Award in 1989; he was also Jones's lover for five years.[9] During this period, he also choreographed and presented his own work.[10]

The impact of being in the Jones/Zane Dance Company on Avilés's career and on his aesthetic/political vision cannot be underestimated: not only did it provide him an entry into professional modern dance, but it involved him (romantically and professionally) with a visionary African American choreographer and dancer (Jones) who was shocking audiences with his bold artistic statements and upfront political ideas on race, sexuality, terminal illness, nudity, and community-building.[11] In fact, Jones's penchant for incorporating advocacy for African Americans, queers, and AIDS and cancer patients as part of his work and the inclusion of many nontraditional dancers in his dance company help to explain the origins of Avilés's own artistic, aesthetic, and community vision: one that accounts for personal histories and includes diverse community members, and that sees art as a vital expression and tool for social change.

In 1996, having separated from the Jones/Zane company and spent a brief period of time in France, Avilés decided to establish his own group, the Arthur Avilés Typical Theatre, which initially was based at The Point Community Development Corporation in Hunts Point in the Bronx. Avilés has stated that the reason the company was named "Typical Theatre" was because one of its goals was to reclaim the cultural and social practices that have been maligned by dominant-class outsiders as "stereotypical," restoring their pertinence to the community and processing them in light of their positive and negative traits.[12] The Typical Theatre now has its home at the Bronx Academy of Arts and Dance, better known as BAAD! Avilés created this space in December of 1998 with his partner, the African American/Puerto Rican playwright and author Charles Rice-González in the American Banknote Building, a landmark factory structure in Hunts Point.[13]

Elizabeth Marrero was born in the Bronx the same year as Avilés but comes from a smaller family; she is the youngest of three children. A former gas station attendant with a high school degree, she went on to become a trust administrator at Chase Manhattan Bank while attending college part-time. Marrero began to collaborate with her first cousin in 1990 with purely amateur credentials; her incredible acting skills, powerful stage presence, varied facial, bodily, and emotional repertoire, and boundless talent for comedy have made her an essential participant in Avilés's productions, a true collaborator in the fullest sense. She has also branched out into her own, one-woman performances, most notoriously in the "Macha" series — *Machataso! A One Woman Cho* (2001), *Macha Does Vegas* (2002), *Petronelia's Finca* (2003), *Petronelia: Her Broadway Cho'* (2004), *The Macha Monologues* (2005), *Santa Macha* (2006), and *Retro Petro* (2008), all directed by Avilés — where she performs a variety of characters in a style reminiscent of John Leguizamo's early work, but with a butch Puerto Rican lesbian twist; she has also done stints as a stand-up comedian in mainstream comedy clubs and in lesbian bars, often performing as the drag king "King Macha."[14] During their Typical Theatre performances, Avilés's brilliance tends to be in the dancing while Marrero speaks in nonstop monologues; yet, as it befits dance-theater, both do a little of everything, and Marrero has also participated in some of the dance-only productions.

In spite of the fact that Avilés and Marrero were both born and raised in New York and are first cousins (as their mothers are sisters), their early life experiences were actually quite dissimilar, given their parents' very different ideas about how to relate to American and Puerto Rican culture. These radically different upbringings deeply inform their successful artistic collaboration, one in which Avilés turns to Marrero (and to other people, such as Jorge Merced) as a source of knowledge in an effort to reconnect to more traditional Puerto Rican experience and use it as a base for his new visions. At the same time, Avilés draws on his professional training, technical expertise, and experience in the performing arts world, acquired as part of a more mainstream integration into American society, and shares this with others. The final product ends up being a synthesis of more recognized forms (or at least ones validated by the arts world) with vernacular, community and family-based artistic knowledge and practices.

Toward a Theory of New York–Rican Cultural Consciousness

Immigrant processes of adaptation to new societies are complex and have far-reaching effects.[15] Puerto Rican immigrants in the United States have historically chosen different strategies for adaptation and incorporation, which can include linguistic and cultural integration or assimilation into mainstream society as well as resistance to and contestation of dominant models and paradigms. Often times, immigrant parents' decisions about how to relate to Puerto Rican and dominant white-Anglo American culture have a profound impact on their children. In the case of Avilés and Marrero, this tension manifested itself through two radically different processes: one, that experienced by Avilés, a parental desire geared toward monolingual, English-only assimilation, entailing a conscious distancing from Puerto Rican culture and from the Spanish language (a model predicated on rejection of bilingualism and biculturalism); the other, that of Marrero, a negotiation or form of colonial resistance that allowed for the maintenance of country-of-origin language and culture and the embrace of bilingualism and biculturalism.

According to Avilés, when he was growing up, his parents frowned upon everything Puerto Rican; his home was a constant battlefield in which American values and customs were presented as superior even when Puerto Rican traditions and habits were followed.[16] This alienation and disjuncture was reinforced in educational settings that also did not validate Puerto Rican experience. This explains why Avilés does not speak much Spanish and does not have much familiarity with autochthonous Puerto Rican culture. Marrero, to the contrary, grew up in an environment in which the values of Puerto Ricanness were instilled, where Spanish was spoken along with English, and where people were not antagonistic toward their heritage nor did they feel compelled to downplay it for the sake of achieving the "American Dream."

Avilés has chosen to identify the first of these two models as what he calls "New York–Rican," an identity or experience he opposes to "Nuyorican." For him, New York–Rican indicates a greater alienation that can be overcome only through a conscious and productive process of engagement with Nuyoricans (or DiaspoRicans) and island-born Puerto Ricans. Avilés has summarized the differences between these immigrant experiences in the program notes to his "dance play" *Arturella* as follows: "Nuyoricans [are] children of Puerto Rican parents who were born in New York and know the island's language and culture, [while] New York–Ricans [are] children of Puerto Rican parents who were born in New York but are estranged from the island's language and culture."

It is precisely this tension between *knowledge* and *estrangement* that makes Avilés and Marrero's work so dynamic; their pieces are an attempt to recuperate, negotiate, and transmit an experience that is not familiar to the entire Puerto Rican community. One also has the sense that Avilés's assimilation narrative has produced strong psychic trauma, which he productively negotiates through diverse means, including social therapy, artistic creation, community building, and activism. As such, his Typical Theatre strives to entertain but also to document and educate, as it effects a personal, social, and community intervention as part of a project of recuperation or preservation and transformation.

This process of critical engagement is somewhat similar to that which other U.S.-born, second-generation queer Puerto Rican artists such as Rose Troche and Erika López have participated in, differing both in its geographic specificity (New York as opposed to Chicago, Philadelphia, or San Francisco) and resolution, as Avilés and Marrero always privilege queer, ghetto, community-centered Puerto Ricanness (or its diasporic incarnation) as the dominant trope of identification, coming closer to López's more recent performance work in *Nothing Left But the Smell: A Republican on Welfare,* where she explores racialized poverty in San Francisco. López in particular has written about the inner tensions produced by this disjuncture, in moving passages in her novel *Flaming Iguanas* (1997) and in her book of comics *Lap Dancing for Mommy* (1997), where she elaborates on what could be identified as "not quite" identities (not quite Puerto Rican, not quite African American, not quite white American, not quite lesbian, not quite a Spanish speaker) that make her identity difficult for herself and for others to grasp.[17] In this context, we can see Avilés's gesture of nomination (giving the name of "New York–Rican" to his identity, which is shared by others) as a strategy to counteract those who tend more toward negation; Avilés's act is a refutation of those who say that people such as he and López "have no culture," perhaps similar to the way in which critics such as Octavio Paz (in his *Labyrinth of Solitude*) accused Pachuco (Mexican American) youth in the 1940s of being "devoid of culture" — specifically Mexican culture — as opposed to recognizing them as a new cultural formation.

Avilés's New York–Ricanness is not necessarily about celebration, so much as it is an acknowledgement of enforced loss and strategic negotiation, and herein lies its intrinsic difference with the way Nuyorican culture has been defined, especially as an artistic movement and identity. According to its leading theoreticians (people such as Miguel Algarín and Juan Flores), Nuyorican cultural consciousness came about in the late 1960s and early 1970s.[18] As a practice of resistance, it entailed the proud affirmation of a new cultural identity, that of Puerto Ricans in the United States, and solidified this through art making, site-specific artistic practices, community organizing, and institution building. It had a political context and content, political visibility (the Young Lords, for example), and was tied to specific neighborhoods (especially Loisaida and El Barrio in Manhattan) as well as to family histories. It was also not especially queer-friendly, even if many of its intellectual founders were queer themselves.

New York–Rican and Suburban-Rican identities (which is a broader or more generalizable, albeit not coterminous manifestation of New York–Ricanness, closer to the experience of Troche and López) are based on models of assimilation that can be voluntarily or accidentally imposed by parents, families, and environments, or self-chosen by individuals who wish to become integrated into mainstream, dominant white American society.[19] These identities do not share the joy of Algarín's Nuyorican,

Tato Laviera's AmeRícan, and Mariposa's DiaspoRican conceptualizations (what Ed Morales refers to as *Living in Spanglish*), and seem to allude more to loss, as in Esmeralda Santiago's memoir *When I Was a Puerto Rican,* i.e., the notion of a past, something left behind or never had, also alluded to (albeit in a very different way) in Negrón-Muntaner's self-reflexive essay "When I Was a Puerto Rican Lesbian," a discussion of her film *Brincando el charco* whose title echoes that of Santiago's text.

The spelling Avilés has chosen for New York-Rican, which separates two orthographically correct terms with a hyphen, also suggests that this is a process of regulation or systematization balanced by grammatically bound punctuation, as opposed to the messy, irreverent neologisms that engage phonetic traits (Nuyorican, Nuyorico, or even the term "faggorican" used in *Maéva de Oz*) or insert non-English language diacritics and capital letters in the middle of words (AmeRícan).[20] New York–Rican's "correctness" as a model of assimilation would seem linguistically if not conceptually closer to Gustavo Pérez Firmat's theorization on the hyphen in relation to Cuban-Americans, as explored in *Life on the Hyphen,* although it also seems closer to the very unusual and still jarring usage of the politically oxymoronic term "Puerto Rican-American," a seemingly redundant term given that all Puerto Ricans have been American citizens since 1917, except for the small minority that has accepted citizenship elsewhere or renounced American citizenship in a symbolic gesture of political emancipation.[21]

To its advantage, the term "New York–Rican" does not share the historical stigma or shame of the word "Nuyorican," which was originally a negative slur. In fact, we could think of New York–Ricanness as a site of utopia or possibility for some (for example, for Avilés's parents), who believe in assimilation into dominant, mainstream, English-language American culture as the key to socioeconomic integration and advancement, something that arguably worked in the case of Avilés but clearly not for all Puerto Ricans who have followed this path. What is interesting or noticeable is that achieving this state (or being molded into it) has negative psychic costs for some, which can then be addressed in other ways; Avilés seems bound by his New York–Ricanness but is actively trying to compensate, move away, or transform its meaning closer into something like Nuyorican.

New York–Rican and Suburban-Rican (or American-Rican) identities have some key basic characteristics, the principal two being limitations in competency regarding Puerto Rican culture (or at the very least, a significant lack of knowledge, recognized by the subject as a problem), and lack of linguistic competency in Spanish. Of course, these can also be features of Nuyorican diasporic identity to different degrees, so perhaps it would be useful or more productive to say that New York–Ricanness entails a more *acute* or *pronounced* lack of linguistic and cultural competency, accompanied by a personal feeling of alienation or distance. Here it would be especially important to be attentive to self-description; so for example, Avilés embraces the term, as he invented it, while artists such as Troche and López have not come up with such words.

Arthur Avilés and Elizabeth Marrero's Ghetto Aesthetics

Avilés and Marrero's work has not only sought to reflect community and individual identities, but also to build, create, and strengthen spaces for queer Puerto Ricans in the United States. They accomplish this by recycling, borrowing, stealing, and reinventing everything around them; they take freely from family and community life and experience as well as from American, Puerto Rican, and global culture. These practices, come to by diverse means, are actually in close synchrony to those of other Latina/o artists working in the United States and to broader Latin American phenomena, especially those occurring in borderlands and contact zones such as the ones explored by scholars such as Néstor García Canclini and Celeste Olalquiaga.[22] They also share some aspects of the Afro-diasporic creative reappropriation practices of hip-hop, specifically evidenced in rap music's borrowings and reworkings of previously recorded music, and the same ghetto environment marked by African American and Puerto Rican interactions, high levels of poverty and crime. They differ significantly in that for the most part (with the exception, perhaps, of some of Marrero's solo work) they do not embrace or advocate hypermasculinity, violence, drugs, or the accumulation of wealth as solutions to urban problems, and have not been incorporated into the dominant cultural industry the way rap has.

One useful way to look at Avilés and Marrero's work is in relation to the Latin American cultural practices that Néstor García Canclini has carefully analyzed in his very influential *Culturas híbridas* (Hybrid cultures, 1990), where he chronicles the experiences of individuals who mix apparently discordant or unrelated materials and produce new works that serve to bridge tradition with modernity. This is not, strictly speaking, simply one more case of a postmodern practice of art for art's sake or of meaningless juxtaposition in a consumerist, media-saturated environment where things are drained of their meaning and put forth as an ironic critique. Rather, it is one that sees this creative reappropriation and reuse as a form of cultural survival and of the maintenance and preservation (but also modernization and reinvention and updating) of lives and cultures that very well might be swept away, minimized, or ignored in cultural contexts where subaltern identities such as theirs are not validated. This strategy is similar to the critical engagement with popular culture that Michelle Habell-Pallán has identified in *Loca Motion* (2005) while discussing the work of Latina/o artists such as El Vez (Robert López) and Marga Gómez.

Celeste Olalquiaga's insights in *Megalopolis* (1992), specifically her attention to the resignification of Latina/o cultural practices through the optic of kitsch, are also a useful way to think of the contemporary art-making practices of some Puerto Ricans in New York that can be extended to Avilés and Marrero. A good comparison is to the fanciful assemblages of the Puerto Rican visual artist Pepón Osorio, who painstakingly glues tchotches or mass-produced or artisanal knick-knacks onto furniture and built environments with strong working-class Latina/o associations.[23] Another is the performances and film work of the Cuban-American Carmelita Tropicana (Alina Troyano) and her sister Ela Troyano, especially the latter's films *Carmelita Tropicana: Your Kunst Is Your Waffen* and *Once Upon a Time in the Bronx*. Tropicana and Troyano's consistent engagement with working-class Latina/o aesthetics and with Puerto Rican communities has at times caused conservative Cuban-Americans to renege associations with them and to assume that the artists are Puerto Rican. Osorio's, Tropicana's, and Troyano's deep attachment to comedy and humor as tools of politization also make them close intellectual allies; Tropicana's lesbianism and queer/camp aesthetic vision — which she shares with her sister — also serve to bring her work into dialogue with Avilés and Marrero, although it would be important to point out that Tropicana and Troyano have more of a link with bohemian downtown avant-gardes (people such as Jack Smith and the feminist WOW Café) while their Bronx counterparts have a rawer, at times less ironic, more "ghetto" (populist, poor, or working-class) stance.

The work of Avilés and Marrero (and to a certain extent, that of people like Osorio, Tropicana, and Troyano) proposes what I would call "ghetto bricolage," the bringing together or assembling of wide-ranging, often incongruous, original and stolen sources, juxtaposed to one another, usually set in a poor, urban, Bronx environment, as an aesthetics of empowerment and community-building, a practice similar in spirit to what Raúl Homero Villa describes as "barriology" in the Chicano context, referring to the positive revalorization of ghetto aesthetics and experience. In the case of Avilés and Marrero, their work is marked by their desire to engage and build communities, to offer alternate models and life stories, fantasies of the possibly real: to create alternate queer Boricua space. Since one of the main objectives is to attract local audiences (including entire multigenerational families), they often integrate well-known references to popular and mass culture, such as *West Side Story, Cinderella, The Wizard of Oz,* and "The Ugly Duckling," that have also been central in their own formation, and thus locate their imaginary utopian spaces within these fantasy fairytale environments.[24]

This hybrid, highly creative, and original production has received the attention of leading dance critics in the United States, who have attempted to understand and validate their work. Ann Daly, for example, quotes Avilés talking about his aesthetics and frames his approach in the context of postmodernism:

> Mr. Avilés is emphatic: "I have no problem being someone who came after Bill [T. Jones]." But then, for [Avilés], the issue of originality is moot. He has taken the post-modern principle of appropriation to its extreme: he openly copies, everything from Disney movies to whole dances from Martha Graham, José Limón, and even Mr. Jones. "If I see something I like, why shouldn't I use it, especially if it inspired me?" he reasons. "Originality is dead, but inspiration is alive. I put myself into that artwork and see what it does for me." (12)

As these comments indicate, Avilés incorporates disparate elements, ranging from classic American modern dance choreographies to mass-media cinematographic productions and literary masterpieces, and filters all of these through a Bronx-centered Nuyorican or New York–Rican gay (and with Marrero, lesbian) optic: an unabashed aesthetics of material and cultural consumption, in which everything is available, in which an absence or distance from traditional Puerto Rican culture and history is subsumed by the juxtaposition of popular and daily practices of the ghetto with high and low art. Concretely, what this means is that Bronx stories (mainly of urban poverty and struggle), Bronx language (Puerto Rican and African American Vernacular English, Puerto Rican Spanish, and Spanglish), and Bronx traditions (a mixture of those brought from Puerto Rico and those of New York) are assembled with current American popular and elite art forms and given a queer twist. While this might resonate with some postmodern practices, it is a very specific kind of postmodernism: a localized, profoundly political, ghetto poor one, what might be more usefully called ghetto bricolage.

Contrary to what we see in first-generation queer diasporic Puerto Rican artists' productions such as those of Manuel Ramos Otero, Luz María Umpierre or Frances Negrón-Muntaner (and much closer to López and Troche), Avilés and Marrero's work focuses almost exclusively on U.S. Puerto Rican experience, and the island of Puerto Rico is something of an abstract referent that has very little to do with daily reality, except for being the far-removed original source.[25] There is no sense of leaving the island; it is never a place inhabited. Instead, the desire will be to either leave the Bronx (because of the repressive traditions of its Puerto Rican community and its myriad social problems) or to reform and change the community of origin. And it is especially in the dance-theater pieces (as opposed to the more strictly dance-only choreographies) in which language, and the stories told, trace an unmistakable identity and belonging to the Bronx.

Nuyorican/New York–Rican Histories

Avilés and Marrero's numerous years of collaborations have resulted in a series of pieces characterized by a recurrent cast of characters, comprising a "typical" Nuyorican/New York–Rican family, who adopt different personalities but always have the same or similar name, often playing with the names of the performers themselves. This critical portrayal attempts to convey and subvert traditional gender roles and highlights the complexities of multiracial Latina/o environments, where siblings born of the same parents may exhibit wide ranges of physical variation and be treated differently because of their skin color, facial features, or type of hair. In this scenario, Marrero often becomes Maéva,[26] an unusually irrepressible, loud Latina mother with many children, described as follows: "Maéva (MA–mother / EVA–earth/Eve) is all the Puerto Rican mothers in the world fused into one outrageous character, the mother of all mothers, a Puerto Rican ghetto matriarch."[27] Arthur becomes Arturo, the oldest son, *el nene lindo* (the pretty boy) or *el rey de la casa* (the king of the house); Blanquita is a beautiful, blue-eyed blond sister who always receives praise and can do no wrong; Triguena is the darker sister, always caught up in her supposedly irrepressible sexuality and blamed for all the ills that accost the family; while China is a daughter with oval eyes that lead people to call her Chinese. The cast members, who resemble a *commedia dell'arte* or Cuban *teatro bufo* troupe, often shed their roles during their performances to interpret other characters, a strategy that serves to disrupt and reorient the potentially pernicious "stereotypes" that the performers satirically portray. In *Arturella* (1996), for example, Marrero plays four different people: Maéva, Evil Step Maéva, Fairy God Maéva, and King Maéva.

Avilés and Marrero's first collaboration, performed in 1991, was called, appropriately enough, *Maéva: A Typical New York–Rican's Ensalada.*[28] Here the reference to *ensalada* (salad) can be seen not only as a type of Spanglish code-switching, but also as referencing a musical style, specifically "a Spanish Renaissance compositional form similar to the quodlibet" (which is to say, an entertaining mixture of different forms).[29] The metaphor suggests a notion of "mess" or disorder but also proposes a somewhat harmonious or at least workable mixture that clearly does not emulate the more hegemonic American "melting pot." The piece incorporates American modern dance and diverse Hispanic Caribbean social dance forms. Commenting on Marrero's performance, dance scholar Jane C. Desmond observes:

> The piece featured as the main character an irrepressible woman, squeezed into a too-small frilly gown, regaling the audience with a non-stop monologue in Spanish and English. Creating a whirlwind of energy with her breathless talking and exuberant posing, she recalled the larger-than-life Carmen Miranda, here both reasserted and caricatured at the same time. She introduces herself with a skein of fifty names, marking the maternity and paternity of past generations, and talks about her fifteen "childrens" as four other dancers crawl around and through her legs to the pulse of Tito Puente music. Periodically, someone offstage yells out "Spic!" but she continues, unflappable, picking up the monologue where she left off, addressing the audience directly with "so, as I was telling you...." Dancers samba around her like back-up singers as she jokes about lazy *caballeros*. At times, the dancers climb on top of her, holding her down, but she always emerges, still talking and gesturing, claiming, in heavily accented English, "What do you mean you won't hire me, I don't have an accent!" (48)

Desmond's engaging description highlights the sheer energy Marrero brings to her stage appearances; the explicit engagement with stereotypical representations of Latinas/os in the United States (the myth and reality of Carmen Miranda); the linguistic components of immigrant experience (how accent and linguistic variation are used to discriminate against people); and the strength and persistence of the mother figure or "ghetto matriarch" who holds her family together in good times and bad. This piece's use of community-based music (Tito Puente) and social dance forms such as salsa and merengue, performed in diverse settings (including outdoors in the rarefied environment of Lincoln Center in New York) by professionally trained modern dancers along with performers with no formal training such as Marrero, also transforms and challenges many tenets of modern dance.

In *Maéva/Middle March* (1991), Avilés reappropriates a choreography of his mentor and former lover Bill T. Jones and transforms the piece, originally intended for Jones and for Lawrence Goldhuber, a large-bodied, 350-pound white man that Jones "wanted to look small against," into one for Marrero and himself. The aphorisms or *Laments* by artist Jenny Holzer that Jones originally read in English in his *Holzer Duet... Truisms* (1985) are now read in Spanish by Marrero.[30] According to Avilés, the title of the piece came from a novel Jones was reading at the time (George Eliot's *Middlemarch*), which Avilés had not read; Avilés describes simply liking the title and taking it, understanding that audiences would probably do the mental work required to link the literary text to his own (something that, at best, was clearly accidental).[31]

Untitled #1 (after Martha Graham) (1994) and *Untitled #2 (after José Limón)* (1994) are two short pieces in which Avilés once again reappropriates classic modern dance choreographies (in this case, by a foundational white woman choreographer and by an equally respected Mexican American male choreographer) and makes them into Nuyorican/New York–Rican performances. *Untitled #1 (after Martha Graham)* is a Puerto Rican retelling of the Joan of Arc story, in which Marrero plays the mother, identified as St. Peter, and Avilés plays Joan of Arc, the son, maiden, warrior, and martyr. Martha Graham's *Seraphic Dialogue* (1955) thus becomes the story of a mother-son relation, of the battle between a Puerto Rican matriarch living in the United States and her gay child.[32] Here Joan of Arc's gender transgression is resignified and reinterpreted as fully relevant for contemporary diasporic Puerto Rican queer subjects.[33]

Untitled #2 (after José Limón) is especially interesting since it is a reelaboration of a piece by José Limón, perhaps the best-known U.S. Latino modern dance choreographer of the twentieth century.[34] Limón's *The Moor's Pavane* (1949), based on Shakespeare's *Othello* and widely disseminated through a TV broadcast of a highly stylized dance film of this piece in 1955, becomes another story of mother and son: this time, Marrero is Othello, who is Maéva; Avilés is Desdemona, who is her son Arturo.[35] Here, Emilia becomes Trigueña and Iago, Blanquita.

In this piece, we notice not only a dramatic gender and relationship inversion, but also an interest in appropriating *Othello,* a classical European text centered on interracial/interethnic dynamics (miscegenation) and violence, and using it to shed light on diasporic Puerto Rican family experience, with possible implications of incest. *Untitled #2* shows the conversion of a traditional heterosexual love story into a mother-son relationship (a central structuring motif in much of Avilés's work) and presents clear manifestations of sibling jealousy, ending in filicide (Maéva's murder of Arturo). If we follow the Shakespearean plot, it also portrays fratricide (Blanquita's murder of Trigueña) as well as the suicide of Maéva. The racialization of the story as Latina/o is consonant with Limón's version, where the Moor character, which is portrayed by Limón himself, can be read as Mexican American, something that dance critic Ramsay Burt has discussed.[36] Avilés's borrowing or adaptation of Limón's *The Moor's Pavane* echoes not only Limón's use of Shakespeare, but Shakespeare's own borrowing of the story from the Italian novelist and poet Cinthio [Giambattista Giraldi Cinzio]'s *Hecatommithi.*[37] Avilés also explores the effects of technological reproduction of dance (dance film as a medium with its own possibilities and restraints), thus commenting on cinema as much as on the terpsichorean form.

Especially relevant to our discussion of a Nuyorican/New York–Rican cultural tradition are the pieces that make specific references to previous representations of Puerto Ricans, as well as to their spatial history in New York City. This is the case of *Typical New York–Rican Workshop #1* (1993), a piece performed outdoors at Lincoln Center in which Maéva (Marrero) comments on what the neighborhood used to look like in the days of *West Side Story,* before the Puerto Rican tenements were razed as part of Robert Moses's "Slum Eradication Program" to make way for the very-white cultural center now there.[38] The reference in this as in other pieces to the famous 1957 Broadway musical, which was also made into an award-winning Hollywood film in 1961, is quite significant given the musical and film's complex valences. As Alberto Sandoval-Sánchez and Frances Negrón-Muntaner have discussed at length, these American cultural productions ostensibly portray Puerto Rican diasporic life but were made almost exclusively (with the important exception of performers such as Chita Rivera on Broadway and of Rita Moreno in Hollywood) by non–Puerto Rican, gay Jewish white men.[39] The fact that Puerto Ricans nevertheless still engage with the musical and the film, and that their lives are often framed in relation to these cultural objects by other people, makes reappropriating them particularly poignant: while the portrayals might have been inaccurate and built on "stereotype," those very same stereotypes can be reconstructed, processed, and resignified as one's own (what Avilés refers to as making "typical," as in the name of his dance company), in a critical act of reception and cultural adaptation.

Arturella (1996), *Maéva de Oz* (1997), *Dorothur's Journey* (1998), and *Super Maéva de Oz* (2000, a synthesis of the previous two), in turn, are rewritings of Walt Disney's *Cinderella* (1950) and Metro-Goldwyn-Mayer's *The Wizard of Oz* (1939). In the first, Avilés (i.e., Arturo, who becomes Arturella) is a poor New York–Rican gay orphan who lives with his evil stepmother Maéva and her many "childrens" in the Bronx and who dreams of going to the princeso's *quinceañero,* or sweet-fifteen birthday party on the day of his own sweet-sixteenth. In the second, Marrero (and more recently, the Nuyorican actress Rhina Valentín) plays Maévacita and Super Maéva as versions of Dorothy, a lesbian Nuyorican who is able to come out of the closet with the help of her faithful dog Arturoto, as they wander down the Bruckner Expressway in their search for Nuyorico. The third features Avilés as Dorothur, incorporating elements from the scarecrow, the tin man, the lion, the wizard, and the good and bad witches as part of his costume, all the while accompanied by his dog Totobeth (Marrero) or Totoína (Valentín), as he travels down the yellow brick road in a search for self-awareness and happiness.

Arturella (1996), Gay Dream Realization, and Ghetto Utopias

Arturella is, without a doubt, one of the most recognizable, well-received works ever produced by the Arthur Avilés Typical Theatre, what *New York Times* dance critic Jennifer Dunning has described as "a blithe signature piece . . . that is typical of Mr. Avilés's gift for Hispanic-and-gay-flavored narrative with all the vivid simplicity and universality of folk art."[40] In addition to its initial two-day run at the Bronx's Hostos Center for the Arts and Culture in 1996, it was restaged for several weeks in 2003 in Manhattan at the Dance Theater Workshop's Bessie Schönberg Theater, and has received numerous positive critical reviews, even if these at times tend toward the infantilizing gestures displayed by the otherwise very generous Dunning.[41] (The *New York Times* critic also partook in an interesting yet tense print debate with Avilés in 1999 and 2000 over her description of his work as "apolitical," a characterization

Painting by Tats Cru ("Nicer"), *Arturella*, 1996. Courtesy of Arthur Avilés.

that the choreographer challenged but also acknowledged as a possible misreading of his intent.[42])

Arturella has a large cast, incorporates a variety of community members (including children), portrays a well-known and liked story, and has a happy ending — albeit with some interesting twists, including a bloody dismemberment sequence near the end that Avilés feels brings the piece closer to the grisly nature of fairytales and also serves as a comment on violence in the ghetto.[43] The piece closely follows the Disney film, in itself a free adaptation of the story as established by Charles Perrault, a seventeenth-century French author who rewrote what is widely acknowledged to be a much older tale dating to classical times.[44] Faithful to the Disney version, the Typical Theatre's rendition includes a series of animal characters (specifically birds, mice, a cat, and a dog), an evil stepmother, two stepsisters, a king, a prince, and a destitute, orphaned youth who suffers but also manages to survive. Here the story of Cinderella, the young damsel who toils amid the cinders, is transformed into that of a young New York–Rican gay man who wants to fall in love. The juxtaposition between Arturella's sweet-sixteenth birthday (a culturally significant moment in American culture for young women) and the *princeso*'s *quinceañero,* or fifteenth birthday (a Latino-specific, much more visible cultural celebration for young women, who are perceived to enter into adulthood) is a good example of the bicultural, hybrid, yet also subversive gender-bending project of this play.[45]

Arturella begins with an act of storytelling, as the narrator (Marrero) comes on stage wearing an elegant purple evening gown with cleavage; she is there to frame the tale and thus tap into a rich cultural archive or repertoire and cross-ethnic, intergenerational, transnational practice, reminiscent of the Puerto Rican tradition of *los cuentos de la abuela* (grandmothers' storytelling), but with a slightly sexualized edge. This gesture inscribes the dance play in a frame of oral transmission of history and culture (Ong, griot), whereby the story is a form of entertainment and a source or repository of knowledge and wisdom, but also acknowledges erotic tensions.

The Typical Theatre's retelling is marked by socioeconomic and cultural adaptation. In Marrero's rendition, "a tiny Kingdom, peaceful, prosperous and rich in romance and tradition" (the site of the Disney film) becomes "a tiny Ghetto, peaceful, you know, with the occasional crime with the *gangas* and the knives, *pero* peaceful all the same: prosperous and rich in romance and tradition." This cultural translation entails a parodical partial destigmatization and resignification of the Spanglish or bilingual ghetto as a site of origin: a place of family and furthermore, of fairytales, one where the word "fairy" acquires a very particular meaning, and where Manhattan (the seat of economic and political power and wealth) is not privileged. Here crime, *gangas,* and knives (yet another reference to *West Side Story*) do not negate the humanity of a place, although it is fair to say that the narration does operate in the realm of paradox when it affirms that this same place is "peaceful." As such, we can say that the piece proposes a tongue-in-cheek momentary suspension of disbelief at the service of very real and pressing political and socioeconomic aspirations, to allow for the envisioning of a different kind of world.

The narration also proceeds on the basis of linguistic and cultural translation and juxtaposition. Some shifts are quite simple as they employ easily understood, linguistically common or frequent cognates (apartment > *apartamento*; gangs > *gangas*) or nonstandard ones such as *princeso* for prince (as opposed to the standard *príncipe*), perhaps used for humorous effect and as a mark of gender and sexual subversion, for its similarity to the word for princess (*princesa*). Parallel structures offering both English and Spanish facilitate the introduction of Puerto Rican vernacular terms charged with complex meanings, as when "a kind and devoted father" is then described as *un papichulo,* an utterance with more affectionate and at times sexual connotations, recognized as such by the audience and marked by their laughter. Other shifts are very specific to New York City queer culture, as when the narrator states that the widowed father went to Henrietta's (a reference to Henrietta Hudson's, a Manhattan lesbian bar) in his search for a new wife. Most dramatically, the substitution of the two stepdaughters' names with a skein of names in Spanish pokes fun at conceptions and stereotypes of large Latino families, a conceit we had already seen in *Maéva: A New York–Rican's Ensalada.* The renaming of the Disney film's stepsisters Anastasia and Drizella Tremaine, who become Ana Cleta and Chancleta de la Rodríguez, is especially funny for Hispanic Caribbean Spanish speakers, who recognize "Anacleta" as an outdated name with rural connotations, see "Chancleta" (literally, flip-flop sandal) as an autochthonous sign of low-brow popular culture — what José Esteban Muñoz has described as *chusma* in relation to Carmelita Tropicana's performances — and recognize "de la Rodríguez" as a nonsensical last name. The persistent use of Spanish by Marrero throughout the piece also renders large parts of her discourse unintelligible to non-Spanish speaking audiences, who presumably can follow the action anyway given the well-known source and serves as an explicit gesture of inclusion and recognition of Spanish-speaking immigrants, particularly Puerto Ricans.

One of the most noticeable moments of cultural translation in *Arturella* occurs in the portrayal of Lucifer, a male cat that is a central character in the Disney film. In the Typical Theatre's adaptation, the cat, renamed "La Chat Duende" in a Franco-Hispanic gesture, is portrayed by a voluptuous, large-bodied woman (Mildred Ruiz) who is dressed in a skin-tight black leotard with open cleavage and wields a large Spanish mantilla with long, dangling frill, which she uses to tease the mice and dog much as a toreador (or *señorita torera*) might use a cape. Ruiz, who is a U.S.-born, Puerto Rican actor and flamenco dancer and singer, culminates her performance by interpreting a song a capella about the personal experience of male solitude ("Solo; / yo voy solo ante la gente / que me mira indiferente / sin sentir curiosidad" which translates as: "Alone; I walk alone among the people who stare at me indifferently, who feel no curiosity"). The song clearly upsets the gender expectations of the audience (the song is in first person, from a male point of view, but is being performed by a woman), but resonates with the more central gender inversion effected by Avilés himself. Ruiz's performance also firmly locates *Arturella* in a Hispanic cultural context marked by language (Spanish) and by references to the musical tradition of the bolero (an androgynous form par excellence) and to flamenco, a folkloric and at times kitsch Spanish cultural institution, also referenced in the Andalusian term *duende* (artistic inspiration or magic). All of this, of course, in a ghetto in the Bronx, suggesting that at times, cultural manifestations of Spanish colonial nostalgia can be useful sites of resistance and affirmation for diasporic Puerto Ricans.[46]

Cultural translation also occurs in *Arturella* with regard to Afro-diasporic practices and beliefs, specifically through religion and music. The dance-play can be read as a metaphor for community strife that is overcome through persistent struggle, with the help of some minor magical intervention, specifically that of a fairy godmother who invokes the Afro-Caribbean religious practice of Santería to accomplish her goals. In one of the most memorable scenes of the play, Fairy God Maéva (played by Marrero) and the entire cast dance in a circle and chant the word "Santería" to the tune of Moses (Charlton Heston) parting the Red Sea in Cecil B. DeMille's *The Ten Commandments* (1956), as the godmother attempts to conjure up an appropriate evening gown for her *ahijado* (godchild) who has been prancing around on-stage naked after his evil stepsisters shredded his dress. As this is a low-budget show — as Fairy God Maéva rhetorically asks, "¿Qué tú te crees, que this is a big Broadway production?" — there are no special effects, so she runs offstage and comes back with the dress in her hands. Asked how he feels, Arturella responds, in a parodical appropriation and subversion of María's speech from *West Side Story,* twirling and finally clenching and raising his right fist in a gesture of politicized revindication: "I feel pretty! Oh so pretty! I feel pretty and witty and gay!" This act is always accompanied by wild audience applause, at least all of the times I have seen the play.

Another key moment of cultural translation or resignification occurs at the ball, when Arturella gets to meet the *princeso,* interpreted by the gay Puerto Rican actor Jorge Merced, who in fact is the artistic director of Pregones Theater and is very well known for his portrayal of a drag queen in *The Bolero Was My Downfall* (1997).[47] The ball scene is marked by a techno/disco musical score by the band Acid, accompanied live by the conga percussion of the Puerto Rican master drummer Angel Rodríguez, who is prominently featured in the front part of the stage. Rodríguez's presence reaffirms the strong Afro-diasporic cultural element in the performance also seen in the mention of Santería and signals the interesting interplay that can be achieved between recorded tracks (the

Jorge Merced and Arthur Avilés in *Arturella*, 1996. Photograph copyright Tom Brazil.

Acid music) and live performers. Jorge Merced also contributed to the Puerto Ricanization of the piece, as he was the one to suggest that Avilés incorporate traditional Puerto Rican *danza* steps into the waltz scene, which Avilés complemented with moves taken from *West Side Story*.[48] The inclusion of a nineteenth-century Puerto Rican bourgeois, creole social dance form (the *danza*), with electronically remastered disco music, an African drum, classical European social dance (the waltz), and Broadway dance moves signal the profoundly postmodern, bricoleur mentality of Avilés, which tends toward pastiche as a form of originality and synthesis. His rewriting is not a simple gender or sexual subversion, like the English choreographer Matthew Bourne's "gay version" of the ballet *Swan Lake* (1995), in which the swans are all portrayed by men and the unhappy prince falls in love with another man before killing himself.[49] Rather, Avilés's version also incorporates a profound racial and ethnic minoritarian perspective.

Elizabeth Marrero's portrayal in *Arturella* of the narrator, Evil Step Maéva, King Maéva, and Fairy God Maéva is marked, as performance scholar Ramón Rivera-Servera has astutely observed, by her butch lesbian physicality as well as by the great humor and strong stage presence that she always brings to her performances. The portrayal of all of these characters, at times simultaneously (for example, in the castle scene, Marrero actually portrays a conversation between the king and his advisor, the grand duke, as a demented soliloquy) introduces not only humor and confusion, but a marked suggestion of schizophrenia, or what in the past would have been referred to as split personality. This unfolding of the self as one actor simultaneously plays several roles is also explored in *Maéva de Oz* and *Dorothur's Journey* to very interesting results. On the one hand, this strategy can be seen (in *Arturella*) as an efficient way to maximize Marrero's participation and make the best use of her talents. In the specific case of the king/grand duke exchange, it avoids having to pit a less effusive performer against her, but more importantly, it breaks realist convention and hints toward the alternative space that the performance is attempting to engage, one that operates outside of the strict boundaries of dominant Western rational thought, as is evidenced by the inclusion of Santería. Finally, it can be read as a subtle reference to the high incidence of mental illness in immigrant Puerto Rican communities, often the result of the stress of immigrant experience and poverty, a topic psychoanalyst Patricia Gherovici and others have carefully explored in the social realm and that many Latina writers such as Julia Alvarez, Cristina García, and Mariana Romo-Carmona have tackled.[50] Yet, of course, in *Arturella,* as in all *Cinderella* stories, it is the plight of the young hapless damsel at the center of the story that most grips our attention. Here the damsel is a boy, albeit one who has a feminized name (Arturella) and who wears dresses when not dancing naked.

The Naked Puerto Rican Faggot's Body

One of Avilés's most distinguishing features, besides his penchant for wearing women's dresses on stage, is his proclivity toward dancing naked, a modality in which he gleefully partook while with Bill T. Jones.[51] In pieces such as *Intoxicating Calm* (1993), premiered in Cannes,[52] or *A Puerto Rican Faggot from America* (1996), both choreographed and performed by Avilés, the dancer's naked body becomes the instrument for the exploration of dance as movement divorced from what some believe is an extraneous element: costume.[53] Of course, the impact or effect of his naked body goes beyond a mere distillation of movement in and of itself and immediately brings myriad other associations, ranging from Hellenic ideals and aesthetics to debates on liberty of expression and pornography. It is, after all, in pornography and in the sex trade where the naked or scantily clad diasporic Puerto Rican male body is most commonly exhibited for public consumption, often for a non–Puerto Rican gay audience. Avilés himself has experienced some of the legal complications of this type of performance, as he was arrested and spent a night in jail in 1996 for working as a go-go dancer in a bar in Chelsea; he describes this experience of incarceration as one of the worst in his life.[54]

Avilés's muscular, sinewy, naked body, frequently displayed on the concert stage and in other spaces as a sexualized, healthy, desiring object in an age of AIDS signals an affront to those who would like to keep Puerto Rican homosexuality in the closet, or to those who advocate a "normalized," sterile, and conservative family-oriented gay agenda. Such is the case surrounding the controversy that occurred at the Hostos Center for the Arts and Culture in 1996 when Avilés first presented *Arturella,* when director Wallace Edgecombe told him the day of the premiere that he could not dance naked, even though he had advised the administration with months of anticipation of his intended plans. Despite the warnings, and to the Center's credit, the performance went on as scheduled.[55]

In *Arturella,* nakedness can be read as a symbol of social defiance, of the individual stripped or placed outside of social hierarchies and conventions; it is a sign of punishment, but also an affirmation of identity. When Mickey Ratón (Gus from the Disney film) first appears, caught in a trap, he is naked; he is in a "state of nature," so to speak, differentiated from humans by a lack of clothing. Arturella is naked while bathing at the beginning of the play and ends up naked as a result of his evil stepsisters Ana Cleta and Chancleta's actions, who rip his first dress to shreds (the one the mice and the birds helped to sew) so that he cannot go to the *princeso*'s ball; the intensity of the dramatic dance that ensues, in which Arturella expresses his great frustration and despair by dancing wildly and crossing the stage in diagonals, often disappearing into the wings, is heightened by his nudity as well as by the booming music and stark lighting. Arturella is still naked when Fairy God Maéva finds him lying, exhausted and defeated, on the stage, and when his *madrina*'s spell breaks, after the clock strikes twelve. The nude body can be seen in these instances as revealing the artifice of social convention and propriety. It can also be seen as an (ever doomed) attempt for transparency and truth: as the French artist Orlan has remarked, the history of the representation of the naked body is so complex and pernicious that it is absolutely impossible to think that a naked body will not always already be full of meaning.[56]

In *Arturella,* the play between drag and nakedness serves to construct a gay Nuyorican or New York–Rican desiring body, whose ultimate wish

Arthur Avilés in *Arturella*, 1996. Photograph copyright Tom Brazil.

will be fulfilled by joining another male, the *princeso.* The waltz scene at the ball consolidates this project of self-creation and affirmation, one that dance critic Ann Cooper Albright has identified as recurrent in this period, in which "more and more dancers and choreographers are asking that the audience see their bodies as a source of cultural identity — a physical presence that moves with and through its gendered, racial, and social meanings" (xxvi). Of course, the cultural legibility of a naked body is questionable and at best complex, especially when one is talking about the Afro-diasporic population of the Caribbean; it is often the naked (or clothed) body in the context of a broader series of cultural practices and signifiers (or geographic locations) what gives it its specific meanings.

While it is undoubtedly a challenge to inscribe "Puerto Ricanness" and, to a lesser degree, "gayness" (particularly if there are no indications of style or mannerisms or other culturally coded gestures) onto a naked body — for example, in *A Puerto Rican Faggot from America,* where there is only movement and there are no words, costume, or music — the fantasy of achieving this motivates the performer, and forces us to think both of why this would be desired and if we are willing to allow it to succeed. Does this identification rely on a very specific racialization of Puerto Ricans or of muscles, for example, as a signifier of gayness? What of Puerto Rican and gay bodies that cannot be easily read? Or is this precisely the point being made by a naked "Puerto Rican faggot from America" dancing "classic" European and North American modern dance?

Reading the naked body for traces of ethnicity or nationality or sexuality is quite a different challenge from that represented by understanding the particularities of language, another socially constructed medium that is often perceived as a marker of cultural specificity. Ultimately, both the naked body and language are elusive, multivalent signs. The consistent and irreverent use of both in *Arturella* helps to define, counteract, and perhaps contradict each other. In *Super Maéva de Oz,* the Typical Theatre will recur to speaking and nonspeaking, fully clothed bodies in its representation of Nuyorican/New York–Rican experience.

Super Maéva de Oz, Schizophrenia, and Queer Diasporic Identities

First presented at The Point in 1997, *Maéva de Oz* (Part I) was performed by Elizabeth Marrero and Arthur Avilés; the dance theater piece is a careful rewriting of the first thirty minutes of the 1939 Metro-Goldwyn-Mayer film *The Wizard of Oz,* which is to say, the parts focusing on

Dorothy's travails in Kansas before and during a tornado, and her experiences in Munchkinland, up until the moment when she embarks on her adventures down the yellow brick road.[57] In the Typical Theatre's version, the lesbian subject is not constituted through gender "inappropriate" clothing (i.e., drag) or through nakedness, and lesbian desire is not signaled by the dancing of two women together. Rather, *Maéva de Oz* is a musical that relies on verbal discourse, songs, and occasional visual markers to create a lesbian Puerto Rican consciousness in the Bronx. Its companion piece or segue, *Dorothur's Journey,* first performed in 1998 by Avilés, Marrero, and Charles Rice-González, is a dance-only number focusing on the yellow brick road sequence that culminates with meeting (and becoming) the Wizard of Oz. These two pieces, along with *Ritual Dance* (2000), have now come to form part of a longer program called *Super Maéva de Oz,* which was presented in Manhattan and the Bronx in 2000, starring Rhina Valentín (instead of Marrero), Avilés, and five additional dancers with live musical accompaniment.[58]

Avilés's rewriting is actually an adaptation of an adaptation, as MGM based its film on L. Frank Baum's extremely popular children's book *The Wonderful Wizard of Oz* (1900), which MGM transformed in diverse ways, for example, changing Dorothy's silver shoes into ruby slippers. Before his death in 1920, Baum had also adapted his own story to the stage and silent screen on numerous occasions and written thirteen additional sequels to his bestseller; other authors such as Ruth Plumly Thompson would continue in his wake, for a total of forty books in the original series.[59] Some of the more recent and best-known adaptations of *The Wizard of Oz* include the African American Broadway musical *The Wiz* (1975–79), made into a motion picture with Diana Ross and Michael Jackson in 1978, and Gregory Maguire's novel *Wicked: The Life and Times of the Wicked Witch of the West* (1995), which was turned into a Broadway musical in 2003.

While Avilés has stated that *The Wiz* was not an influence on his piece and that his only referent was the original 1939 film,[60] the Harlem and New York–based, African American version should still be seen as an important precedent. As a racialized, class-specific rewriting of a classic American tale, *The Wiz* serves as a counterpoint to the all-white MGM original and clearly affects the reception of Avilés's queer Nuyorican/New York–Rican production. The fact that *The Wizard of Oz* has also been widely received by gay audiences as a queer text and turned into an icon of gay liberation, notably because of Judy Garland's star persona, the utopian bent of the plot, the colorful musical numbers, and the explicit weaknesses and fey performances of the scarecrow, tin man, and especially the lion, who is described as a "sissy," is also profoundly relevant; the film critic Alexander Doty has offered an unusual queer reading of the film focusing on Dorothy as a lesbian.[61]

Maéva de Oz's central conceit or structuring device is the cultural, linguistic, and geographic translocation of *The Wizard of Oz*'s story-line to a Bronx-oriented, multilingual, Spanglish Puerto Rican space, along with the compression or condensation of the film's numerous protagonists into two main figures: Maévacita (based on Dorothy), who portrays all of the other speaking roles in the film as schizophrenic dimensions of herself, and her dog Arturoto (Toto), who dances around her and occasionally pants, howls, and barks. These two characters are complemented by five actors who serve at times as kurokos (silent Japanese kabuki-theater stagehands, all dressed in black, a device also used by Avilés in *Arturella*) and who at other times become a singing and dancing collective chorus (an embodiment of the Munchkins), dressed in colorful peasants' clothes, as if a rainbow assortment of Puerto Rican mountainside *jíbaros*, with no personal individuation. The interplay between Maévacita and Arturoto propels the lesbian quest storyline, which is also an exploration of the divided (closeted, socially repressed) self, affected by schizophrenia and other mental illnesses such as depression. The play's unsettling journey (its at times quite frankly confusing enactment of the story through one speaking actor) ultimately proposes a process of social healing that allows queer Nuyorican/New York–Rican subjects to overcome social and environmental factors that lead to their unhappiness, and to create new spaces of tolerance.

In the play, Maévacita (Marrero/Valentín) changes intonation, pitch, and body position to indicate character shifts but does not engage in more typical physical displacements or pauses that usually help theater spectators understand that one actor is portraying several characters. Furthermore, she is in fact trying to convey multiple characters as dimensions of herself, suggesting a person who is not in control of her emotions, who seems to undergo radical shifts in a matter of seconds and who is living in a reality all of her own, possibly because of the mixed messages and social pressures she experiences as a person who cannot reveal her true self. This is most clearly indicated in the script by the fact that the main character refers to all of these dimensions of herself as "I," an I that has become a collective embodiment of the entire rural Kansas (or South Bronx) community portrayed in the opening scenes of *The Wizard of Oz,* of all the residents of Munchkinland (Nuyorico), and the two witches.

Elizabeth Marrero and Arthur Avilés in *Maéva de Oz*, 1997. Photograph copyright Tom Brazil.

One way this dissonant tension manifests itself is with regard to the treatment of Arturoto: in some of Maévacita's guises, she loves her pet, while in others she becomes quite physically and vocally abusive toward him.

Spectators who have expectations of viewing a realist representation will be either very confused by *Maéva de Oz*, or interpret what they are seeing as the portrayal of a person with mental illness, an assessment that will be validated explicitly as the play progresses. Other reactions have included accurate observations such as those by *Village Voice* dance critic Deborah Jowitt, who praises the piece but also indicates that it would have benefited from having a dramaturge or the director "fine-tune it into coherence." At the same time, if spectators are able to discern that what they are viewing is in fact the compression of all characters into one, then they will find it amusing.

This radical, jarring staging strategy locates this performance as part of what Sally Banes has usefully identified as postmodern dance and, more specifically, as a postmodern fairy tale, something also applicable to *Arturella*.⁶² Here familiarity with the original referent (in the case of *Super Maéva de Oz,* the MGM film) allows viewers to recuperate emotions and feelings associated with the original cultural artifact, while also appreciating or relating to the new one. The inclusion of specific cultural elements will make the piece particularly attractive or meaningful to queer Bronx Nuyorican/New York–Rican audiences, as well as to those who are familiar with the original film.

Cultural shifts in the revised storyline contribute to making *Maéva de Oz* a profoundly Nuyorican/New York–Rican production. In keeping with the translocation from a Kansas farm to the Bronx ghetto, the hogs from the barnyard become roast *perniles* (pork shoulders), a cut of meat that is highly prized in Puerto Rican cuisine. This shift from a rural farm to an urban housing project apartment and to culinary metaphors is especially developed in the rewording of the classic tune "Over the Rainbow," which becomes "¡Algo en la cocina!" (Something in the kitchen). The original song, composed by Harold Arlen with lyrics by E. Y. Harburg and performed by Judy Garland, stressed a belief in the existence of a utopian place "somewhere over the rainbow," a place mentioned in lullabies, where dreams come true and problems no longer trouble the soul; the only food mentioned in the original lyrics is lemon drops, a type of candy. In Arlen and Harburg's version, the speaking subject indicates her desire to be like bluebirds, who can fly over the rainbow. The Typical Theatre's rendering is oddly pedestrian in comparison, focusing on real lived experience, nostalgia, and the comfort of the familiar, although it also plays with the grotesque, as bluebirds become something to be consumed when cooked into a pie. The lyrics read as follows:

[*Maévacita sings to the tune of "Over the Rainbow"*]

¡Algo en la cocina me llama!
Las ollas están esperando para cocinar.
Algo en la cocina se tiene que lavar.
Si no, las cucarachas se lo van a llevar.

Some day I'll wish upon a star
que yo supiera la receta de viandas, ¡pero que easy!
Con ñame y yautía y batata
y mucho barbecue upon the chimney tops, ¡ay pero qué recipe!

¡Algo en la cocina, faltan dos!
El sabor del sofrito que yo, o que yo adoro.
If happy little bluebird pie
were baked with love por tú and you et moi!

Something in the kitchen is calling me!
The pots are waiting to cook.
Something in the kitchen must be washed.
If not, the cockroaches will take it away.

Someday I'll wish upon a star
That I would know the recipe for *viandas,* but how easy!
With *ñame* and *yautía* and *batata,*
and lots of barbecue upon the chimney tops, oh, what a recipe!

Something in the kitchen, we are missing two!
The taste of the *sofrito* that I, oh that I adore.
If happy little bluebird pie
were baked with love por tú and you et moi!

The bilingual (or, more accurately, trilingual) lyrics for this song stress island cooking ingredients (*viandas* or tubers such as *ñame,* a type of yam, *yautía,* and *batata,* a type of sweet potato), seasonings (*sofrito,* a typical cooking base made by sautéing onions, garlic, tomato, and additional herbs and spices), cooking styles (barbecue, a popular Southern — but more broadly, all American — style of grilling, which in fact has its etymological roots in a Taíno word), and even references to common kitchen pests such as *cucarachas* (cockroaches), which are also strongly culturally coded and humorous because of the famous Spanish-language folk song or corrido "La cucaracha."[63] "¡Algo en la cocina!" serves as a marker of nostalgia, indicated through absence ("faltan dos"). The song concludes dramatically with the mention of bluebird pie, a food item that would result rather unsavory to the American mainstream — particularly to New Yorkers, as the bluebird is the official state bird — and which also plays with the near homophone "blueberry pie"; neither of these are Puerto Rican dishes. Rather, Avilés's culinary image is a parodic resignification of the MGM song (specifically, of Harburg's lyrics) as a mark of grotesque difference.

The importance of the kitchen as a space of sociability and of food as a cultural marker for Puerto Rican immigrants in the Bronx has been widely noted by other Nuyorican writers such as Nicholasa Mohr and the openly lesbian performer and playwright Janis Astor del Valle. Mohr's book *El Bronx Remembered* (1975) begins with a story, "A Very Special Pet," which humorously showcases the travails of a family that has a pet chicken named after Joan Crawford; the mother is forced to kill "Joncrofo la gallina" while the children are out, so that she may put food on the table. In another story, "Mr. Mendelsohn," Mohr presents the moving tale of a lonely, elderly Jewish man who is "adopted" by his Puerto Rican neighbors, who feed him garlicky *pernil* but tell him it is chicken, so that he can pretend to keep his kosher laws. In her one-woman show *Transplantations: Straight and Other Jackets para Mí* (1997), which also openly addresses madness as a metaphor for immigrant frustrations, Janis Astor del Valle describes her *abuelita*'s kitchen in the Bronx (and the making of *sofrito*) as spaces of comfort and cultural affirmation, which she opposes to the sterile environment of the middle-class suburb in Connecticut to which her family has relocated. Astor del Valle's play *I'll Be Home para la Navidad* (1994), which centers on the lesbian Puerto Rican protagonist's experiences going to Connecticut for Christmas, also takes place in the family kitchen.

Central to *Maéva de Oz*'s plot is its attempt to redefine perceptions and meanings of lesbianism and of womanhood, predicated on the individual (from closeted to openly gay) but also as part of a geographically defined collective that partakes of a social change. This shift occurs after the storm sequence, in moving from the "Old South Bronx" to the "New South Bronx" or Nuyorico, and from old attitudes and values to the new. Maévacita's initial frustrations as she confronts the world of adults who do not understand her and who are too busy to help culminates during the tornado, when she runs for shelter into the closet (as indicated by a cardboard sign carried by kurokos), rather that into her bedroom, as in the film. In addition to the flying cows and knitting grandmother from the movie's oneiric sequence, a large cardboard gun and a syringe appear as signifiers of the Bronx's reality. And instead of waking up in Munchkinland, she awakens in Nuyorico, that utopian Puerto Rican place located somewhere beyond the Bruckner Expressway; as she tells Arturoto, "I have a feeling we're not in the South Bronx anymore."

In Maévacita's new world, being "straight as an arrow" (a pun for heterosexual but also for repressed) is portrayed as something undesirable and bad, and as something from the past: "that wicked straight as an arrow image I created for myself in the Old South Bronx." To the contrary, in Nuyorico, being a "bitch" and a "marimacha" (mannish) are portrayed as good. The protagonist's personal transformation is seen as part of a collective process with wider implications ("Let the fiesta de Lesbos be spread!"), in which other people should also participate. Just as in *Arturella, Maéva de Oz* emphasizes that not all of the problems of the Nuyorican community respond to outside factors; some, such as homophobia, stem from within.

Maévacita's process of achieving personal maturity is signaled in the play through a visual change: both the filmic background projection or images on TV monitors and Maévacita's clothes go from black-and-white to color; the background is in fact a television rainbow-like grid. This shift echoes the MGM film, which goes from sepia to Technicolor once Dorothy arrives in Munchkinland. The transformation of the characters' costumes, which were created by close-collaborator Liz Prince, is very notable: Maévacita begins with a hand-painted black-and-white checker-cloth dress, and ends up with a shiny, irregular, yellow- and blue-squared one (in the 1997 production) or with a red dress overlayed with black and white checker-cloth (in 2000). Arturoto's dog costume also changes, from black and white to golden. One of the clearest indications of the lesbian nature of this change (at least in the 1997 production) was that Maévacita received rainbow-colored ankle ribbons (referred to as *cinturones*), much like Arturella, who received them instead of glass slippers. Here Avilés takes advantage of the current use of the rainbow flag as a symbol of the global LGBT movement to connect with a central Oz metaphor.[64] In a funny culminating speech shortly after coming out of the closet, Maévacita affirms that it is not necessary to be ugly or bad to be not a witch, as in the film, but rather, a lesbian.

Maévacita's coming-out process makes her into a role model or leader ("I am their heroine, mi amor. It's all right! I can come out now!"). Here Avilés plays with the possibilities for double-entendre in relation to Glinda the Good Witch's song "Come out, come out, wherever you are" (addressed to the Munchkins) and in a parodic or camp gesture, turns Maévacita into "un star":

> [*sings to the tune of "Come out, come out, wherever you are"*]
>
> I'm coming out, I'm coming out, from wherever I was!
> And you can meet me, yo soy un star!

Part of Maévacita's change entails finding new words, or redefining and resignifying those words that are in current usage. This happens when she refuses labels and insists on individuation ("Am I a good dyke or a bad lesbian? I'm not a homosexual at all! I'm Maévacita from the Old South Bronx") or engages in tactical repetition of stereotypes ("I already said, I'm not a *cachapera* at all! Muff-divers are old and ugly . . . "); though community pressure ("Oh, the Cubans and the Chicanos are laughing because I am Maévacita, the good marimacho of the New South Bronx"); through redefinition ("Only bad queers are ugly"); and through surprise ("Oh, I am? I beg your pardon! I never thought I could be a beautiful butch before").

This shift or reorientation is also discussed in the form of a narrative song describing the coming-out process. This song replaces Dorothy's standard narrative explaining how her house was picked up by a tornado and dropped in Munchkinland on the Wicked Witch of the East, killing her. The narrative stresses self-choice and makes many references to well-known lesbians, establishing a public framework for Maévacita's actions:

> *Maévacita*:
> It really was no miracle, what happened was just this:
> I chose to be a bitch — in a world we made for Juan Mitch!
> And suddenly I said to myself, us girls want a niche.
> Just then, Bessie Smith — to supply me with a hint —
> Went flying by my window singing all her hits.
>
> *Ensemble*:
> And oh, what happened then was rich!
> Mi apartamento began to pitch — my heart melted like kitsch!
> And suddenly I ran to the phone to call my friend Anne Heche.
> Which was such a healthy scene, to which I reached to kiss her lips.
> Mi apartamento began to pitch — I kept depression at a distance!
> k.d. lang-ed on this Wicked Witch and I wanted to get hitched!
> Which was such a healthy scene, I could be dead, in a ditch.
> And begin to twitch, spit on and kicked, beat up, then lit.
> To think that I could be someone like Margarita López!

In this song, Maévacita is portrayed as being friends or having contact with well-known lesbians or bisexual women such as the African American blues singer Bessie Smith, the Hollywood actress Anne Heche (famous at the time for being Ellen DeGeneres's lover), and the Canadian rock singer k.d. lang. She also has Puerto Rican role models such as openly lesbian city councilwoman Margarita López and talks about the risks of depression and of being the victim of dramatic physical violence.[65] The world is described as made for men (the allusion to the fictional character of "Juan Mitch") and choosing to be a "bitch" and searching for a "niche" implies rebelling against dominant conformity. Finally, it is suggested that she is the Wicked Witch herself, and that she is killing or transforming that manifestation of her own self (perhaps by listening to or engaging with k.d. lang) in order to be happy.

In addition to the diverse allusions to mental illness that I have commented on above (Maévacita's quite literal mental "disorder" as she portrays numerous characters at the same time; her passing comments on depression), the play also offers an explicit mention of schizophrenia and sees it (along with depression) as tied to socioeconomic oppression and repression, including homophobia and rigid sex and gender norms and expectations. The links between depression, mental "breakdowns" and environment come across quite clearly in a sequence sung by the entire cast to the tune of "Ding-Dong! The Witch Is Dead" in which gay liberation (represented through rainbow ribbons) and coming out of the closet are portrayed as a solution:

> [*to the melody of "Ding-Dong! The Witch Is Dead"*]
>
> Suppressed, oppressed, depressed and dead,
> repressed I said, dead in my head,
> fed a bunch of crap with wicked lead!
>
> I'm waking up, what a sleepy head,
> Need to dry my eyes and get out of bed,
> Happy, blessed, getting dressed, just took a step!
>
> I'll lead you where the children grow so fly,
> rainbow ribbons in the sky,
> soaring high, that ain't no lie,
> who cares!
>
> I know why! A breakdown is where I'd go,
> I'd get so high, then sink so low,
> suppressed, oppressed, depressed, repressed, and dead!

Maéva de Oz, the first part of *Super Máeva de Oz,* concludes with a triumphant celebration of having overcome adversity and becoming a new person. Here the protagonist affirms her new identity and is joined by the chorus in singing a hymn of affirmation:

> [*To the tune of "We're Off to See the Wizard"*]
>
> I'm becoming Maéva,
> Super Maéva de Oz!
> Ma equals mother and Eva is Eve,
> I'm the one who created Adam and Steve!
> My life's on the fringe,
> So don't fuck with my love!
> I will break through that glass in that ceiling above.
> And know that my stance is defiant yet pliant because—
> Because when I demand, I stand rounded and grounded and founded!
> I am becoming Maéva,
> Super Maéva de Oz!
> Maéva de Oz!

At this moment, all of the kurokos and Arturoto raise Maévacita, who has become Super Maéva de Oz and seems to fly off with her new super-powers (yet another allusion to popular culture, here in the form of superhero cartoons), signaling the end of part one.

It is legitimate to question why there is such a difference in approach to the constitution of gayness in *Arturella* and lesbianism in *Maéva de Oz,* as well as such different end results. In the first, a celebration of a youth's body and his agony of facing adversity culminates in a traditional storybook love affair, even if it is one tainted by an alternate gory ending (dismemberment). In the second, the individual child's quest ends in a process of self-identification and consciousness-raising, a coming-to-being as a liberated individual (and a superhero), but not an explicit corporeal celebration of the lesbian body or of lesbian relationships. I believe the difference in these pieces has to do with the divergent film models followed, with the particularities of Avilés's and Marrero's (and Valentín's) training and skills, and with the possibly different meanings of a naked female body on-stage.[66] It may also have to do with the fact that, while the creative process often occurs in tandem, Avilés ultimately controls the artistic direction of the pieces. The camp nature or campiness of the plot should also be considered, since Avilés is not proposing a realist representation, but rather a humorous yet politicized form of entertainment. I find both pieces satisfactory, but I am aware that some people are not pleased with these differences.

Dorothur's Journey, the companion piece to *Maéva de Oz,* shifts the action away from Maévacita and the spoken word to a different realm. Strongly centered on a campy seventies disco aesthetic, the piece has no dialogue and the plot is constructed exclusively through dance. Here Dorothur (Avilés) incorporates the other characters of *The Wizard of Oz* (the scarecrow, the tin man, the lion, the good witch Glinda, the Wicked Witch of the West, and the wizard) as part of his costume, something that also occurs in a less noticeable fashion to Maévacita in *Maéva de Oz.* While Dorothur dances with his dog, a kuroko dressed as Link from *The Mod Squad* (Rice-González, sporting hot pants and a large Afro hairstyle) comes on stage and slowly dresses him with different garments (at times just a sleeve) alluding to the previously mentioned characters.[67] As Avilés has stated, each one of these is seen as embodying certain attributes such as love, hate, being cowardly or being brave, that every individual typically should have access to:

> It was about receiving all of these things: love, hate, power, all that stuff, and putting them on one person, and this person not really understanding that he has all of these things, and not being able to control it. . . . We had a big deconstructed disco ball put over my head, and that's when I became the Wizard. . . . You feel like such a powerful person now because you realize that you can choose to love when you want to love, you can choose to hate when you want to hate, you can choose to be smart or dumb, in whatever situation you can do that in. I think that for Latino people that's a really important thing to understand because I think that a lot of us at least who were born in New York feel stupid, you know? Just stupid, rather than realizing that, "Oh shit, you know?" We make decisions about where it is we want to be smart and cunning, and where it is we want to be stupid. We *make* those decisions. We're not just stupid. And that's where I speak from a very working-class, actually, a very poor-class situation, where you feel like shit all the time. And through social therapy, I feel very empowered. I feel as if, "Oh shit, I could love, and I could hate, and I could feel stupid and I could feel smart whenever I want to, not whenever *it* takes over *me.*"[68]

By embodying all of *The Wizard of Oz*'s characters, Avilés proposes to gain control over his identity and the full range of emotions and talents at his disposal. Avilés's theorization of stupidity as a tool of oppression (and resistance) tied to poverty reveals a grasp of the workings of hegemonic power over racialized minorities; his use of the term "poor-class" as a vernacular counterpoint to the euphemism of "working-class" is particularly noticeable. Here the scarecrow's lack of a brain (a central motif in *The Wizard of Oz*) is restructured into a contingent, street-smart tactic or perhaps even a strategy of empowerment. Stupidity, as the literary critic Avital Ronell has signaled, is hardly exclusive to those who lack intelligence: it is a complex emotion or performance with its own weight, used for good and evil, and profoundly imbedded with social implications.

Dorothur's Journey presents an entertaining quest for self-fulfillment. It ends on a light, inspiring note, as the dancers create a tableau simulating the 1970s TV program *Charlie's Angels* (the three dancers as glamorous, pistol-wielding, empowered women detectives) and the disco film *Saturday Night Fever.* Avilés describes John Travolta's signature disco pose from this movie as simultaneously pointing toward the sky (reaching up high) with one arm and toward the ground (indicating a sense of being grounded) with the other, a combination that sums up well the dynamic efforts of artists and activists such as Avilés and Marrero, who are trying to raise their community but also maintain a strong sense of roots.

The performances of Arthur Avilés and Elizabeth Marrero represent a radical new form of Puerto Rican diasporic cultural production, a dramatic departure not only from historic negative portrayals of the Puerto Rican Bronx such as those of René Marqués (in his best-known play *La carreta,* 1952) or infamous Hollywood renditions such as *Fort Apache, The Bronx* (1981), but also from the more nuanced (yet at times also depressing) views of Nuyorican artists such as Nicholasa Mohr, Abraham Rodríguez Jr., and Janis Astor del Valle, who have also discussed the Bronx experience in their work. They do not correspond neatly to any of the categories that Juan Flores offers in his essays on Nuyorican cultural consciousness, although they interestingly borrow diverse aspects, particularly a utopian vision, manifested in fantasy Hollywood-inspired scenarios (or archetypes) rather than more realist-based narratives. Avilés and Marrero resignify strong ideological master narratives and inflect them with local, realist content, a gesture that makes them seem more closely associated to Latina/o and Latin American hybrid productions such as those of Luis Alfaro and Carmelita Tropicana (specifically her rewriting of the Cucarachita Martina story in *With What Ass Does the Cockroach Sit?*), or the Puerto Rican Javier Cardona, who rewrote the *Sleeping Beauty* tale in his performance *You Don't Look Like* as a racialized (queer) Puerto Rican search for identity.

Avilés and Marrero's postmodern aesthetics reflect the artists' simultaneous rejection and embrace of traditional classic forms, such as canonical American modern dance, and of mass-media texts within a rich Bronx Nuyorican/New York–Rican context. Most significantly, their commitment to a Latino community in the Bronx means that most of the productions I have discussed are presented in community centers and other locations that are accessible to their desired audience. In this sense, Avilés and Marrero's work is a radical departure from traditional modern dance, an elite form performed for select groups, and becomes a popular theatrical or performance modality, whose aspirations are to critically present and reflect on the reality of Nuyoricans and New York–Ricans, and gay and lesbian ones specifically.

Acknowledgments

THIS BOOK IS AN EXTENSION and significant revision of my Ph.D. dissertation, written in the Department of Spanish and Portuguese at Columbia University in the city of New York under the supervision of Jean Franco, a visionary feminist Latin American cultural critic and scholar with whom I had the privilege to study for a number of years. It is also the result of important intellectual mentorship of other faculty, notably of Roger Lancaster, whose anthropological work on gender and sexuality in Nicaragua and Latin America decisively shaped my thinking. I thank all of my professors at Columbia and Barnard, especially Licia Fiol-Matta and Flor María Rodríguez-Arenas, for their generous support, as well as my graduate cohort (at Columbia and New York University), whose encouragement has been legendary, especially Margarita Saona, Betina Kaplan, Andrea Parra, Guillermina de Ferrari, William Childers, Celinés Pimentel, Sonya Canetti Mirabal, Arnaldo López-Maldonado, and Magdalena Sagardía.

Research for this book was sponsored by the Social Science Research Council's International Migration Program Minority Summer Dissertation Workshop Fellowship. I thank the SSRC for its vision and generosity, and my fellow fellows for their comments and camaraderie that summer in Chapel Hill. My writing was also facilitated by a Columbia University Graduate School of Arts and Sciences Merit Fellowship for Historically Underrepresented Ph.D. Students. Sabbaticals and nurturance leaves at Rutgers, the State University of New Jersey, New Brunswick, and most recently at the University of Michigan, Ann Arbor, allowed me to substantially advance this project. A Woodrow Wilson National Fellowship Foundation Career Enhancement Fellowship for Junior Faculty finally allowed me to finish the book. To all of these institutions, my profound appreciation.

I especially thank my colleagues in the Program in American Culture and the Department of Romance Languages and Literatures at the University of Michigan, many of whom prodded me mercilessly to ensure that this book was as good as it could be. To Catherine

Benamou, María Cotera, Carroll Smith-Rosenberg, Jesse Hoffnung-Garskof, Jarrod Hayes, Gustavo Verdesio, Cristina Moreiras, Peggy McCracken, Gareth Williams, Javier Sanjinés, Paulina Alberto, Silvia Pedraza, Amy Sara Carroll, Anthony P. Mora, Magdalena Zaborowska, Alan Wald, Sarita See, Nadine Naber, and Evelyn Alsultany, my heartfelt thanks. To my colleagues who have since left — particularly Jossianna Arroyo, Lucía Suárez, Ifeoma Nwankwo, Andy Smith, María Carla Sánchez, and María Montoya — you made my life so much richer and are greatly missed.

It would have been absolutely impossible to write this book without the most generous cooperation of numerous queer diasporic Puerto Rican artists: Rane Arroyo, Janis Astor del Valle, Arthur Avilés, Erika López, Angel Lozada, Elizabeth Marrero, Nemir Matos-Cintrón, Jorge Merced, Frances Negrón-Muntaner, Charles Rice-González, Angel Rodríguez-Díaz, Luz María Umpierre, and Alfredo Villanueva-Collado, you are lights on my path. The spirit of Manuel Ramos Otero has accompanied me in profound and mysterious ways since I began this journey; as I am a queer Rican artist, in many ways this book is about me, but, Manuel, it is most explicitly about you and for you.

At the University of Minnesota Press, Richard Morrison has been a kind and sympathetic editor, and I am greatly in his debt for his patience. I also appreciate the help of his editorial assistant, Adam Brunner, and of John Eagleson, for the copyediting and typesetting of *Queer Ricans*. A most generous group of fellow academics, friends, and mentors, has joined me on the very long voyage of this book: Silvia Alvarez Curbelo, Frances Aparicio, Luis Aponte-Parés, José Aranda, Efraín Barradas, Daniel Balderston, Ruth Behar, Emilio Bejel, Emilie Bergmann, Mary Pat Brady, George Chauncey, Daisy Cocco de Filippis, Elizabeth Crespo Kebler, Arnaldo Cruz-Malavé, María DeGuzmán, Juanita (Ramos) Díaz-Cotto, Jorge Duany, Brad Epps, Lowell Fiet, Juan Flores, David William Foster, Myrna García Calderón, Juan G. Gelpí, Dara Goldman, Gayatri Gopinath, Laura G. Gutiérrez, Judith Halberstam, María Herrera-Sobek, Gladys Jiménez, Miriam Jiménez Román, E. Patrick Johnson, Miranda Joseph, Lázaro Lima, Heather Love, Agnes Lugo-Ortiz, Eithne Luibhéid, Martin Manalansan, Elena M. Martínez, Sylvia Molloy, Oscar Montero, José Esteban Muñoz, Suzanne Oboler, Ricardo Ortíz, José Quiroga, Julio Ramos, Tey Diana Rebolledo, Nelly Richard, Rubén Ríos Avila, Raquel Z. Rivera, Ramón Rivera-Servera, Eliana Rivero, Juana María Rodríguez, Malena Rodríguez-Castro, Carlos Rodríguez-Matos, Josie Saldaña, Virginia Sánchez Korrol, Alberto Sandoval-Sánchez, Mayra Santos-Febres,

Ben. Sifuentes-Jáuregui, Paul Julian Smith, Doris Sommer, Diana Taylor, Daniel Torres, Lourdes Torres, Silvio Torres-Saillant, Sandy Soto, Yvonne Yarbro-Bejarano, George Yúdice, and Patricia Zavella, you have all inspired me and taught me what it means to be a great scholar. To David Román, my thanks for being a most generous reader of this manuscript and giving me useful advice and encouragement. Yolanda Martínez–San Miguel read so many versions of this book that I have lost count; you are a role model in more ways than I can describe, and a kind friend to boot. Nunca te podré agradecer lo suficiente toda tu ayuda.

During 1998–99, my generous colleagues at the Ohio State University made Columbus a welcoming place. Particular thanks to Elizabeth Davis, Maureen Ahearn, Ileana Rodríguez, Mayra Bonet, Ignacio Corona, Fernando Unzueta, Dieter Wanner, Julia Watson, and Gregor Hens. From my years at Rutgers, I thank Asela Rodríguez de Laguna, Ana Yolanda Ramos-Zayas, Camilla Stevens, César Braga-Pinto, Susan Martin-Márquez, Mary Lee Bretz, Elpidio Laguna Díaz, Olga Jiménez de Wagenheim, Luis Martínez-Fernández, Carmen Whalen, Mónica Licourt, Édgar Rivera Colón, Cheryl Clarke, and the wonderful faculty and staff of the Department of Women's and Gender Studies and the Institute for Research on Women and Gender, particularly Barbara Balliet, Ed Cohen, Harriet Davidson, Beth Hutchison, Jasbir Puar, Joanna Regulska, and Louisa Schein. My thanks to Aldo Lauria for inviting me to share my work on Erika López at Rutgers in 2006, and to Zaire Dinzey Flores for her insights on race. My fellow board members at the Center for Lesbian and Gay Studies at the City University of New York during 1999–2002 were often sources of inspiration. Among them I most want to thank Amber Hollibaugh, Esther Newton, Robert Reid-Pharr, Paisley Currah, and Alisa Solomon. The board members of Latino Gay Men of New York were a most kind and supportive group, and I am especially thankful to Jimmy López-Acosta, Roberto Martínez, and Mark Reyes. I also wish to thank Andrés Duque for his outstanding job as the coordinator of Mano a Mano at the Latino Commission on AIDS. Support from the Center for Puerto Rican Studies at Hunter College, City University of New York, was also crucial. I thank Xavier Totti, José de Jesús, and Anthony de Jesús.

I have been blessed with many extraordinary friendships since I began this project. The late Leticia Stella Serra was for a long time my biggest fan and greatest source of inspiration: may this book serve as a small tribute to her memory. Aravind Enrique Adyanthaya, Carlos Arroyo,

Isolina Ballesteros, Javier Cardona, Angel Cienfuegos, Nayda Collazo-Lloréns, Jorge Ignacio Cortiñas, Marcial Godoy Anativia, Kelly Keating, Javier Laureano-Pérez, Carmen Oquendo-Villar, Alfredo Torres, Mark Trautman, Michael Witt, Thomas Uldrick and Towfiq Awwal, Rafael Rosario-Laguna and David Lounsbury, you have all been kind friends. The remarkable Eugenio Frías-Pardo took it upon himself to call me periodically for years to check on my progress. More recently, I have benefited from several new and renewed friendships in Ann Arbor, Detroit, and elsewhere. I thank Michael Woodford, Lori Brooks and Laura Wernick, Christian Willauer and HyeJohn Chung, Sebastián José Colón-Otero, Jim Leija, Holly Hughes, Tim Retzloff and Rick Yuille, Atef Said, Ricardo Domínguez, Jason Wright, Leo Ogata, Lorgia García-Peña, Mariam Colón Pizarro and Rafael Boglio, Radost Rangelova, Jessica Piney, Beatriz Ramírez Betances, Cristina Míguez, Danny Méndez, Celiany Rivera-Velázquez, Jessi Gan, Laura Halperín, Isabel Córdova, Julio Domínguez and Dave Hill, Sam Consiglio, Alvarito Jurado, Fausto and Patricia Fernós, Marc Felion, and the entire cast of the Feast of Fools podcast for keeping me sane and relatively happy. My neighbors Jackie Byars, Carl Michel, Mike Sivak, and Julie Renfro deserve a special thanks for looking after me and nurturing me in so many different ways.

Finally, I thank my family, which has been patient and supportive. My parents, Mona and Don La Fountain, have not always understood what I do but have never wavered in their support. Marion and Peter Stark have been my East Coast parents in exile, while Nick and Maria Stokes have been my Cali comrades in arms. Connie Santoni has always had a kind word. My cousins Eric, Sara, and Damien Stark, Dorian Santoni, and Trevor and Jason Stokes have always been true. My sister, Michele, and my brother-in-law, Rodrigo Leo Ortiz Arroyo, and niece, Julieta Omikua, are a great delight. It probably all began because of my grandmother's storytelling, and that is why this book is dedicated to her. Thanks.

Notes

Introduction

1. Sexuality is also a key factor provoking non-Latina/o, white American migration to Puerto Rico and return migration of diasporic Puerto Ricans to the island, topics I will not explore in this book.

2. See Altman; Binnie; Carrillo; Epps et al.; Espín; Gopinath; Luibhéid; Luibhéid and Cantú; Manalansan; Patton and Sánchez-Eppler; Puar; Reddy; Warner.

3. See Acosta-Belén and Santiago; Díaz Quiñones (*La memoria rota*); Duany; Flores; Grosfoguel; Laó-Montes; C. Rodríguez; Torre et al.; Torres and Velázquez; Whalen and Vázquez-Hernández.

4. I have attended performances at the American Crafts Museum, New York City; Bronx Academy of Arts and Dance, Hunts Point, New York; Bessie Schönberg Theater, Dance Theater Workshop, New York City; Douglass Student Center, Rutgers, the State University of New Jersey, New Brunswick; Hostos Center for the Arts and Culture, Bronx, New York; Nuyorican Poets Café, New York City; Performance Space 122, New York City; Pregones Theater, Bronx, New York; and WOW Café Theatre, New York City. The dance-theater performances of Arthur Avilés for the most part do not have written scripts, as the actors simply memorize all the lines. I transcribed *Arturella* and *Maéva de Oz* for this book.

5. Archives and libraries consulted for this research include Archibald S. Alexander Library and Douglass Library, Rutgers, the State University of New Jersey, New Brunswick; Bronx Academy of Arts and Dance, Hunts Point, New York; Centro Library and Archives, Center for Puerto Rican Studies, Hunter College, New York City; Colección Puertorriqueña, Biblioteca José M. Lázaro, and Seminario Federico de Onís, Facultad de Humanidades, University of Puerto Rico, Río Piedras; Elmer Holmes Bobst Library, New York University, New York City; Harlan Hatcher Graduate Library, Shapiro Undergraduate Library, and Special Collections Library, University of Michigan, Ann Arbor; New York Public Library for the Performing Arts, New York City; Nicholas Murray Butler Library and Lehman Social Sciences Library, Columbia University, New York City; Walter Royal Davis Library, University of North Carolina, Chapel Hill.

6. See Warner, *Fear of a Queer Planet*. For discussions of the applicability and translatability of queer as a conceptual tool into other linguistic and cultural contexts, see Johnson (" 'Quare' Studies' "); Llamas; Louro; Moreno.

7. See C. Vázquez, "Citizen Queer."

8. See La Fountain–Stokes, "Queer Ducks"; Martorell, "Nominación"; Murray and Dynes.

9. Manalansan addresses these issues with regard to Tagalog and English in *Global Divas*, 21–61.

173

10. Negrón-Muntaner's *Boricua Pop* (2004) includes significant discussions of queer diasporic Puerto Rican culture, but does not explicitly focus on LGBT issues as its primary methodological or intellectual concern. Guzmán's *Gay Hegemony/Latino Homosexualities* (2006) is a sociological study that centers on diasporic Puerto Rican gay men, although the author does not indicate this in the title. Cruz-Malavé's *Queer Latino Testimonio, Keith Haring, and Juanito Xtravaganza* (2007) is a major contribution to our understanding of queer Nuyorican lived experience.

11. See Fiske; Schechner; R. Williams.

12. On Puerto Rican queer and LGBT issues, see D. Acevedo et al. (*Los otros cuerpos*); Aponte-Parés ("*Outside/In*"); Aponte-Parés and Merced; Aponte-Parés et al.; Ardín Pauneto; J. Arroyo; Asencio; Baerga Santini; Barradas; Bleys; Crespo Kebler; Cruz-Malavé; Dávila-Caballero; Lía Fiol-Matta; Licia Fiol-Matta; Liza Fiol-Matta; Gelpí; Guzmán; Hidalgo ("Puerto Rican Lesbian"); Hidalgo and Hidalgo Christensen; Iglesias; F. Jiménez; La Fountain–Stokes; Lugo-Ortiz; Martínez–San Miguel ("Beyond Homonormativity" and *Caribe Two Ways*); Morales-Díaz; Muñoz (*Disidentifications*); Muñoz-Laboy; Negrón-Muntaner; Oliver; Quiroga (*Tropics of Desire*); Ramírez; Juanita Ramos; Reyes; Ríos Avila; Rivera Lassén and Crespo Kebler; Rivera-Servera; J. M. Rodríguez; Rodríguez Allende; Rodríguez Madera; Rodríguez-Matos; Sandlin; Sandoval-Sánchez; D. Torres; L. Torres; Trelles Hernández; Umpierre ("Lesbian Tantalizing"); Vidal-Ortiz.

13. See Aponte-Parés et al., "Puerto Rican Queer Sexualities," for a useful summary and bibliography of this field, as well as articles in a special issue of *CENTRO Journal* 19, no. 1 (Spring 2007).

14. See Johnson, " 'Quare' Studies"; Ferguson.

15. See del Puente; La Fountain–Stokes, "1898"; Rosado; Vega.

16. See La Fountain–Stokes, "1898"; Negrón-Muntaner, "Echoing Stonewall."

17. See Delgado Castro.

18. See del Puente.

19. On police arrests, see Laureano Pérez. See Acevedo on progressive Protestant theology in Puerto Rico.

20. Gopinath discusses queerness as unnamable and unimaginable in the South Asian context in *Impossible Desires*.

21. On the open negotiation of the closet, see Decena ("Tacit Subjects"); Lancaster ("Tolerance and Intolerance"); Sedgwick.

22. See Ramírez.

23. I view Antonio S. Pedreira's harangue against effeminate men in *Insularismo* (1934) and René Marqués's comments regarding Puerto Rican men's "docility" (*El puertorriqueño dócil*) as characterizations of unmanly behavior and homosexuality as threats to the nation.

24. See Braulio, Crespo Kebler, Dávila-Caballero, and J. M. Rodríguez ("Getting F**ked").

25. The Reverend Margarita Sánchez de León was one of the main leaders responsible for the elimination of Article 103 of the Puerto Rican Penal Code, which penalized consensual, adult, male and female same-sex relations with up to ten years of imprisonment (see La Fountain–Stokes, "1898").

26. See J. M. Rodríguez ("Getting F**ked") for an insightful analysis of the (in)significance of this three-day precedent.

27. This is certainly the case of how the American gay male migration to Puerto Rico in the 1960s was looked at; to this day, most gay-owned businesses on the island belong to non–Puerto Ricans. See Negrón-Muntaner ("Echoing Stonewall"), La Fountain–Stokes ("1898"). In René Marqués's novel *La mirada* (1976), there is a subtext that the prevalence of homosexuality on the island is directly linked to the North American sexual liberation movement, and that as such, Americans are to blame for its preponderance.

28. Associations of male homosexuality and foreignness also occur in the very etymology of the words used to describe male homosexuals. In Spain, for example, and by extension all of Latin America, the term "bugarrón" (used to refer to the "active" partner in same-sex male intercourse) originates from the Latin term *bulgarus*, or Bulgarian. See Cela.

29. See Haeberle.

30. See Arenas; Lumsden; Peña ("Visibility and Silence"); and Young.

31. Duany ("The Rough Edges") is an exception.

32. See Peña ("Visibility and Silence") for a useful critique of Alejandro Portes.

33. See Stychin.

34. Manolo Guzmán describes sexile as follows: "A *sexile* is a neologism of mine that refers to the exile of those who have had to leave their nations of origins on account of their sexual orientation" (" 'Pa la Escuelita,' " 227). More recently, Jaime Cortez has created an HIV/AIDS-prevention graphic novel called *Sexilio/Sexile*, based on the life experiences of Adela Vázquez, a transgender Cuban/Mariel refugee in California.

35. Epps et al., *Passing Lines;* Cruz-Malavé and Manalansan, *Queer Globalizations;* Luibhéid and Cantú, *Queer Migrations*. Also see Eng, "Out Here"; Otalvaro-Hormillosa; Puar.

36. On migration to Canada, see Crary; Fox. On internal U.S. migration, see "New Virginia Law."

37. Epps quotes a passage from Robert J. Foss stating that the exclusion was on medical rather than moral grounds ("Passing Lines," 109); other authors differ. See, especially, Luibhéid (*Entry Denied* and "Introduction" to Luibhéid and Cantú, *Queer Migrations*, ix–xlvi).

38. See Luibhéid ("Obvious Homosexuals") for a history of this period, and MacLean for a case of expulsion.

39. The most notable current case of exclusion is that of foreigners who are HIV positive or have AIDS. While there is no longer automatic exclusion on the grounds of homosexuality, it is becoming harder and harder to gain asylum on the basis of persecution due to sexual orientation. To receive such asylum, individuals must prove that they are subjected to harassment and violence for belonging to a "social group or organization." See J. M. Rodríguez, "The Subject on Trial" (*Queer Latinidad*, 84–113).

40. See Ingram et al. and Bell and Valentine for a thorough discussion of lesbian and gay geographies.

41. See Gil, 55–79.

42. See Soto, *En busca*.

43. See Soto, "La cautiva" (*Spiks*); Vivas Maldonado, "La última la paga el diablo" (*A vellón las esperanzas o Melania*); Díaz Valcárcel, *Harlem todos los días;* L. R. Sánchez, *La guagua aérea.*

44. See Díaz; La Fountain–Stokes, "Tomboy Tantrums"; Negrón-Muntaner, "Magali García Ramis."

45. See Cruz-Malavé, "What a Tangled Web!"

46. See J. Miller.

47. On queer characters in Ortiz Cofer's work, see Reyes, "Recuerdos 'parciales.' " Abraham Rodríguez Jr.'s novel *Spidertown* is full of references to queers as a sign of abjection. Ernesto Quiñónez's novel *Changó's Fire* features an exemplary effeminate homosexual *babalao,* or Santería priest, as one of its principal secondary characters; unfortunately, this character is killed off at the end.

48. "1.5" generation, as defined by Rubén Rumbaut and Gustavo Pérez Firmat, refers to immigrants who leave their home country and go to their host country as children (usually because their parents are first-generation migrants) and, as such, have intimate connections to both places during their formative years. They differ from second-generation immigrants, who are born in the host country and do not have early life experiences in the family's country of origin. See Pérez Firmat.

49. I wish to thank Rita González and Ondine Chavoya for sharing their research on Rodríguez-Soltero. Also see Suárez.

50. On Rivera, see Duberman; Gan; Retzloff; Shepard.

51. See Flores, "Puerto Rican Literature in the United States: Stages and Perspectives" (*Divided Borders,* 142–53) and " 'Qué assimilated, brother, yo soy asimilao': The Structuring of Puerto Rican Identity" (ibid., 182–95).

1. The Persecution of Difference

1. See Ochoa.

2. See Butler, *Gender Trouble.*

3. See Fiet.

4. On stigma, see Goffman. On the management of sex/gender stigma by effeminate men in Latin America, see Lancaster, esp. "Guto's Performance" and *Life Is Hard* (235–78).

5. See Ramírez on the relational nature of masculinity and effeminacy. See Castillo on the virgin/whore paradigm.

6. See J. Arroyo, "Manuel Ramos Otero"; Cruz-Malavé, " 'What a Tangled Web!' "; Lugo-Ortiz, "Community at Its Limits." Also see Perivolaris (99–109).

7. See Barradas, *Para leer,* 65–80, and "Sobre la cuentística"; Cachán; Feliciano Fabre; Figueroa, esp. chapter 4; and Gelpí, "La cuentística antipatriarcal."

8. For a review of the film, see Trelles.

9. See Barradas, *Para leer,* and J. Ortega.

10. See Aparicio, *Listening to Salsa;* J. Arroyo, "Desde la vellonera"; Cruz-Malavé, "Towards an Art of Transvestism"; Foster, *Latin American Writers,* 401–4; Gelpí, *Literatura y paternalismo.* I use the term "semicloseted" to acknowledge Sánchez's negotiation of the public disclosure of his sexual orientation. See my discussion of the "open secret" in the Introduction (xvii).

11. Sánchez, "¡Jum!" 55; Sánchez, "Hum!" 131. All text in Spanish quoted from Sánchez, *En cuerpo de camisa.* Text in English quoted from translation by Rose M. Sevillano, *Grand Street,* except when indicated.

12. Foster incorrectly states that the protagonist's name is Jum and that he is a boy (*Latin American Writers,* 401).

13. Sánchez, "¡Jum!" 55; my translation to the English. Sevillano offers the following translation: "That Trinidad's son was tightening his cheeks until he suffocated his asshole" (Sánchez, "Hum!" 131).

14. See Almaguer; Lancaster; Ramírez.

15. Barradas, *Para leer,* 75.

16. The Nicaraguan novelist Sergio Ramírez quotes the following passage from Carpentier's novel: "Negras eran aquellas hermosas señoras, de firme nalgatorio, que ahora bailaban la rueda en torno a una fuente de tritones."

17. Also see Rodríguez Ramírez. For a critique of the objectification of black Puerto Rican women, see Ramos Rosado.

18. I do not agree with Perivolaris's reading of Trinidad's son as *mulato;* I find no compelling evidence of this in the story.

19. See "El cuerpo de nuestro nuevo Narciso" (Zenón Cruz, *Narciso,* 2: 30–115). I wish to thank Miriam Jiménez Román for informing me of the discussion of homosexuality in this book, and Ana Irma Rivera Lassén and Elizabeth Crespo Kebler for their insights on the legacy of Zenón Cruz.

20. See Omi and Winant.

21. My translation of all Zenón Cruz texts. Zenón Cruz, *Narciso,* 2: 17.

22. Zenón Cruz, *Narciso,* 2: 17.

23. See section entitled "Las nalgas y las caderas" (Zenón Cruz, *Narciso,* 2: 100–108).

24. For example, Zenón Cruz agrees with Ortiz's "historicization" of the black female body, which entails citing the Venus Calipigia as "biological evidence" of black woman's physiognomy (*Narciso,* 2: 108). On the complexity of Ortiz's legacy, see J. Arroyo, *Travestismos culturales.*

25. Zenón Cruz, *Narciso,* 1: 108–11.

26. Sánchez, "¡Jum!" 55; Sánchez, "Hum!" 131.

27. See La Fountain–Stokes, "Queer Ducks."

28. See Moliner (*Diccionario de uso,* 2: 1508) on the links between the color green, sex, and immorality. Vaquero and Morales cite Claudio de la Torre's similar definition of "viejo verde" (775).

29. Sánchez, "Hum!" 131.

30. Salessi comments on how "compadritos" and "canfinfleros" were chastised in early twentieth-century Buenos Aires for dressing like the rich, which in this case implied accusations of effeminacy and narcissism (383). Also see La Fountain–Stokes, "Leyendo el secreto abierto."

31. Clarke offers a useful critique of Hernton's heterosexism and homophobia.

32. Also see Arlene Torres.

33. See Gates Jr. and Harper. Note should be made of the struggle of black lesbian and gay individuals to achieve recognition within their own community: Langston Hughes, James Baldwin (most notably attacked for his sexual orientation by Eldridge Cleaver in his 1968 work *Soul on Ice*), Audre Lorde, Marlon Riggs, Essex Hemphill,

Isaac Julien, and Cheryl Dunye, to name a few. See Chauncey for a history of black gay and lesbian figures during the Harlem Renaissance.

34. See J. Arroyo, *"Mirror, Mirror on the Wall"* and "Sirena canta boleros," as well as articles in the special dossier on *Sirena Selena* in *CENTRO Journal* 15, no. 2 (Fall 2003).

35. All references to Lugo-Ortiz in this chapter are to her landmark essay "Community at Its Limits."

36. Sánchez, "Hum!" 131; Sánchez "¡Jum!" 55.

37. I would like to think that perhaps *aporrear* alludes to *porra* (the Brazilian slang for sperm), in which case the violence implied would have a definitive masculinist stance. On hate speech, see Butler's *Excitable Speech.*

38. See Salessi's analysis on the distinction between *marica* and *maricón* (282), which he makes in agreement with María Moliner's definitions. Also see La Fountain–Stokes, "Queer Ducks."

39. *Madamo,* a masculinization of the French *madame* (most commonly employed as a term of courtesy between unequal speakers in relations of servitude), also implies certain allegations of class disparity between Trinidad's son and the women. Angel Lozada suggests that it can also refer to the figure of the *madame* or medium in Puerto Rican espiritismo, a version of Allan Kardek's Spiritism, as well as of Santería (personal communication).

40. Sánchez, "Hum!" 132.

41. Sánchez, "¡Jum!" 56; Sánchez, "Hum!" 132.

42. Muñoz, *Disidentifications,* 114–15.

43. Sánchez, "¡Jum!" 57; Sánchez, "Hum!" 132. This "false piety" among women in one of the main elements of Federico García Lorca's *La casa de Bernarda Alba,* where the protagonist justifies all of her actions on the grounds of public decency and religious morality in an attempt to cloak her easily visible mundane preoccupations regarding social gossip (*el qué-dirán social*).

44. Sánchez, "¡Jum!" 60; Sánchez, "Hum!" 135.

45. Also see Santos-Febres's "Hebra rota" (1996), on a girl's desire to have her hair straightened and the life of a beautician renowned for straightening curly hair. This story has been made into a short film by Sonia Fritz.

46. Sánchez, "¡Jum!" 59; Sánchez, "Hum!" 134.

47. See J. Arroyo, "Historias de familia"; Cruz-Malavé, "Towards an Art of Transvestism"; Villanueva-Collado.

48. Sánchez, "¡Jum!" 60; Sánchez, "Hum!" 135.

49. See Sifuentes-Jáuregui, 87–118.

50. See Amícola on Puig's role in the novel's film adaptation.

51. For example, J. Arroyo writes: "Sin embargo, para el hijo de Trinidad, el negro homosexual de '¡Jum!' la única salida es el suicidio" ("Manuel Ramos Otero," 312). Foster (*Latin American Writers,* 401), Mira (648), and Ramos Rosado (124) also describe his death as a suicide; Mira claims that *se abre las venas* (he opens his veins).

52. See Rodríguez-Matos, "Acts of Love," in which the author credits Olmo Olmo for discovering Fonseca's poem in *Alma Latina* (31); Cruz-Malavé, "Towards an Art," 137.

53. See Umpierre, "Lesbian Tantalizing."

2. Autobiographical Writing and Shifting Migrant Experience

1. See interview with Costa (59); García Ramis, "La mayor de las muertes." All translations of Ramos Otero are my own.

2. For valuable biographical and critical summaries of these authors, see entries in Foster, *Latin American Writers.*

3. For a comparison of Arenas and Ramos Otero, see Ríos Avila, "Caribbean Dislocations."

4. See J. Arroyo, "Exilio y tránsitos," "Historias de familia," "Itinerarios de viaje," "Manuel Ramos Otero"; Cruz-Malavé, "Para virar al macho," "Towards an Art of Transvestism," " '*What a Tangled Web!*' "; Gelpí, "Conversación," "Historia y literatura," *Literatura y paternalismo, "Página en blanco y staccato"* (book review); Martínez–San Miguel, *Caribe Two Ways;* Reyes, "Modernism."

5. See Cañas, 140–42.

6. On the relationship between writing and exile, see Cady; Said.

7. Gelpí, "*Página en blanco,*" 248. All translations of Gelpí are my own.

8. "El desplante y el solipsismo que caracteriza a los personajes de los primeros cuentos," the result of "la conmoción inicial sufrida por todo exiliado o emigrado" (Gelpí, "*Página en blanco,*" 248.)

9. Ibid., 248.

10. Ibid., 250. See Franco, "Narrator, Author, Superstar," on the importance of the figure of the storyteller as an embodiment of collective knowledge and tradition in a contemporary Latin American literary context.

11. Sotomayor, "Genealogías."

12. Cruz-Malavé, "Para virar al macho."

13. See Barradas, " 'Epitafios' "; Cruz-Malavé, "Para virar al macho"; Gelpí, *Literatura y paternalismo.*

14. Ramos Otero, *El libro de la muerte,* 44–62.

15. This is the case, for example, of Ramos Otero's engagement with Cortázar in "Inventario mitológico del cuento," as Cruz-Malavé has lucidly demonstrated ("Para virar al macho").

16. W. Hernández, "Política homosexual."

17. See Torres-Saillant.

18. See Díaz Quiñones, *Conversación.*

19. For a more extensive biography of Ramos Otero, see Gelpí, "Conversación."

20. See Quiñones Santiago.

21. "Aquello que te censuren, cultívalo, porque eso eres tú" (Ramos Otero, "La ética," 17).

22. García Ramis, *Felices días, tío Sergio,* 80 (my translation). Also see La Fountain–Stokes, "Tomboy Tantrums."

23. See Santiago, 25–28; Bhabha, 36–39. Mexican performance artist Guillermo Gómez-Peña also offers interesting theorizations on this subject in his *The New World Border.*

24. See Ríos Avila, "The End of Gay Culture?"

25. See Ramos Otero, "Lorca" (in *El libro de la muerte,* 45–46).

26. Ferré comments: "El número 7 [de *Zona de carga y descarga*], en el cual salieron nuestros dos cuentos sobre Isabel la Negra ... fue un golpe moralmente mortal para la sociedad puertorriqueña. Las señoras del Condado los compraban por resmas en Tottis Drug Store y hacían fogatas con él en los traspatios de sus casas. Eladio Rodríguez Otero dijo en el Ateneo que se trataba de una revista del demonio, y que había que exorcisar con agua bendita los sitios donde se vendía.... El número ocho fue también un shock, pero esta vez el luto fue mayor.... El número lo boicotearon; se quedó sin vender en los estantes. El obispo declaró que el que lo leyera quedaría excomulgado. Todavía tengo guardados más de quinientos números en el garaje de mi casa." See "Los pasos en el polvo."

27. See D. Torres, "El 'hombre de papel' " and *Verbo y carne*.

28. See Gelpí, "*Página en blanco,*" and especially *Literatura y paternalismo*, 137–54.

29. With regard to the characters' gender ambiguity, it can be said that this is a valid (if trepidatious) form of experimentation; classic texts of transgender literature such as Leslie Feinberg's *Stone Butch Blues* have used this strategy to great success. It is also possible that Ramos Otero assumed they would be understood to be male narrators.

30. Cruz-Malavé, "Para virar al macho"; J. Arroyo, "Exilio y tránsitos."

31. "Y le escribo desde Ceilán y San Petersburgo ... y le escribo desde un punto remoto de Africa negra" (Ramos Otero, *Concierto de metal*, 75). It is odd that, in a story written around 1970, the narrator uses the colonial (Ceylon instead of Sri Lanka) and prerevolutionary names of geographic locations (St. Petersburg for Leningrad), as well as engages in an exoticizing reduction of Africa. It perhaps suggests that the geographic knowledge of the character mostly stems from literary readings and not from actual travel or current newspapers.

32. Currently, middle-class migration has become as prevalent as working-class migration. See Aranda; Duany, *Puerto Rican Nation;* García Ramis, "Los cerebros que se van"; Ramos-Zayas, *National Performances*.

33. See Ramos Otero's conversation with Manuel Puig and Olga Nolla, published in *Cupey* (Ramos Otero et al., "Escritura y ensoñación") as well as "Ficción e historia."

34. For a history of the Hotel Christopher, located at 180 Christopher Street, see "Greenwich Village: A Gay History," http://www.huzbears.com/nychistory/gv.html.

35. Other works that center on night are José Donoso's *El obsceno pájaro de la noche* (1970) and Mariana Romo-Carmona's *Living at Night* (1997). For a comparison of these two novels, see DeGuzmán, "Night Becomes 'Latina.' "

36. Palés Matos's poetic muse is known to have been a professor of literature at the University of Puerto Rico, Río Piedras. Her epithet brings together the Greek for love or friendship (*philia*) and the French for mixed (*mêlé*), which can be seen as a reference to race. See Ríos Avila, *La raza cómica*, 136–40.

37. Ramos Otero, *El cuento de la Mujer*, 102.

38. This would be the case especially if we think of the syllabic division of the word "Palés" as Pal/és as opposed to the more standard Pa/lés. See Prosper-Sánchez for an insightful discussion of *l* and *r* in Puerto Rican Spanish, particularly of rhotacism (l > r, 186–87).

39. See Cruz-Malavé, "Para virar al macho."

40. Ramos Otero comments profusely on his relation to English in his interview with Costa. Regarding his involvement in the New York gay world, he states: "[E]l mundo homosexual en el que me movía era exclusivamente en inglés" (Costa, 64).

41. A notable exception is when the narrator states: "Once upon a time on Christopher Street" (*El cuento de la Mujer*, 103). This interesting shift alludes to the fairy-tale or constructed nature of the lover's narrations (its paralleling of *The 1001 Nights*); it detracts from any "reality" effect and emphasizes their poetic value. The other notable case is the following passage: " 'cruising the corner, watching the night of an August moon go by, waiting again for the other man, on Christopher Street' (la calle Cristóbal es más sabia, más silenciosa, más cercana al sueño del amor)" (*El cuento de la Mujer*, 103). This is an unusual instance of Christopher Street as poetic, utopian space, as opposed to its more general dark description.

42. Falcón discusses the diverse socioeconomic provenances of early diasporic Puerto Rican writers in New York.

43. This interpretation is substantiated by the reception gay and lesbian groups received at the Puerto Rican Day Parade during the 1970s. A notable exception to this homophobic exclusion was the conduct of some of the Young Lords, who advocated international gay and lesbian liberation as part of their general agenda.

44. For the history of the Village as a gay space, see Chauncey. Other notorious gay areas have included Riverside Drive (mentioned, for example, in García Ramis's *Happy Days, Uncle Sergio*) and Forty-Second Street, immortalized as a gay space by Rechy in *City of Night*. Also see Duberman for a discussion of Sylvia Rivera's political and social involvement in the Times Square area.

45. See Hanhardt on current-day racial and class tensions on Christopher Street regarding queer-of-color youths. The Ecuadorian–Puerto Rican gay performance poet Emanuel Xavier has written in his poem "Chelsea Queen" (*Pier Queen*, 27–28) and in his articles in the gay press about racism in Chelsea. The Chelsea-clone muscular body type is captured well in the $50 doll known as Billy, a pumped-up, blonde (or brunette), anatomically correct version of Barbie's Ken (Quiroga, *Tropics of Desire*, 173–81). Shortly after his appearance, Billy acquired a diasporic Puerto Rican boyfriend, Carlos, who is distinguished by his goatee, body hair, and the fact that he is uncircumcised. The Latino gay-activist coalition "Mano a Mano" has mounted campaigns against the racist portrayal of Latinos in the gay social press as drug-addicted, violent homeboys. See Aponte-Parés, "*Out*side/In."

46. The trope of the invisible city is long-standing in Western culture, having its origins in St. Augustine and Thomas Aquinas. It is usually used as a signifier for utopias, something that is not evident in Ramos Otero but which could be related, perhaps as a utopia gone wrong, or antiutopia. A more recent elaboration of the invisible city is found in Italo Calvino's work, *Invisible Cities* (1972).

47. Gelpí, *Literatura y paternalismo*, 143–48.

48. See Flores, *From Bomba to Hip-Hop*, 114–39; R. Rivera.

49. See Algarín, "Introduction: Nuyorican Language."

50. For a history of the deindustrialization of New York City (particularly of the waterfront areas) see Gastil. For a more general analysis of deindustrialization in the United States, see Bluestone.

51. See Gelpí, "Conversación."

52. The black gay filmmaker Marlon Riggs also stresses this point in *Tongues Untied*.

53. See J. Arroyo, "Itinerarios de viaje," 865–66.

54. "Hay un lector, medio ideal, pero no necesariamente escribo para él. Se trata del lector puertorriqueño. A pesar de que mi literatura brega con una referencialidad cultural puertorriqueña, también trabajo con temas del ser humano como el amor, la muerte, la sexualidad, la libertad" (Costa, 64).

55. This was pointed out to me by Arnaldo Cruz-Malavé.

56. For a more recent account, see I. López.

57. This conference, which was organized by Asela Rodríguez de Laguna (and, according to Angel Rodríguez-Díaz, by Manuel Ramos Otero), was called the First National Conference on Puerto Rican Literature, and held on April 7–9, 1983, at Rutgers University, Newark. The selected proceedings were published by Rodríguez de Laguna as *Images and Identities: The Puerto Rican in Two World Contexts*.

58. See Cruz-Malavé, "El simulacro"; Montero; Rodríguez-Díaz.

59. See Martínez–San Miguel, "Juan Antonio Ramos."

60. See "16 (number)," *Wikipedia*, http://en.wikipedia.org/wiki/Sixteen.

61. See Sontag on the cultural stigma of AIDS.

62. See Abu-Lughod; Maffi; Mele.

63. It is not surprising that the first two national publicly elected gay and lesbian Puerto Rican politicians, former New York City Council member Antonio Pagán and former Council member Margarita López, were from this district. See La Fountain–Stokes, "1898."

64. See Cruz-Malavé, "'*What a Tangled Web!*'" Algarín's well-known poem "Mongo Affair" is perhaps an exception, in its subtle portrayal of (non-sexual) affect between a younger and older man; yet the key image of the poem, "mongo" (flaccid), is precisely a suggestion of impotence (sexual and otherwise).

65. See Vidal-Ortiz on the links between homosexuality and Santería.

66. Quiroga, *Tropics of Desire*, 145–68. Also see La Fountain–Stokes, "Trans/Bolero."

67. Aparicio, *Listening to Salsa*; Flores, *From Bomba to Hip-Hop*; Glasser, *My Music Is My Flag*.

68. See Anzaldúa, 82–83; Morales, 149–75; Pérez Firmat.

69. This suicide attempt is also brought up in the poem "Metáfora contagiosa" (Ramos Otero, *Invitación al polvo*, 50).

70. García Ramis mentions this accident in "La mayor de las muertes."

71. Costa, 59.

72. According to Rodríguez-Díaz, Ramos Otero later apologized for using the image without permission and without acknowledgment (personal communication, June 2006).

73. I do not know of any Puerto Rican or Nuyorican author of Chinese descent, but there are numerous artists of Asian heritage in Latin America, the Cuban painter Wilfredo Lam being the most famous. There were no openly gay Nuyorican poets in the 1970s, to my knowledge.

74. See essays in Anderson and Lee (*Displacement and Diasporas*) and Wilson for a discussion of Chinese migration to the Caribbean. The Cuban-American novelist Cristina García has explored the topic in *Monkey Hunting* (2003).

75. Commonalities in cuisine, specifically the daily consumption of rice, is possibly one of the best known links between some Asian and Caribbean peoples, as UCLA's Center for Intercultural Performance "The Art of Rice Traveling Theater" showed. See www.wac.ucla.edu/cip/artofrice/index.html.

76. Ramos Otero was quite up-front about his hesitation and slight discomfort regarding writing in English, even when he felt that he had an adequate command of the language. See his comments to this respect in his interview with Costa.

77. Fragoso, who also lived in New York, was the first gay Puerto Rican poet to die of AIDS. His book *Ser islas/Being Islands* was published by Ramos Otero's publishing house, El Libro Viaje, in 1976. Ramos Otero makes direct mention of him in another story of *Página en blanco y staccato,* "Descuento." See Barradas, "Fragoso" and "Todo"; Rodríguez-Matos, "Fernández-Fragoso."

78. See McNamara for a discussion of male hustling in Times Square. On bisexuality, see Muñoz-Laboy.

79. The implicit basis of this speculation is that Sam Fat somehow has served (or stands in for others who served) to transmit the epidemic. It is understood that in many cases, this transmission was in no way malicious in intent nor conscious but rather the result of unprotected sexual encounters or drug use; it was not until several years into the epidemic that somewhat effective means of prevention became better known and publicly disseminated.

80. *Ekphrasis* refers to poetry or poetic writing that talks vividly about visual arts.

81. In Puerto Rico, *echar un polvo* means to engage in sexual relations. See Vaquero and Morales, 626.

82. On Cuban-Puerto Rican gay ties, see La Fountain–Stokes, "De un pájaro."

3. Women's Bodies, Lesbian Passions

1. Luz María Umpierre's full name is Dr. Luz María Umpierre-Herrera and her nickname is Luzma. See her website at www.luzmaumpierre.com.

2. On Matos-Cintrón, see Rodríguez-Matos, "Matos-Cintrón"; Sotomayor, *De lengua, razón y cuerpo,* 54–57. Matos-Cintrón is also famous for the controversy she and Yolanda V. Fundora engaged in with Manuel Ramos Otero, who wrote a negative review of their book. See Ramos Otero, "La luna ultrajada"; Matos-Cintrón and Fundora, "Carta abierta." Carmen de Monteflores and Luisita López Torregrosa are much more reserved about their lesbian experience, although both discuss it openly. For a scathing assessment of de Monteflores, see Sánchez González, 141–48, 158–60. For a more positive valuation, see Keating.

3. See Duque; Juan González; Lavietes; R. Ortega; L. Torres ("Boricua Lesbians").

4. Ramos discusses her personal experiences in her essay "Bayamón, Brooklyn y yo" (*Compañeras,* 89–96).

5. Avotja and Hidalgo have important essays in *Compañeras,* including Hidalgo's rousing manifesto "¡Fuera del clóset, boricua!" (Juanita Ramos, 62–64).

6. This coincides in interesting ways with Crespo Kebler's findings for Puerto Rican women on the island.

7. Also see Ardín Pauneto, "Elyíbiti" and *Elyíbiti* (video); Crespo Kebler; Negrón-Muntaner, "Echoing Stonewall."

8. In *Borderlands/La frontera,* Anzaldúa states: "I am a turtle, wherever I go I carry 'home' on my back" (43).

9. See Acosta-Belén.

10. See L. Torres, "Boricua Lesbians."

11. Sandlin, "Julia de Burgos."

12. Umpierre has published two books of literary criticism (*Ideología y novela en Puerto Rico* and *Nuevas aproximaciones críticas*) in addition to numerous scholarly essays, interviews, and book reviews. Her articles on de Burgos ("Metapoetic Code"), Esteves ("La ansiedad de la influencia," "El diálogo poético"), and Sutton ("Breaking of Form") are especially important in terms of establishing women writer complicities and solidarities. Umpierre has talked about this in numerous interviews. See DiFrancesco; Fortis; E. Martínez, "An Interview"; Pérez-Erdelyi.

13. Also see Balch; Vázquez-Hernández.

14. See Aparicio, "La vida." Also see Carmen Haydée Rivera.

15. All translations of Umpierre and Matos-Cintrón are my own.

16. There is an extensive bibliography dealing with mental health issues of immigrant communities. In *Medicalizing Ethnicity,* Santiago-Ortiz has explored the ways in which Latino culture has been pathologized by the dominant psychiatric establishment, at times by Latino mental health practitioners themselves. In her essay "Esta risa no es de loca," Souza has written eloquently about how multiple pressures as a Puerto Rican female immigrant have also challenged her mental health. Also see Irene Vilar's memoirs, initially published as *A Message from God in the Atomic Age* and reprinted in paperback as *The Ladies Gallery: A Memoir of Family Secrets,* and her work-in-progress *Abortion Addict* (also listed as "Impossible Motherhood"), as well as Halperín. For a diasporic Puerto Rican lesbian vision, see Astor del Valle, "Transplantations."

17. E. Martínez, *Lesbian Voices,* 169.

18. Umpierre, "Lesbian Tantalizing."

19. I have respected Esteves's non-standard spelling of *borrinqueña* with two R's (as opposed to the more common *borinqueña*) in keeping with the idea that U.S. Puerto Rican Spanish exhibits autonomous patterns.

20. Umpierre, "El diálogo poético."

21. See Azize Vargas, "A Commentary"; Horno-Delgado; E. Martínez, *Lesbian Voices;* C. Rivera, 126–31.

22. See Luis, *Dance,* 74–80; "María C(h)ristina Speaks."

23. See Umpierre's short story "La veintiuna" for a fictionalized account of her childhood environment.

24. Umpierre, "El diálogo poético."

25. E. Martínez, *Lesbian Voices,* 168. Also see Lima, who, inspired by Cruz-Malavé's scholarship, reads Umpierre's book as a counter-discourse to Pedreira's *Insularismo* (*Latino Body,* 130–40).

26. A *danza* is a European-style, classically inspired Puerto Rican musical composition meant for ballroom dancing. *Danzas* are widely heralded as an autochthonous, creole cultural form, particularly by the upper class and bourgeoisie that favored them. Many *danza* musicians and composers were black or *mulato.*

27. Sutton, the author of *SAYcred LAYdy* (1975), was possibly the first Nuyorican-identified woman to publish a book of poetry, but she is relatively unknown today.

See Barradas, "Introducción," 15–16 (footnote 5); Esteves, "Feminist Viewpoint"; Umpierre, "Breaking of Form."

28. For accounts of Umpierre's grievance with Rutgers (including national media coverage in the *Advocate*), problems at other universities, and general biographical information, see Freiberg; Klawitter; Carmen Haydée Rivera; Carmen S. Rivera, 107–12; Umpierre, "Whose Taboos?"; Vosburg.

29. I wish to thank Carroll Smith-Rosenberg for this and other observations on Umpierre's work.

30. On masturbation, see Bennett and Rosario; Laqueur.

31. Latina lesbian mother/daughter bonds and lesbian motherhood have also been explored by Cherríe Moraga, both in *Loving in the War Years* and *Waiting in the Wings*.

32. See Bergmann; Esquibel.

33. Umpierre's description of the female moon as hero or rescuer ("La luna, que es siempre mujer, / ayudará esta noche / permitiendo sacar de aquel Castillo / la eme que suena en los corridos de aquel, otro país / que tiene la tequila de brebaje" [32]), echoes Sor Juana's elaboration of the role of the moon providing clarity to the soul in the *Primero Sueño* (see Franco, *Plotting Women* 23–54, especially 32–33). See Carrión (*Arquitectura y cuerpo*) on the relationship between architecture and the body in the work of Santa Teresa de Jesús.

34. On the U.S. invasion of Mexico City, see DeGuzmán, *Spain's Long Shadow,* 88–89. Umpierre links Sor Juana and Ana Castillo in a brief poem written in the style of an office memo, "Título: En que trata de lo que es y no hay mah ná' " (*Margarita Poems,* 27).

35. Martínez–San Miguel, "Bitextualidad" and *"Boricua* (Between) Borders."

36. On Puerto Ricans in New Jersey, see Hidalgo (*Puerto Ricans in Newark*); Jiménez de Wagenheim.

37. E. Martínez, *Lesbian Voices,* 194.

38. See Lima, 135.

39. "lenguaje o discurso enrevesado e incomprensible; lenguaje informal usado por cierta clase de persona" (Moliner, 187).

40. Vaquero and Morales cite this definition from Gabriel Vicente Maura: "Juego de niños que consiste en intercalar la partícula ché o chí entre cada una de las sílabas de una palabra, al hablar" (434).

41. For variations, see "Jerigonza," (http://es.wikipedia.org/wiki/Jerigonza).

42. Many critics have translated "garita" as garret, but this is inaccurate.

43. Coll y Toste's retelling of the story centers on an orphaned *mestiza* named Dina, who is of Taíno and Spanish parentage and lives with her elderly, sick aunt, and with Dina's infatuation with an Andalusian guitar-playing soldier called Sánchez, nicknamed "Flor de Azahar" (Orange blossom), who serves in the Castillo de San Cristóbal, located at the entrance to the walled city of San Juan, and not at the Morro (the largest and most important colonial fort), as Umpierre suggests.

44. This emphasis on the island as dominant trope has been carefully analyzed by Dara Goldman, who traces the development of the idea of insularism and insularity throughout the Hispanic Caribbean and its diaspora. On Mendieta, see Quiroga, *Cuban Palimpsests,* 173–96.

45. See Aponte-Parés, "What's Yellow"; Flores, *From Bomba to Hip-Hop,* 63–77.

46. Braschi also flirts with lesbianism, female bisexuality, and transvestism in her earlier work, *El imperio de los sueños* (1988), translated by Tess O'Dwyer as *Empire of Dreams* (1994). See M. Carrión, "Geographies"; La Fountain–Stokes, "Pop-Shock."

47. See Sánchez, "¡Jum!"; Marqués, *La mirada*; Lozada, *La patografía*; Varo, *Rosa Mystica.*

4. Visual Happenings, Queer Imaginings

1. For a different generational analysis of diasporic Puerto Rican lesbian production, see La Fountain–Stokes, "Pop-Shock."

2. For example, both Negrón-Muntaner ("Watching *Tongues Untie(d)*") and Umpierre (*Margarita Poems*) have expressed strong identification with and debt to the work of Audre Lorde.

3. Aldo Alvarez is an example of a first-generation adult migrant who does not write in Spanish, clearly favors a non-Hispanic gay white American audience, and does not center issues of Puerto Ricanness in his work. See his *Interesting Monsters.* The novelist Angel Lozada does follow Negrón-Muntaner's model.

4. On U.S. Third World feminism and its relation to second-wave feminism, see Alarcón; Mohanty; C. Sandoval. On third-wave feminism, see Baumgardner and Richards; Heywood and Drake.

5. For more background information, see interviews with Aguilar Castro; Juhasz, *Women of Vision*, 276–89; D. Rodríguez. Also see Rodríguez-Matos, "Negrón-Muntaner."

6. Juhasz, *Women of Vision*, 280–81.

7. Ibid., 279.

8. *AIDS in the Barrio* is distributed by Cinema Guild, www.cinemaguild.com. *Brincando el charco* is distributed by Women Make Movies, www.wmm.com.

9. Erika López also presents Latinas in Philadelphia but does not explore their social issues, something she has done more recently in relation to San Francisco, specifically in her performance piece *Nothing Left but the Smell.*

10. Flores, *Divided Borders*, 189–91.

11. Laviera, 51–87. See Aparicio (*Listening to Salsa*), Otero Garabís, Quintero Herencia, Quintero Rivera, and Santos-Febres ("Salsa as Translocation") for interesting considerations on politics, identity, gender, and literature in relation to salsa.

12. Negrón-Muntaner further discusses issues of AIDS in the Philadelphia Latina/o community in a conversation with Juan David Acosta and Robert Vázquez-Pacheco. See Negrón-Muntaner, "Surviving Cultures."

13. Thirty Puerto Rican activists took over the Statue of Liberty on October 25, 1977, to protest the continued imprisonment of four pro-independence nationalist sympathizers. See Ocasio Rivera.

14. Sarah Miller, 11.

15. See Rodríguez-Matos, "Mena-Santiago."

16. Romo-Carmona is also the author of an important novel focusing on a Puerto Rican lesbian youth in Connecticut, *Living at Night* (1997), as well as of a book of

short stories, *Speaking Like an Immigrant* (1998). See DeGuzmán, "Night Becomes 'Latina' "; La Fountain–Stokes, "Pop-Shock."

17. For scholarly analyses of *Brincando el charco,* see Cvetkovich; La Fountain–Stokes, "Cultures," 290–94; Negrón-Muntaner, "When I Was"; Quiroga, *Tropics of Desire,* 193–95; Sandoval-Sánchez, "Imagining."

18. See Azize Vargas, "Otro modo de ver"; Negrón-Muntaner, "Drama Queens" and "Of Lonesome Stars."

19. This metaphor was a dominant trope employed in 1940s and 1950s Puerto Rican populist political discourse.

20. On Muñoz Marín, see Rodríguez Juliá, *Las tribulaciones de Jonás.*

21. See Negrón-Muntaner, "When I Was"; Juhasz, *Women of Vision.*

22. Negrón-Muntaner ("When I Was," 512) goes to great lengths to insist that the large American flag that appears in this sequence is queer, with fifty-one stars arranged in a circle: an American flag that incorporates the lone Puerto Rican star.

23. See interview by D. Rodríguez.

24. Sadie Benning is an example of a white lesbian filmmaker who regularly appears in her autobiographical experimental videos.

25. See Anzaldúa and Moraga, *This Bridge;* Juanita Ramos, *Compañeras;* Trujillo, *Chicana Lesbians;* Latina Feminist Group, *Telling to Live.* Also see Cruz-Malavé, *Queer Latino Testimonio.*

26. For a discussion of veracity in filmmaking and the genre of mock-documentary, see Juhasz and Lerner, *F Is for Phony;* Roscoe and Hight, *Faking It.*

27. See Negrón-Muntaner ("When I Was," 515–16) for an extensive discussion of this scene.

28. "I constructed the scene as a parody of melodrama: a visual compression of religious, political, and dominant representations of Puerto Rican culture's homophobia." Negrón-Muntaner, "When I Was," 516.

29. Personal communication, Yolanda Martínez–San Miguel, June 2006. Also see Negrón-Muntaner, "Surviving Cultures," 115.

30. Licia Fiol-Matta, "Latina Identities"; Ríos Avila, personal communication, June 2007.

31. Negrón-Muntaner refers to it as a " 'foundational' romance" ("When I Was," 519).

32. Personal communication.

33. See La Fountain–Stokes, "1898."

34. See Grosfoguel ("Divorce") and Grosfoguel and Laó-Montes ("El proyecto") for a discussion of the central tenets of the "radical democratic project" at the heart of the *estadidad radical* (radical statehood) proposal.

35. On Hayworth, see Ríos Avila, "El show de Cristina."

36. See Rodríguez Madera on transgender issues in Puerto Rico. Georgie Irizarry discusses Hayworth's role in organizing the first Pride Parade in Puerto Rico in Ardín Pauneto's documentary *Elyíbiti.*

37. Negrón-Muntaner's lack of explicit recognition of her intellectual interlocutors also occurs in *Boricua Pop,* where she tends to bury the names of many fellow scholars in the endnotes. Negrón-Muntaner has claimed that she engages in this strategy to avoid "cluttering" her prose with names that would make her writing "less accessible" (and less marketable) to a mainstream audience.

38. This film can be viewed for free at www.scenariosusa.org, the Scenarios, USA website.

39. Negrón-Muntaner and Troche publicly discussed their differences at a Women in the Director's Chair film festival panel in March 1995 in Chicago; see Wilmington. According to Negrón-Muntaner, they had a heated argument and did not see eye to eye (personal communication, September 2006).

40. On Troche, see Patricia Juliana Smith; Sloane; Stukin. Lo offers an excellent analysis of Latina (mis)representation in *The L Word*.

41. However, *Curve* magazine has indicated that Troche adapted the Puerto Rican drag queen Holly Woodlawn's autobiography *A Low Life in High Heels* for the screen (Anderson-Minshall).

42. On *Go Fish* see J. Carr; Francke; Maslin; B. Ruby Rich; Romney; Willis. For more extended academic, scholarly treatment, see L. Henderson; Hollinger; C. Jones; Pramaggiore.

43. See Turner and Troche, 13–14; Willis.

44. See Vachon and Edelstein (*Shooting to Kill*) and Vachon and Bunn (*A Killer Life*) for a discussion of Vachon's experiences producing *Go Fish*. Also see Pierson for a detailed account of his involvement with the film, specifically at the Sundance Film Festival (279–98), and for a breakdown of the expenses related to the film (311–18).

45. Pierson (who also funded Spike Lee's film) claims responsibility for generating the comparison between Troche and Lee (286). Similar comments appear in Holden; Levy ("Girl Meets Girl," 94); and "Let the Summer Begin."

46. Some notable exceptions of critics who do highlight the Puerto Rican elements include Escalona, García (xli), Henderson, and B. Ruby Rich.

47. Achy Obejas, personal communication, October 2006. The specificity of the neighborhood is very important. According to Troche, "Wicker Park was mainly a Latino area with artists, gays and lesbians moving in, as well as unwelcome yuppies who were attracted by the low real estate costs" (Turner and Troche, 17). See Ramos-Zayas for homophobic reactions from Latino residents ("All This," 83).

48. On Puerto Ricans in Chicago, see de Genova and Ramos-Zayas; Lennon; M. Martínez; Padilla; Pérez; Ramos-Zayas; Rinaldo; Toro-Morn; and the articles in *CENTRO Journal* 13, no. 2 (Fall 2001). Padilla identifies the gentrification of Wicker Park as something that occurred in the mid-1970s (*Puerto Rican Chicago*, 216–17).

49. On Troche's suburban experience, see B. Ruby Rich (15), Stukin ("Rose," 56).

50. See Ramos-Zayas for very insightful observations on the meanings of "whiteness" for Puerto Ricans and Latinas/os in Chicago, and for a discussion of the "inner city"/suburb divide.

51. "There weren't any Puerto Rican writers. Puerto Ricans didn't write books. Miguel had never even seen one" (A. Rodríguez Jr., *Spidertown*, 62).

52. Pramaggiore also defends *Go Fish*'s radical nature, but fails to account for the problematic representation of race and ethnicity in the film, a surprising elision given that the main thrust of her article (besides discrediting the analytic category of "New Queer Cinema") is to compare *Go Fish* with Maria Maggenti's *The Incredibly True Adventure of Two Girls In Love* (1995), a film that focuses on an interracial lesbian relationship between a wealthy African American teenage girl and a working class white girl.

53. Guzmán, *Gay Hegemony*, 25–29.

54. I share Henderson's apprehension that the older, more knowledgeable, black Kia at times comes across as a "mammy" figure in her interaction with the younger, inexperienced, white Max (56, note 12).

55. For example, see Lennon's study of Protestant and Catholic Puerto Ricans in Chicago.

56. Ramos-Zayas, "All This," 83.

57. Achy Obejas, personal communication, October 2006. See Obejas's novel *Memory Mambo* (1996) for a literary portrayal of a lesbian relationship between a Cuban and a Puerto Rican in Logan Square (Chicago).

58. Ramos-Zayas, "All This," 82.

59. See Martínez–San Miguel, "Bitextualidad" and "*Boricua* (Between) Borders."

60. See La Fountain–Stokes, "Tomboy Tantrums."

61. Ging offers an interesting analysis of Troche's use of sound in this film, specifically analyzing this scene.

62. See Paz Brownrigg's very insightful article on the history of the lynching of Latinos in the United States.

63. The topic of queer Latinas/os' relationships to their families has been extensively discussed by many queer Latina/o authors, including Gloria Anzaldúa and Robert Vázquez-Pacheco. See Negrón-Muntaner, "Surviving Cultures."

64. On *The Watermelon Woman*, see Juhasz, "Phony Definitions," 13–18; Keeling; Reid-Pharr, "Makes Me Feel"; Sullivan; Winokur. None of these scholars brings up *Go Fish* as a relevant intertext. Sullivan goes so far as to describe *Go Fish* as a "white" film. On Dunye, see interviews in Juhasz (*Women of Vision*, 290–304) and Mauceri.

65. On the complex meanings of Carmen Miranda's life and myth, see Helena Solberg's extraordinary documentary *Carmen Miranda: Bananas Is My Business* (1994) as well as the essay by O'Neil.

66. I am writing López with an accent on the *o* in accordance with Spanish-language rules and out of personal preference. I would like to acknowledge that the artist herself typically spells her last name with no accent mark.

67. The comparison with Pietri seems especially if we consider his penchant for humor based on the absurd.

68. Michele Serros's *Chicana Falsa* is another example of a work by a younger Latina writer that reacts against older, more rigid, dogmatic models.

69. On *Flaming Iguanas*, see Cooper; Laffrado; Solomon; L. Torres.

70. See Ramos Otero, *Página en blanco*, 49–68. On Puerto Ricans in California, also see U.S. Commission on Civil Rights.

71. See Garber.

72. Negrón-Muntaner states, "To photograph Ray, then, sets up a complex erotics of male gay sexuality and creative cannibalism" ("When I Was," 515).

73. See "Chiquita Brands International," *Wikipedia*, http://en.wikipedia.org/wiki/Chiquita_Brands_International.

74. See López's website as well as "Postcards."

5. Nuyorico and the Utopias of the Everyday

1. I am writing Avilés with an accent on the *e* in accordance with Spanish-language rules and out of personal preference. I would like to acknowledge that the artist himself typically spells his last name with no accent mark or with an accent on the *i* (Avíles).

2. On Alfaro, also see Habell-Pallán (81–111). On Tropicana, see Muñoz, *Disidentifications* and "No es fácil."

3. See Jonnes; Kleiman; Rivera-Servera; Rosenthal; Siegal; Vásquez (*Pregones Theatre*). For a general history of the Bronx, see E. González.

4. Pregones Theater's *The Bolero Was My Downfall*, their Asunción Playwrights Project, and the numerous BAAD! festivals such as "BAAD Ass Women" and "Out Like That" have been some of the most successful initiatives. See La Fountain-Stokes, "Trans/Bolero" and "Pregones"; Merced; Rivera-Servera; Vásquez (*Pregones Theatre*).

5. Interethnic and racial tensions are especially noticeable in Marrero's solo work (for example, *Machataso*), which I do not discuss here at length.

6. See Nieves.

7. Kisselgoff, " 'Cinderella.' "

8. See Dunning ("Arthur Avilés's Life in Dance") for more biographical information and discussion of his training. Nieves and Rose also offer interesting biographical details.

9. Avilés became Jones's lover after Arnie Zane's death (La Fountain-Stokes, "Naked Puerto Rican," 318–19). Jones describes their personal and professional relationship in *Last Night on Earth* (see 191–92, 228–30). For reviews of Avilés's work with Jones, see Dunning, "Arthur Avilés's Life," "New Works"; Tobias.

10. See J. Anderson; J. Lewis; Solomons; Sulcas; Supree; Zimmer.

11. On Jones, see articles in special issue of *TDR: The Drama Review* 49, no. 2 (Summer 2005).

12. Arthur Avilés, personal communication, January 1998.

13. See La Fountain-Stokes, "Come on Down"; Siegal, "Long-Vacant Plant."

14. See Marrero's MySpace page, " 'King Macha' — Drag King," www.myspace .com/kingmacha.

15. See Portes and Rumbaut.

16. Arthur Avilés, personal communication, January 1998.

17. See E. López, *Flaming Iguanas*, 28–29; *Lap Dancing*, 180–83. Also see L. Torres, "Boricua Lesbians."

18. See Algarín, "Introduction: Nuyorican Language"; Flores, *Divided Borders* and *From Bomba to Hip-Hop*.

19. These "American-Rican" identities come closer to the early positions of the Chicano Richard Rodríguez in *Hunger of Memory* and of Linda Chávez, but are marked by the acknowledgement of loss.

20. I should point out, however, that Avilés (or whomever prepares the programs at BAAD!) also writes "New York Rican" at times without a hyphen.

21. Flores signals his disagreement with Pérez Firmat's "life on the hyphen" and with Ilan Stavans's "life in the hyphen" in his essay "Life Off the Hyphen" (*From Bomba to Hip-Hop*, 167–88).

22. For useful discussions of borderlands and contact zones, see Anzaldúa; Pratt.

23. See Indych.

24. See Lee.

25. For a complex account of Avilés and Marrero's performances in Puerto Rico, see Homar, La Fountain–Stokes ("A Naked Puerto Rican").

26. I am reproducing the Typical Theatre's spelling of Maéva (and Maévacita) with an accent over the *e* out of respect for their idiosyncratic usage. This spelling does not follow Spanish-language rules of accentuation.

27. Program notes, Celebrate Brooklyn! Performing Arts Festival, Prospect Park Bandshell, August 1, 1998.

28. See Solomons for a review of this piece.

29. "Ensalada," *Wikipedia,* http://en.wikipedia.org/wiki/Ensalada. Webster's defines "ensalada" as "a burlesque madrigal consisting of several popular tunes sung as a quodlibet that was cultivated in Spain in the 16th century."

30. See J. Anderson, "In New Works."

31. La Fountain–Stokes, "A Naked Puerto Rican," 317–18.

32. On Graham's *Seraphic Dialogue,* see McGehee, Siegel.

33. For a different contemporary reinterpretation of the Joan of Arc story, see the experimental German lesbian filmmaker Ulrike Ottinger's feminist revision in *Johanna D'Arc of Mongolia* (1989).

34. On Limón, see Dunbar; Pollack; Woodford.

35. *The Moor's Pavane* was transmitted by the Canadian Broadcasting Company on March 6, 1955, and is currently available on VHS and DVD.

36. Burt, 121–27. Limón's interest in racial narratives is also evident in other filmed pieces such as his *The Emperor Jones* (1956), a dance based on a play by Eugene O'Neill about an African American fugitive from a chain-gang turned emperor in the Caribbean.

37. "Othello," *Wikipedia,* http://en.wikipedia.org/wiki/Othello.

38. See Zimmer ("West Side Stories") for a superficial review of Avilés's piece. On Moses, see Cook. Goodman offers an ironic appraisal of the development of Lincoln Center.

39. See Sandoval-Sánchez, *José, Can You See?* 62–82; Negrón-Muntaner, *Boricua Pop,* 58–84.

40. Dunning, "Art Out of the Closet."

41. See Dunning ("New Spin on 'Cinderella'") for a review of the 1996 production of *Arturella* and Kisselgoff for a review of the 2003 restaging.

42. See Dunning, "Fast-Spinning Steps"; "Different Styles."

43. See La Fountain–Stokes, "A Naked Puerto Rican," 322–24.

44. "Cinderella," *Wikipedia,* http://en.wikipedia.org/wiki/Cinderella.

45. See J. Alvarez, *Once Upon a Quinceañera.* For a queer Chicano-centered film version, see Richard Glatzer and Wash Westmoreland's *Quinceañera* (2006).

46. See DeGuzmán, *Spain's Long Shadow.*

47. See La Fountain–Stokes, "Trans/Bolero."

48. La Fountain–Stokes, "A Naked Puerto Rican," 324.

49. See S. L. Foster for a discussion of Bourne's highly commercial, very popular, and fairly conservative ballet.

50. See Halperín on Alvarez and García. On Romo-Carmona, see DeGuzmán ("Night Becomes 'Latina' "), La Fountain–Stokes ("Pop-Shock").

51. See, for example, the 1988 photograph of *Absence* in B. Jones (187).

52. See Sulcas, 98.

53. See La Fountain–Stokes, "A Naked Puerto Rican," 320–22.

54. See ibid., "A Naked Puerto Rican," 323–26.

55. See Dunning, "New Spin."

56. Orlan, personal communication, March 2006.

57. See Gladstone for a synopsis of *Maéva de Oz* and what later became *Dorothur's Journey,* and La Fountain–Stokes ("Arthur Avilés") for a review of the piece.

58. *Super Maéva de Oz* was presented in April 2000 at BAAD! and in June 2000 at the Here Arts Center in Manhattan as part of the "Queer at Here" Festival. I did not attend these performances in 2000 but have worked with videos of both, which I transcribed, as there are no written scripts of the play.

59. See "L. Frank Baum," *Wikipedia,* http://en.wikipedia.org/wiki/L._Frank_Baum; "List of Oz Books," *Wikipedia,* http://en.wikipedia.org/wiki/Oz_books; Swartz.

60. La Fountain–Stokes, "A Naked Puerto Rican," 326–27.

61. Vito Russo cites *The Wizard of Oz* in an epigraph in the opening pages of his classic *The Celluloid Closet.* Also see Conner et al., 349; Hopcke; Stewart, 273.

62. See Banes, especially "Happily Ever After? The Postmodern Fairytale and the New Dance" (280–90).

63. See Pietri, "Suicide Note," for a satirical Nuyorican cockroach version.

64. On the importance of the rainbow and rainbow flag as LGBT symbols (including their links to *The Wizard of Oz*), see Conner et al., 278–79; Hogan and Hudson, 470–71; Rowlett; Stewart, 211.

65. On Margarita López, see La Fountain–Stokes, "1898."

66. For example, 1970s and 1980s feminist film theorists such as Laura Mulvey argued that all representations of women were subject to the male gaze, while other feminists such as Andrea Dworkin and Catharine MacKinnon blamed pornography for violence against women (a view challenged by Camille Paglia and Susie Bright). See Duggan and Hunter.

67. See La Fountain–Stokes, "A Naked Puerto Rican," 328–29.

68. Ibid., 327–28.

Bibliography

Abbe, Elfrieda. "Creating Images Where There Were None." Interview with Frances Negrón-Muntaner. *Angles: Women Working in Film and Video* 3, no. 2 (January 1997): 8–12.

Abu-Lughod, Janet L., ed. *From Urban Village to East Village: The Battle for New York's Lower East Side.* Oxford: Blackwell Publishers, 1994.

Acevedo, Carlos Aníbal. *Cristianismo y homosexualidad: Una perspectiva puertorriqueña.* [Vega Alta, P.R.: Taller Gráfico Gongolí,] 1992.

Acevedo, David Caleb, Moisés Agosto Rosario, and Luis Negrón, eds. *Los otros cuerpos: Antología de temática gay, lésbica y queer desde Puerto Rico y su diáspora.* San Juan: Editorial Tiempo Nuevo, 2007.

Acosta-Belén, Edna, ed. *The Puerto Rican Woman: Perspectives on Culture, History, and Society.* New York: Praeger Publishers, 1986.

Acosta-Belén, Edna, and Carlos E. Santiago. *Puerto Ricans in the United States: A Contemporary Portrait.* Boulder, Colo.: Lynne Rienner, 2006.

Agosto-Rosario, Moisés. Interview by Sarah Schulman, December 14, 2002. ACT UP Oral History Project. New York: MIX/The New York Lesbian and Gay Experimental Film Festival, 2003.

———. *Nocturno y otros desamparos.* San Juan: Terranova Editores, 2006.

Aguilar Castro, Jaditza A. "Frances Negrón-Muntaner." Interview. In *Cine y video puertorriqueño "Made in USA": Un proyecto de historia oral,* ed. Ana María García, 176–90. Río Piedras: Programa de Estudios de Honor, Universidad de Puerto Rico, 2000.

Alarcón, Norma. "The Theoretical Subject(s) of *This Bridge Called My Back* and Anglo-American Feminism." In *Feminist Theory Reader,* ed. Carole R. McCann and Seung-Kyung Kim, 404–14. New York: Routledge, 2003.

Alarcón, Norma, Ana Castillo, and Cherríe Moraga, eds. *Third Woman: The Sexuality of Latinas.* Berkeley: Third Woman Press, 1989.

Albright, Ann Cooper. *Choreographing Difference: The Body and Identity in Contemporary Dance.* Middletown, Conn.: Wesleyan University Press; Hanover, N.H.: University Press of New England, 1997.

Algarín, Miguel. "Introduction: Nuyorican Language." In *Nuyorican Poetry: An Anthology of Puerto Rican Words and Feelings,* ed. Miguel Algarín and Miguel Piñero, 9–20. New York: William Morrow, 1975.

———. *Love Is Hard Work: Memorias de Loisaida.* New York: Scribner Poetry, 1997.

———. *Mongo Affair: Poems.* New York: Nuyorican Poet's Café, 1978.

Almaguer, Tomás. "Chicano Men: A Cartography of Homosexual Identity and Behavior." In *The Lesbian and Gay Studies Reader,* ed. Henry Abelove, Michèle Aina Barale, and David M. Halperin, 255–73. New York: Routledge, 1993.

Altman, Dennis. *Global Sex.* Chicago: University of Chicago Press, 2001.

Alvarez, Aldo. *Interesting Monsters: Fictions.* St. Paul, Minn.: Graywolf Press, 2001.

193

Alvarez, Julia. "Freeing La Musa: Luzma Umpierre's *The Margarita Poems*." In *The Margarita Poems*, by Luz María Umpierre, 4–7. Bloomington, Ind.: Third Woman Press, 1987.

———. *Once upon a Quinceañera: Coming of Age in the USA*. New York: Viking, 2007.

Amícola, José. "*Hell Has No Limits*: de José Donoso a Manuel Puig." In *Desde aceras opuestas: Literatura/cultura gay y lesbiana en Latinoamérica*, ed. Dieter Ingenschay, 21–36. Madrid: Iberoamericana; Frankfurt: Vervuert, 2006.

Anderson, Benedict. *Imagined Communities: Reflections on the Origin and Spread of Nationalism*. London: Verso, 1991.

Anderson, Jack. "In New Works, Laughter, the Alphabet, and Old Saws." *New York Times*, September 25, 1991, C18.

———. "New Works from 4 Choreographers." *New York Times*, November 12, 1989, 72.

Anderson, Wanni W., and Robert G. Lee, eds. *Displacement and Diasporas: Asians in the Americas*. New Brunswick, N.J.: Rutgers University Press, 2005.

Anderson-Minshall, Diane. "Whatever Happened to Her?" *Curve* 12, no. 4 (June 2002). Accessed electronically.

Anzaldúa, Gloria. *Borderlands/La frontera: The New Mestiza*. 2nd ed. San Francisco: Aunt Lute Books, 1999 [1987].

Aparicio, Frances. *Listening to Salsa: Gender, Latin Popular Music, and Puerto Rican Culture*. Hanover, N.H.: Wesleyan University Press; University Press of New England, 1998.

———. "La Vida es un Spanglish Disparatero: Bilingualism in Nuyorican Poetry." In *European Perspectives on Hispanic Literature in the United States*, ed. Genevieve Fabre, 147–60. Houston: Arte Público Press, 1988.

Aponte-Parés, Luis. "*Outside/In*: Crossing Queer and Latino Boundaries." In *Mambo Montage: The Latinization of New York*, ed. Agustín Laó-Montes and Arlene Dávila, 363–85. New York: Columbia University Press, 2001.

———. "What's Yellow and White and Has Land All Around It?" *CENTRO Journal* 7, no. 1 (Winter–Spring 1994–95): 8–19.

Aponte-Parés, Luis, and Jorge B. Merced. "Páginas Omitidas: The Gay and Lesbian Presence." In *The Puerto Rican Movement: Voices from the Diaspora*, ed. Andrés Torres and José E. Velázquez, 296–315. Philadelphia: Temple University Press, 1998.

Aponte-Parés, Luis, coedited with Jossianna Arroyo, Elizabeth Crespo-Kebler, Lawrence La Fountain–Stokes, and Frances Negrón-Muntaner. "Puerto Rican Queer Sexualities: Introduction." *CENTRO Journal* 19, no. 1 (Spring 2007): 4–24.

Aranda, Elizabeth M. *Emotional Bridges to Puerto Rico: Migration, Return Migration, and the Struggles of Incorporation*. Lanham, Md.: Rowman & Littlefield, 2007.

Ardín Pauneto, Aixa A. "Elyíbiti: Historia del activismo LGBTT en Puerto Rico desde los 70 a mediados de los 90." Senior thesis, Universidad de Puerto Rico, Río Piedras, 2001.

———, dir. *Elyíbiti*. Video (DVD). Oakdale, Minn.: Imation Enterprises Corp., 2002.

Arenas, Reinaldo. *Before Night Falls*. Trans. Dolores M. Koch. New York: Viking, 1993.

Arrillaga, María. *Yo soy Filí Melé: Obra poética*. San Juan: Editorial de la Universidad de Puerto Rico, 1999.

Arroyo, Jossianna. "Desde la vellonera: Masculinidad y diálogos transnacionales en *La importancia de llamarse Daniel Santos.*" Paper presented at the 2nd Puerto Rican Studies Association Conference, San Juan, P.R., September 26–29, 1996.

———. "Exilio y tránsitos entre la Norzagaray y Christopher Street: Acercamientos a una poética del deseo homosexual en Manuel Ramos Otero." *Revista Iberoamericana* 67, no. 194–95 (January–June 2001): 31–54.

———. "Historias de familia: Migraciones y escritura homosexual en la literatura puertorriqueña." *Revista Canadiense de Estudios Hispánicos* 26, no. 3 (Spring 2002): 361–78.

———. "Itinerarios de viaje: Las otras islas de Manuel Ramos Otero." *Revista Iberoamericana* 71, no. 212 (July–September 2005): 865–85.

———. "Manuel Ramos Otero: Las narrativas del cuerpo más allá de *Insularismo.*" *Revista de Estudios Hispánicos* (Río Piedras, P.R.) 21 (1994): 303–24.

———. " 'Mirror, Mirror on the Wall': Performing Racial and Gender Identities in Javier Cardona's 'You Don't Look Like.' " In *The State of Latino Theater in the United States,* ed. Luis A. Ramos-García, 152–71. New York: Routledge, 2002.

———. "Sirena canta boleros: Travestismo y sujetos transcaribeños en *Sirena Selena vestida de pena.*" *CENTRO Journal* 15, no. 2 (Fall 2003): 38–51.

———. *Travestismos culturales: Literatura y etnografía en Cuba y Brasil.* Pittsburgh: University of Pittsburgh, Instituto Internacional de Literatura Iberoamericana, 2003.

Arroyo, Rane. *Pale Ramón.* Cambridge, Mass.: Zoland Books, 1998.

Asencio, Marysol. *Sex and Sexuality among New York's Puerto Rican Youth.* Boulder, Colo.: Lynne Rienner Publishers, 2002.

Astor del Valle, Janis. *I'll Be Home para la Navidad.* In *Torch to the Heart: Anthology of Lesbian Art and Drama,* ed. Sue McConnell-Celi, 97–113. Red Bank, N.J.: Lavender Crystal, 1994.

———. "Transplantations: Straight and Other Jackets para Mí." In *Action: The Nuyorican Poets Cafe Theater Festival,* ed. Miguel Algarín and Lois Griffith, 373–93. New York: Simon and Schuster, 1997.

Avilés, Arthur. *Arturella.* Performance. Hostos Center for the Arts and Culture, The Bronx, New York, November 1–2, 1996.

———. *Dorothur's Journey.* Performance. American Crafts Museum, New York City, March 15, 1998.

———. *Intoxicating Calm.* Performance. Cannes International Dance Festival, France, 1993.

———. *Maéva: A Typical New York–Rican's Ensalada.* Performance. Dance Chance Series, Dance Theatre Workshop, New York City, January 24–27, 1991.

———. *Maéva de Oz.* Performance. The Point Community Development Corporation, Hunts Point, The Bronx, New York, May 10–18, 1997.

———. *A Puerto Rican Faggot from America.* Performance. Food for Thought, Danspace Project, New York City, October 11, 1996.

Azize Vargas, Yamila. "A Commentary on the Works of Three Puerto Rican Women Poets in New York." In *Breaking Boundaries: Latina Writing and Critical Readings,* ed. Asunción Horno-Delgado, Eliana Ortega, Nina M. Scott, and Nancy Saporta Sternbach, 146–65. Trans. Sonia Crespo Vega. Amherst: University of Massachusetts Press, 1989.

———. "Poetas puertorriqueñas en Nueva York." *Cupey* 4, no. 1 (1987): 17–24.

———. "Otro modo de ver: El documental desde la perspectiva feminista." *Hómines* 17, no. 1–2 (1993–94): 224–31.

Baerga Santini, María del Carmen. "Cuerpo subversivo, norma seductora: Un capítulo de la historia de la heterosexualidad en Puerto Rico." *OP. CIT.* 14 (2002): 49–95.

Balch Institute for Ethnic Studies of the Historical Society of Pennsylvania. *Latino Philadelphia: Our Journeys, Our Communities/Filadelfia Latina: Nuestros Caminos, Nuestras Comunidades. A Community Profile.* Philadelphia: Historical Society of Pennsylvania, 2004.

Banes, Sally. *Writing Dancing in the Age of Postmodernism.* Hanover, N.H.: Wesleyan University Press, University Press of New England, 1994.

Barradas, Efraín. "Concierto de metal para un recuerdo y otras orgías de soledad." *Sin nombre* 3 (1972): 108–10.

———. " 'Epitafios': El canon y la canonización de Manuel Ramos Otero." *La Torre* 7, no. 27–28 (1993): 319–38.

———. "Fragoso, Víctor, El reino de la espiga: Canto al coraje de Walt y Federico." *Ventana* 12 (1974): 35–40.

———. "Fragoso, Víctor, Ser islas/Being Islands." *Sin nombre* 9, no. 4 (1979): 91–93.

———. "Introducción." In *Herejes y mitificadores: Muestra de la poesía puertorriqueña en los Estados Unidos,* ed. Efraín Barradas and Rafael Rodríguez, 11–30. Río Piedras: Ediciones Huracán, 1980.

———. "El machismo existencialista de René Marqués: Relecturas y nuevas lecturas." *Sin nombre* 8, no. 3 (1977): 69–81.

———. *Para leer en puertorriqueño: Acercamiento a la obra de Luis Rafael Sánchez.* Río Piedras: Editorial Cultural, 1981.

———. *Partes de un todo: Ensayos y notas sobre literatura puertorriqueña en los Estados Unidos.* Río Piedras: Editorial de la Universidad de Puerto Rico, 1998.

———. "Sobre la cuentística de Luis Rafael Sánchez." In *El cuento hispanoamericano,* ed. Enrique Pupo-Walker, 473–92. Madrid: Editorial Castalia, 1995.

———. " 'Todo lo que dijo es cierto' . . . : En memoria de Víctor Fernández Fragoso." *Revista Chicano-Riqueña* 10, no. 3 (1982): 43–46.

Barrientos, Tanya. "If Filmmaking Doesn't Pan Out, She Can Always Get a Ph.D. In the Meantime, Frances Negrón-Muntaner's Screen Work Has Impressed Some Important Folks." *Philadelphia Inquirer* June 14, 1995. NewsBank/Access World News.

Baumgardner, Jennifer, and Amy Richards. *Manifesta: Young Women, Feminism, and the Future.* New York: Farrar, Straus, and Giroux, 2000.

Behar, Ruth, ed. *Bridges to Cuba/Puentes a Cuba.* Ann Arbor: University of Michigan Press, 1995.

Bell, David, and Gill Valentine, eds. *Mapping Desire: Geographies of Sexualities.* London: Routledge, 1995.

Bennett, Paula, and Vernon A. Rosario II, eds. *Solitary Pleasures: The Historical, Literary, and Artistic Discourses of Autoeroticism.* New York: Routledge, 1995.

Bergmann, Emilie. "Abjection and Ambiguity: Lesbian Desire in Bemberg's *Yo, la peor de todas.*" In *Hispanisms and Homosexualities,* ed. Sylvia Molloy and Robert McKee Irwin, 229–47. Durham, N.C.: Duke University Press, 1998.

Bersani, Leo. "Is the Rectum a Grave?" *October* 43 (Winter 1987): 197–222.

Bhabha, Homi K. *The Location of Culture.* London: Routledge, 1994.

Binnie, Jon. *The Globalization of Sexuality.* London: SAGE, 2004.

———. "Invisible Europeans: Sexual Citizenship in the New Europe." *Environment and Planning A* 29 (February 1997): 237–48.

Bleys, Rudi C. *Images of Ambiente: Homotextuality and Latin American Art, 1810–Today.* London: Continuum, 2000.

Bluestone, Barry. *The Deindustrialization of America: Plant Closings, Community Abandonment, and the Dismantling of Basic Industry.* New York: Basic Books, 1982.

Bourdieu, Pierre. *Outline of a Theory of Practice.* Trans. Richard Nice. Cambridge: Cambridge University Press, 2004.

Brady, Mary Pat. *Extinct Lands, Temporal Geographies: Chicana Literature and the Urgency of Space.* Durham, N.C.: Duke University Press, 2002.

Braschi, Giannina. *El imperio de los sueños.* San Juan: Editorial de la Universidad de Puerto Rico, 1999 [1988]. Trans. Tess O'Dwyer as *Empire of Dreams.* New Haven, Conn.: Yale University Press, 1994.

———. *Yo-Yo Boing!* Pittsburgh: Latin American Literary Review Press, 1998.

Braulio, Mildred. "Challenging the Sodomy Law in Puerto Rico." *NACLA Report on the Americas* 31, no. 4 (January–February 1998): 33–34.

La Bruja [Caridad de la Luz]. *Brujalicious.* Mixed by DJ Precision (X-ecutioners). De La Luz Records 007 (2005).

Burt, Ramsay. *The Male Dancer: Bodies, Spectacle, Sexualities.* London: Routledge, 1995.

Butler, Judith. *Excitable Speech: A Politics of the Performative.* New York: Routledge, 1997.

———. *Gender Trouble: Feminism and the Subversion of Identity.* New York: Routledge, 1990.

Cachán, Manuel. "*En cuerpo de camisa* de Luis Rafael Sánchez: La antiliteratura alegórica del otro puertorriqueño." *Revista Iberoamericana* 162–63 (1993): 177–86.

Cady, Joseph. "Gay and Lesbian Writers in Exile." In *Literary Exile in the Twentieth Century,* ed. Martin Tucker, 10–22. New York: Greenwood Press, 1991.

Cañas, Dionisio. *El poeta y la ciudad: Nueva York y los poetas hispanos.* Madrid: Cátedra, 1994.

Cant, Bob, ed. *Invented Identities? Lesbians and Gays Talk about Migration.* London: Cassell, 1997.

Cardona, Javier. *Ah mén!* Performance. 45to Festival de Teatro Puertorriqueño, Sala Experimental Carlos Marichal, Centro de Bellas Artes, Santurce, Puerto Rico, May 13–16, 2004.

———. *You Don't Look Like.* *Conjunto* 106 (May–August 1997): 47–49.

Carr, Jay. "Rose Troche Reels in a Winner with *Go Fish.*" *Boston Globe,* July 1, 1994, 48.

Carr, Norma. "Image: The Puerto Rican in Hawaii." In *Images and Identities: The Puerto Rican in Two World Contexts,* ed. Asela Rodríguez de Laguna, 96–106. New Brunswick, N.J.: Transaction Books, 1987.

Carrillo, Héctor. "Sexual Migration, Cross-Cultural Sexual Encounters, and Sexual Health." *Sexuality Research and Social Policy* 1, no. 3 (2004): 58–70.

Carrión, María M. *Arquitectura y cuerpo en la figura autorial de Teresa de Jesús.* Barcelona: Anthropos, 1994.

———. "Geographies, (M)Other Tongues and the Rôle of Translation in Giannina Braschi's *El imperio de los sueños.*" *Studies in Twentieth Century Literature* 20, no. 1 (Winter 1996): 167–91.

Castillo, Ana. *Massacre of the Dreamers: Essays on Xicanisma.* Albuquerque: University of New Mexico Press, 1994.

Cela, Camilo José. *Diccionario del erotismo.* Barcelona: Grijalbo, 1982.

Chauncey, George. *Gay New York: The Making of the Gay Male World, 1890–1940.* New York: Basic Books, 1994.

Cinderella. Film. Clyde Geronimi, Wilfred Jackson, and Hamilton Luske, dirs. Walt Disney Studios, 1950.

Clarke, Cheryl. "The Failure to Transform: Homophobia in the Black Community." In *Dangerous Liaisons: Blacks, Gays, and the Struggle for Equality,* ed. Eric Brandt, 31–44. New York: New Press, 1999.

Coll y Toste, Cayetano. "La Garita del Diablo (1790)." In *Leyendas y tradiciones puertorriqueñas,* 86–90. Río Piedras: Editorial Cultural, 1975.

Conner, Randy P., David Hatfield Sparks, and Mariya Sparks. *Cassell's Encyclopedia of Queer Myth, Symbol, and Spirit: Gay, Lesbian, Bisexual, and Transgender Lore.* London: Cassell, 1997.

Cooper, Sara. "Queer Family and Queer Text in *Flaming Iguanas." CiberLetras* 16 (January 2007). www.lehman.cuny.edu/ciberletras/v16/cooper.html.

Cook, Fred J. "Robert Moses, Glutton for Power." *Dissent* 8, no. 3 (1961): 312–20.

Cora, María. "Nuestras Auto-Definiciones/Our Self-Definitions: Management of Stigma and Identity by Puerto Rican Lesbians." M.A. field study report, San Francisco State University, 2000.

Cortez, Jaime. *Sexilio/Sexile.* New York and Los Angeles: Institute for Gay Men's Health, 2004.

Costa, Marithelma. "Entrevista: Manuel Ramos Otero." *Hispamérica* 20, no. 59 (1991): 59–67.

Crary, David. "Some Americans Will Go Canadian." *Philadelphia Gay News* July 25, 2003: 14.

Crespo Kebler, Elizabeth. " 'The Infamous Crime against Nature': Constructions of Heterosexuality and Lesbian Subversion in Puerto Rico." In *The Culture of Gender and Sexuality in the Caribbean,* ed. Linden Lewis, 190–212. Gainesville: University of Florida Press, 2003.

Cruz-Malavé, Arnaldo. "The Oxymoron of Sexual Sovereignty: Some Puerto Rican Literary Reflections." *CENTRO Journal* 19, no. 1 (Spring 2007): 50–73.

———. "Para virar al macho: La autobiografía como subversión en la cuentística de Manuel Ramos Otero." *Revista Iberoamericana* 59, no. 162–63 (1993): 239–63.

———. *Queer Latino Testimonio, Keith Haring, and Juanito Xtravaganza: Hard Tails.* New York: Palgrave Macmillan, 2007.

———. "El simulacro de la revelación." *Cupey* 10, no. 1–2 (1992): 41–44.

———. "Towards an Art of Transvestism: Colonialism and Homosexuality in Puerto Rican Literature." In *¿Entiendes? Queer Readings, Hispanic Writings,* ed. Emilie Bergmann and Paul Julian Smith, 137–67. Durham, N.C.: Duke University Press, 1995.

———. " 'What a Tangled Web!': Masculinity, Abjection, and the Foundations of Puerto Rican Literature in the United States." In *Sex and Sexuality in Latin America,* ed. Daniel Balderston and Donna J. Guy, 234–49. New York: New York University Press, 1997.

Cruz-Malavé, Arnaldo, and Martin Manalansan, eds. *Queer Globalizations: Citizenship and the Afterlife of Colonialism.* New York: New York University Press, 2002.

Cvetkovich, Ann. "Transnational Trauma and Queer Diasporic Publics." In *An Archive of Feeling: Trauma, Sexuality, and Lesbian Public Cultures,* 118–55. Durham, N.C.: Duke University Press, 2003.

Daly, Ann. "When Dancers Move on to Making Dances." *New York Times*, April 6, 1997, C12+.

Dávila, Angela María. *Animal fiero y tierno*. Río Piedras: QeAse, 1977.

Dávila-Caballero, José. "El denominado estatuto de sodomía de Puerto Rico." *Revista Jurídica de la Universidad de Puerto Rico* 69 (2000): 1185–1266.

———. "Entre el silencio y lo criminal: La orientación sexual, el clóset, y el derecho puertorriqueño." *Revista Jurídica de la Universidad de Puerto Rico* 68 (1999): 665–76.

de Burgos, Julia. "Farewell in Welfare Island." In *Yo misma fui mi ruta*, ed. María M. Solá, 158. Río Piedras: Ediciones Huracán, 1986.

———. *El mar y tú*. 2nd ed. Río Piedras: Ediciones Huracán, 1981 [1954].

———. "Río Grande de Loíza." In *Poema en veinte surcos*, 13–14. 3rd ed. Río Piedras: Ediciones Huracán, 1997 [1938].

Decena, Carlos Ulises. "Queering the Heights: Dominican Transnational Identities and Male Homosexuality in New York City." Ph.D. diss., New York University, 2004.

———. "Tacit Subjects." *GLQ: A Journal of Lesbian and Gay Studies* 14, no. 2–3 (2008): 339–59.

de Certeau, Michel. "Practices of Space." In *On Signs*, ed. Marshall Blonsky, 122–45. Baltimore: Johns Hopkins University Press, 1985.

de Diego Padró, José Isaac. *En babia, el manuscrito de un braquicéfalo: Novela*. San Juan: Biblioteca de Autores Puertorriqueños, 1940.

de Genova, Nicholas, and Ana Yolanda Ramos-Zayas. *Latino Crossings: Mexicans, Puerto Ricans, and the Politics of Race and Citizenship*. New York: Routledge, 2003.

DeGuzmán, María. "Night Becomes 'Latina': Mariana Romo-Carmona's *Living at Night* and the Tactics of Abjection." *CENTRO Journal* 19, no. 1 (Spring 2007): 90–115.

———. *Spain's Long Shadow: The Black Legend, Off-Whiteness, and Anglo-American Empire*. Minneapolis: University of Minnesota Press, 2005.

de Monteflores, Carmen. "Invisible Audiences." *Outlook* 3, no. 2 (1990): 64–68.

———. *Singing Softly/Cantando bajito*. San Francisco: Spinsters/Aunt Lute Press, 1989.

Deleuze, Gilles, and Félix Guattari. *Kafka: Toward a Minor Literature*. Trans. Dana Polan. Minneapolis: University of Minnesota Press, 1997 [1975].

———. *Nomadology: The War Machine*. [From *A Thousand Plateaus*.] Trans. Brian Massumi. New York: Semiotext(e), 1986.

Delgado Castro, Ileana. "Nadie se escapa." *La Revista. El Nuevo Día* (San Juan, P.R.), April 29, 2007. Accessed electronically.

del Puente, José Ramón. *El homosexualismo en Puerto Rico: ¿Crimen, pecado, o enfermedad?* Río Piedras: n.p., 1986.

Desmond, Jane C. "Embodying Difference: Issues in Dance and Cultural Studies." In *Meaning in Motion: New Cultural Studies of Dance*, ed. Jane C. Desmond, 29–54. Durham, N.C.: Duke University Press, 1997.

Díaz, Luis Felipe. "Ideología y sexualidad en *Felices días, tío Sergio* de Magali García Ramis." *Revista de Estudios Hispánicos* (Río Piedras, P.R.) 21 (1994): 325–41.

Díaz Quiñones, Arcadio. *Conversación con José Luis González*. Río Piedras: Ediciones Huracán, 1977.

———. *La memoria rota: Ensayos de cultura y política*. Río Piedras: Ediciones Huracán, 1993.

Díaz Valcárcel, Emilio. *Harlem todos los días*. Río Piedras: Ediciones Huracán, 1978.

DiFrancesco, Maria. "Poetic Dissidence: An Interview with Luz María Umpierre." *MELUS* 27, no. 4 (Winter 2002): 137–54.

Donoso, José. *El lugar sin límites.* 4th ed. Barcelona: Seix Barral, 1987 [1966].

Doty, Alexander. "'My Beautiful Wickedness': *The Wizard of Oz* as Lesbian Fantasy." In *Flaming Classics: Queering the Film Canon,* 49–78. New York: Routledge, 2000.

Duany, Jorge. *The Puerto Rican Nation on the Move: Identities on the Island and in the United States.* Chapel Hill: University of North Carolina Press, 2002.

———. "The Rough Edges of Puerto Rican Identities: Race, Gender, and Transnationalism." *Latin American Research Review* 40, no. 3 (2005): 177–90.

Duberman, Martin. *Stonewall.* New York: Plume, 1994.

Duggan, Lisa, and Nan D. Hunter. *Sex Wars: Sexual Dissent and Political Culture.* New York: Routledge, 1995.

Dunbar, June, ed. *José Limón: The Artist Re-viewed.* Amsterdam: Harwood Academic, 2000.

Dunning, Jennifer. "Art Out of the Closet in the South Bronx." *New York Times,* February 9, 2003, AR 25.

———. "Arthur Avilés's Life in Dance: Nonstop Exhilaration." *New York Times,* March 24, 1989, C3.

———. "Different Styles Stirred into a South Bronx Stew." *New York Times,* October 15, 2000, AR 10.

———. "Fast-Spinning Steps That Reveal a Vivid Imagination." *New York Times,* November 23, 1999, E5.

———. "New Spin on 'Cinderella': Prince Finds a Dream Guy." *New York Times,* November 5, 1996, C16.

———. "New Works for a Benefit." *New York Times,* May 31, 1991, C3.

Dunye, Cheryl, dir. *The Watermelon Woman.* Film. First Run Features, 1996.

Duque, Andrés. "She Is Survived by Her Partner: An Op-Ed Piece by Andrés Duque." *Gay and Lesbian Alliance Against Defamation.* April 1, 2002. www.glaad.org/publications/resource_doc_detail.php?id=3104.

Dyer, Richard. "Believing in Fairies: The Author and the Homosexual." In *Inside/Out: Lesbian Theories, Gay Theories,* ed. Diana Fuss, 185–201. New York: Routledge, 1991.

Ellis, Robert Richmond. *The Hispanic Homograph: Gay Self-Representation in Contemporary Spanish Autobiography.* Urbana: University of Illinois Press, 1997.

———. *They Dream Not of Angels but of Men: Homoeroticism, Gender, and Race in Latin American Autobiography.* Gainesville: University Press of Florida, 2002.

Eng, David L. "Out Here and Over There: Queerness and Diaspora in Asian American Studies." *Social Text* 52–53 (Fall–Winter 1997): 31–52.

———. *Racial Castration: Managing Masculinity in Asian America.* Durham, N.C.: Duke University Press, 2001.

Epps, Brad. "Passing Lines: Immigration and the Performance of American Identity." In *Passing: Identity and Interpretation in Sexuality, Race, and Religion,* ed. María Carla Sánchez and Linda Schlossberg, 92–134. New York: New York University Press, 2001.

Epps, Brad, Keja Valens, and Bill Johnson González, eds. *Passing Lines: Sexuality and Immigration.* Cambridge, Mass.: David Rockefeller Center for Latin American Studies and Harvard University Press, 2005.

Escalona, Judith. "Our Latin Thing: The Nuyorican Experience in Narrative Film" (1999). *Puerto Rico and the American Dream.* www.prdream.com/film-index .html.

Espín, Oliva M. "Crossing Borders and Boundaries: The Life Narratives of Immigrant Lesbians." In *Ethnic and Cultural Diversity among Lesbians and Gay Men*, ed. Beverly Greene, 191–215. Thousand Oaks, Calif.: SAGE Publications, 1997.

———. "The Immigrant Experience in Lesbian Studies." In *The New Lesbian Studies: Into the Twenty-First Century*, ed. Bonnie Zimmerman and Toni A. H. McNaron, 79–85. New York: The Feminist Press at the City University of New York, 1996.

———. *Latina Realities: Essays on Healing, Migration, and Sexuality.* Boulder, Colo.: Westview Press, 1997.

———. *Women Crossing Boundaries: A Psychology of Immigration and Transformations of Sexuality.* New York: Routledge, 1999.

Esquibel, Catrióna Rueda. "Sor Juana and the Search for (Queer) Cultural Heroes." In *With Her Machete in Her Hand: Reading Chicana Lesbians*, 66–90. Austin: University of Texas Press, 2006.

Esteves, Sandra María. "A la Mujer Borrinqueña." In *Yerba Buena*, 63. Greenfield Center, N.Y.: Greenfield Review Press, 1980.

———. "The Feminist Viewpoint in the Poetry of Puerto Rican Women in the United States." In *Images and Identities: The Puerto Rican in Two World Contexts*, ed. Asela Rodríguez de Laguna, 171–77. New Brunswick, N.J.: Transaction Books, 1987.

———. "So Your Name Isn't María Cristina." In *Bluestown Mockingbird Mambo*, 32–33. Houston: Arte Público Press, 1990.

Falcón, Rafael. *La emigración a Nueva York en la novela puertorriqueña.* Valencia: Albatros Hispanófila, 1983.

———. *La emigración puertorriqueña a Nueva York en los cuentos de José Luis González, Pedro Juan Soto y José Luis Vivas Maldonado.* New York: Senda Nueva de Ediciones, 1984.

Farmer, Paul. *AIDS and Accusation: Haiti and the Geography of Blame.* Berkeley: University of California Press, 1993.

———. *Infections and Inequalities: The Modern Plagues.* Berkeley: University of California Press, 2001.

Feliciano Fabre, Mariano A. "Luis Rafael Sánchez y sus cuentos de seres marginados." In *Luis Rafael Sánchez: Crítica y bibliografía*, ed. Nélida Hernández Vargas and Daisy Caraballo Abreu, 51–61. Río Piedras: Editorial de la Universidad de Puerto Rico, 1985.

Ferguson, Roderick A. *Aberrations in Black: Toward a Queer of Color Critique.* Minneapolis: University of Minnesota Press, 2004.

Ferré, Rosario. "Los pasos en el polvo." *Claridad* (San Juan, P.R.), November 9–15, 1990, 19.

———. "Ramos Otero o la locura versus la libertad." *El mundo* (San Juan, P.R.), June 12, 1977, A16.

Fiet, Lowell. *Caballeros, vejigantes, locas y viejos: Santiago Apóstol y los performeros afropuertorriqueños.* Carolina, P.R.: Terranova Editores, 2007.

Figueroa, Alvin Joaquín. *La prosa de Luis Rafael Sánchez: Texto y contexto.* New York: Peter Lang, 1989.

Fiol-Matta, Lía. "Análisis sobre el control de la sexualidad de la mujer: Estudio del lesbianismo en Puerto Rico." Master's thesis, Universidad de Puerto Rico, Río Piedras, 1986.

Fiol-Matta, Licia. Panelist, "Latina Identities: Racial and Sexual Issues. Film Presentation: *Brincando el charco* by Puerto Rican Filmmaker Frances Negrón-Muntaner." *Brincando el charco*/Caribbean Women, One Day Literary Conference, New School for Social Research, New York, April 19, 1996.

———. *A Queer Mother for the Nation: Gabriela Mistral and the State*. Minneapolis: University of Minnesota Press, 2002.

Fiol-Matta, Liza. "Beyond Survival: A Politics/Poetics of Puerto Rican Consciousness." In *Telling to Live: Latina Feminist Testimonios*, by the Latina Feminist Group, 148–55. Durham, N.C.: Duke University Press, 2001.

———. "Después de tanto guardar silencio: A Poetics of Puerto Rican Consciousness." Ph.D. diss., Union Institute, Ohio, 1996.

Fiske, John. *Reading the Popular*. Boston: Unwin Hyman, 1989.

———. *Understanding Popular Culture*. Boston: Unwin Hyman, 1989.

Flores, Juan. *The Diaspora Strikes Back: Caribeño Tales of Learning and Turning*. New York: Routledge, 2009.

———. "The Diaspora Strikes Back: Nation and Location." In *None of the Above: Puerto Ricans in the Global Era*, ed. Frances Negrón-Muntaner, 211–16. New York: Palgrave Macmillan, 2007.

———. *Divided Borders: Essays on Puerto Rican Identity*. Houston: Arte Público Press, 1993.

———. *From Bomba to Hip-Hop: Puerto Rican Culture and Latino Identity*. New York: Columbia University Press, 2000.

Fortis, Marie José. "When Sappho Suffers...: Marie José Fortis Talks to Luzma Umpierre." *Collages and Bricolages* 7 (1993): 55–61.

Foster, David William, ed. *Latin American Writers on Gay and Lesbian Themes: A Bio-Critical Sourcebook*. Westport, Conn.: Greenwood Press, 1994.

Foster, Susan Leigh. "Closets Full of Dances: Modern Dance's Performance of Masculinity and Sexuality." In *Dancing Desires: Choreographing Sexualities On and Off the Stage*, ed. Jane C. Desmond, 147–207. Madison: University of Wisconsin Press, 2001.

Foucault, Michel. *The History of Sexuality*. Vol. 1, *An Introduction*. Trans. Robert Hurley. New York: Vintage, 1980.

Fox, Justin. "Dispirited Gay Americans Are Leaving." *New York Blade*, November 26, 2004. EBSCO GLBT Life Database.

Fragoso, Víctor F. *El reino de la espiga: Canto al coraje de Walt y Federico*. New York: Nueva Sangre, 1973.

———. *Ser islas/Being Islands*. Trans. Paul Orbuch. New York: El Libro Viaje, 1976.

Francke, Lizzie. "Go Fish." *Sight and Sound* 4, no. 7 (July 1994): 42–43.

Franco, Jean. "Narrator, Author, Superstar: Latin American Narrative in the Age of Mass Culture." In *Critical Passions: Selected Essays*, 147–68. Durham, N.C.: Duke University Press, 1999.

———. *Plotting Women: Gender and Representation in Mexico*. New York: Columbia University Press, 1989.

Freiberg, Peter. "Lesbian Professor Charges Bias at N.J. University." *Advocate*, December 8, 1987, 15–16.

Gan, Jessi. "Still at the Back of the Bus: Sylvia Rivera's Struggle." *CENTRO Journal* 19, no. 1 (Spring 2007): 124–39.

Garber, Marjorie. *Vice Versa: Bisexuality and the Eroticism of Everyday Life.* New York: Simon and Schuster, 1995.

García, Ana María, ed. *Cine y video puertorriqueño "Made in USA": Un proyecto de historia oral.* Río Piedras: Programa de Estudios de Honor, Universidad de Puerto Rico, 2000.

García Canclini, Néstor. *Hybrid Cultures: Strategies for Entering and Leaving Modernity.* Trans. Christopher L. Chiappari and Silvia L. López. Minneapolis: University of Minnesota Press, 1995.

García Ramis, Magali. "Los cerebros que se van y el corazón que se queda." In *La ciudad que me habita,* 9–19. Río Piedras: Ediciones Huracán, 1993.

———. *Felices días, tío Sergio.* 5th ed. Río Piedras: Editorial Antillana, 1992 [1986]. Trans. Carmen C. Esteves as *Happy Days, Uncle Sergio.* Buffalo: White Pine Press, 1995.

———. "La mayor de las muertes (Breve semblanza de Manuel Ramos Otero)." In *La ciudad que me habita,* 121–32. Río Piedras: Ediciones Huracán, 1993.

Gastil, Raymond W. *Beyond the Edge: New York's New Waterfront.* New York: Princeton Architectural Press, 2002.

Gates Jr., Henry Louis. "The Black Man's Burden." In *Fear of a Queer Planet: Queer Politics and Social Theory,* ed. Michael Warner, 230–38. Minneapolis: University of Minnesota Press, 1993.

Gelpí, Juan G. "Conversación con Manuel Ramos Otero: Nueva York, 3 de mayo de 1980." *Revista de Estudios Hispánicos* (Río Piedras, P.R.) 27, no. 2 (2000): 401–10.

———. "La cuentística antipatriarcal de Luis Rafael Sánchez." *Hispamérica* 15, no. 43 (1986): 113–20.

———. "Historia y literatura en *Página en blanco y staccato,* de Manuel Ramos Otero." In *Enfoques generacionales/Rumbos postmodernos,* ed. Carmen Cazuro García de la Quintana and Mario R. Cancel Sepúlveda, 51–60. Aguadilla, P.R.: Quality Printers, 1997.

———. *Literatura y paternalismo en Puerto Rico.* San Juan: Editorial de la Universidad de Puerto Rico, 1993.

———. "Página en blanco y staccato." *La Torre* (nueva época) 4, no. 14 (1990): 245–50.

Gherovici, Patricia. *The Puerto Rican Syndrome.* New York: Other Press, 2003.

Gil, Carlos. *El orden del tiempo: Ensayos sobre el robo del presente en la utopía puertorriqueña.* San Juan: Editorial Postdata, 1994.

Gilroy, Paul. *The Black Atlantic: Modernity and Double Consciousness.* Cambridge, Mass.: Harvard University Press, 1993.

Ging, Debbie. "The Politics of Sound and Image: Eisenstein, Artifice and Acoustic Montage in Contemporary Feminist Cinema." In *The Montage Principle: Eisenstein in New Cultural and Critical Contexts,* ed. Jean Antoine-Dunne and Paula Quigley, 67–96. Amsterdam: Rodopi, 2004.

Gladstone, Valerie. "Avilés in Oz: Nuyorican Choreographer Gets to the Point." *Village Voice,* May 13, 1997, 95.

Glasser, Ruth. *My Music Is My Flag: Puerto Rican Musicians and Their New York Communities, 1917–1940.* Berkeley: University of California Press, 1995.

Godreau, Isar P. "Peinando diferencias, bregas de pertenencia: El alisado y el llamado 'pelo malo.'" *Caribbean Studies* 30, no. 1 (2002): 82–134.

Goffman, Erving. *Stigma: Notes on the Management of Spoiled Identity.* Englewood Cliffs, N.J.: Prentice Hall, 1963.

Goldman, Dara E. *Out of Bounds: Islands and the Demarcation of Hispanic Caribbean Identity.* Lewisburg, Pa.: Bucknell University Press, 2008.

Gonzalez, Evelyn. *The Bronx.* New York: Columbia University Press, 2004.

González, José Luis. *Puerto Rico: The Four-Storeyed Country and Other Essays.* Trans. Gerald Guinness. Maplewood, N.J.: Waterfront Press, 1990 [1980].

González, Juan. "Puerto Ricans Mourn an Inspiration." *New York Daily News,* May 30, 2002, 40.

Goodman, Percival. "Lincoln Center, Emporium of the Arts." *Dissent* 8, no. 3 (1961): 333–38.

Gopinath, Gayatri. *Impossible Desires: Queer Diasporas and South Asian Public Cultures.* Durham, N.C.: Duke University Press, 2005.

Grosfoguel, Ramón. *Colonial Subjects: Puerto Ricans in a Global Perspective.* Berkeley: University of California Press, 2003.

———. "The Divorce of Nationalist Discourses from the Puerto Rican People: A Sociohistorical Perspective." In *Puerto Rican Jam: Essays on Culture and Politics,* ed. Frances Negrón-Muntaner and Ramón Grosfoguel, 57–76. Minneapolis: University of Minnesota Press, 1997.

Grosfoguel, Ramón, and Agustín Laó-Montes. "El proyecto neocolonialista del imperio." *La Revista, El Nuevo Día* (San Juan, P.R.), July 22, 2007. Accessed electronically.

Guzmán, Manolo. *Gay Hegemony/Latino Homosexualities.* New York: Routledge, 2006.

———. " 'Pa' La Escuelita con Mucho Cuida'o y por la Orillita': A Journey through the Contested Terrains of the Nation and Sexual Orientation." In *Puerto Rican Jam: Essays on Culture and Politics,* ed. Frances Negrón-Muntaner and Ramón Grosfoguel, 209–28. Minneapolis: University of Minnesota Press, 1997.

Habell-Pallán, Michelle. *Loca Motion: The Travels of Chicana and Latina Popular Culture.* New York: New York University Press, 2005.

Haeberle, Erwin J. "Swastika, Pink Triangle and Yellow Star — The Destruction of Sexology and the Persecution of Homosexuals in Nazi Germany." *Journal of Sex Research* 17, no. 3 (August 1981): 270–87.

Halperín, Laura. "Narratives of Transgression: Deviance and Defiance in Late Twentieth Century Latina Literature." Ph.D. diss., University of Michigan, Ann Arbor, 2006.

Hanhardt, Christina. " 'Safe Space': Sexual Minorities, Uneven Urban Development, and the Politics of Anti-Violence." Ph.D. diss., New York University, 2007.

Harper, Phillip Brian. "Eloquence and Epitaph: Black Nationalism and the Homophobic Impulse in Responses to the Death of Max Robinson." In *Fear of a Queer Planet: Queer Politics and Social Theory,* ed. Michael Warner, 239–63. Minneapolis: University of Minnesota Press, 1993.

Henderson, Lisa. "Simple Pleasures: Lesbian Community and *Go Fish.*" *Signs* 25, no. 1 (Spring 1999): 37–64.

Henderson, Mae G. *Borders, Boundaries, and Frames: Essays in Cultural Criticism and Cultural Studies.* New York: Routledge, 1995.

Herek, Gregory M. *"AIDS in the Barrio: Eso no me pasa a mí."* [1997–2004] *Video AIDS.* www.videoAIDS.org.

Hernández, Wilfredo. "Homosexualidad, rebelión sexual, y tradición literaria en la poesía de Manuel Ramos Otero." In *Sexualidad y nación,* ed. Daniel Balderston, 225–41. Pittsburgh: Instituto Internacional de Literatura Iberoamericana, 2000.

———. "Política homosexual y escritura poética en Manuel Ramos Otero." *Chasqui* 29, no. 2 (November 2000): 73–95.

Hernton, Calvin C. *Sex and Racism in America.* Garden City, N.Y.: Doubleday, 1965.

Heywood, Leslie, and Jennifer Drake, eds. *Third Wave Agenda: Being Feminist, Doing Feminism.* Minneapolis: University of Minnesota Press, 1997.

Hidalgo, Hilda. "The Puerto Rican Lesbian in the United States." In *Women-Identified Women*, ed. Trudy Darty and Sandee Potter, 105–15. Palo Alto, Calif.: Mayfield, 1984.

———. *The Puerto Ricans in Newark, N.J.* Newark: Aspira, Inc., 1971.

Hidalgo, Hilda, and Elia Hidalgo Christensen. "The Puerto Rican Cultural Response to Female Homosexuality." In *The Puerto Rican Woman*, ed. Edna Acosta-Belén and Elia Hidalgo Christensen, 110–23. New York: Praeger, 1979.

———. "The Puerto Rican Lesbian and the Puerto Rican Community." *Journal of Homosexuality* 2, no. 2 (Winter 1976–77): 109–21.

Hocquenghem, Guy. *Homosexual Desire.* Trans. Daniella Dangoor. Durham, N.C.: Duke University Press, 1993 [1972].

Hogan, Steve, and Lee Hudson. *Completely Queer: The Gay and Lesbian Encyclopedia.* New York: Henry Holt and Company, 1998.

Holden, Stephen. "Critic's Choice/Film: AIDS Patients on Life and Death." *New York Times*, May 13, 1994, C28.

Hollinger, Karen. *In the Company of Women: Contemporary Female Friendships in Film.* Minneapolis: University of Minnesota Press, 1998.

Homar, Susan. "Rompeforma: Unusually Exciting, Emotional." *San Juan Star* (Puerto Rico) March 30, 1996: 31.

Hopcke, Robert H. "Dorothy and Her Friends: Symbols of Gay Male Individuation in *The Wizard of Oz.*" *Quadrant* 22, no. 2 (1989): 65–77.

Horno-Delgado, Asunción. " 'Señores, Don't Leibol Mi, Please!! Ya soy Luz María Umpierre.' " In *Breaking Boundaries: Latina Writing and Critical Readings*, ed. Asunción Horno-Delgado, Eliana Ortega, Nina M. Scott, and Nancy Saporta Sternbach, 136–45. Trans. Janet N. Gold. Amherst: University of Massachusetts Press, 1989.

Iglesias, Anthony, dir. *Gay Ricans Speakin' Out.* Film. New York, 1995.

Indych, Anna. "Nuyorican Baroque: Pepón Osorio's Chucherías." *Art Journal* 60, no. 1 (Spring 2001): 72–83.

Ingram, Gordon Brent, Anne-Marie Bouthillette, and Yolanda Retter, eds. *Queers in Space: Communities, Public Spaces, Sites of Resistance.* Seattle: Bay, 1997.

Jiménez, Félix. *Las prácticas de la carne: Construcción y representación de las masculinidades puertorriqueñas.* San Juan: Ediciones Vértigo, 2004.

Jiménez de Wagenheim, Olga. "From Aguada to Dover: Puerto Ricans Rebuild Their World in Morris County, New Jersey, 1948 to 2000." In *The Puerto Rican Diaspora: Historical Perspectives*, ed. Carmen Teresa Whalen and Víctor Vázquez-Hernández, 106–27. Philadelphia: Temple University Press, 2005.

Johnson, E. Patrick. *Appropriating Blackness: Performance and the Politics of Authenticity.* Durham, N.C.: Duke University Press, 2003.

———. " 'Quare' Studies, or (Almost) Everything I Know about Queer Studies I Learned from My Grandmother." In *Black Queer Studies: A Critical Anthology*, ed. E. Patrick Johnson and Mae G. Henderson, 124–57. Durham, N.C.: Duke University Press, 2005.

Jones, Bill T., and Peggy Gillespie. *Last Night on Earth.* New York: Pantheon, 1995.

Jones, Chris. "Lesbian and Gay Cinema." In *An Introduction to Film Studies*, ed. Jill Nelmes, 279–318. 3rd London: Routledge, 2003.

Jonnes, Jill. *South Bronx Rising: The Rise, Fall, and Resurrection of an American City.* 2nd ed. New York: Fordham University Press, 2002.

Jowitt, Deborah. "New Storytelling." *Village Voice,* April 4, 2000, 71.

Juhasz, Alexandra. "Phony Definitions." In *F Is for Phony: Fake Documentary and Truth's Undoing,* ed. Alexandra Juhasz and Jesse Lerner, 1–18. Minneapolis: University of Minnesota Press, 2006.

———. *Women of Vision: Histories in Feminist Film and Video.* Minneapolis: University of Minnesota Press, 2001.

Juhasz, Alexandra, and Jesse Lerner, eds. *F Is for Phony: Fake Documentary and Truth's Undoing.* Minneapolis: University of Minnesota Press, 2006.

Julien, Isaac, dir. *Frantz Fanon: Black Skin, White Mask.* Film. San Francisco: California Newsreel, 1995.

Kanellos, Nicolás. "An Overview of Hispanic Literature of the United States." In *Herencia: The Anthology of Hispanic Literature of the United States,* ed. Nicolás Kanellos, 1–32. Oxford: Oxford University Press, 2002.

Keating, AnnLouise. "Monteflores, Carmen de." In *Latin American Writers on Gay and Lesbian Themes: A Bio-Critical Sourcebook,* ed. David William Foster, 248–50. Westport, Conn.: Greenwood Press, 1994.

Keeling, Kara. " 'Joining the Lesbians': Cinematic Regimes of Black Lesbian Visibility." In *Black Queer Studies: A Critical Anthology,* ed. E. Patrick Johnson and Mae G. Henderson, 213–27. Durham, N.C.: Duke University Press, 2005.

Kisselgoff, Anna. " 'Cinderella' Set in a Puerto Rican Ghetto." *New York Times,* February 3, 2003, E6.

Klawitter, George. "Umpierre-Herrera, Luz María." In *Latin American Writers on Gay and Lesbian Themes: A Bio-Critical Sourcebook,* ed. David William Foster, 434–36. Westport, Conn.: Greenwood Press, 1994.

Kleiman, Neil Scott, and Center for an Urban Future. "South Bronx." *The Creative Engine,* New York City Policy Research Report (November 2002): 29–30. www.nycfuture.org.

Laffrado, Laura. "Postings from Hoochie Mama: Erika López, Graphic Art, and Female Subjectivity." In *Interfaces: Women, Autobiography, Image, Performance,* ed. Sidonie Smith and Julia Watson, 406–29. Ann Arbor: University of Michigan Press, 2002.

La Fountain–Stokes, Lawrence. "1898 and the History of a Queer Puerto Rican Century: Imperialism, Diaspora, and Social Transformation." *CENTRO Journal* 11, no. 1 (Fall 1999): 91–110. First published in *Chicano/Latino Homoerotic Identities,* ed. David William Foster, 197–215. Westport, Conn.: Greenwood Press, 1999.

———. "Arthur Avilés y *Maéva de Oz.*" *Claridad* (San Juan, P.R.), August 22–28, 1997, 26.

———. "Come on Down to the Boogie-Down Bad BAAD! Bronx!" *Ollantay Theater Magazine* 15, no. 29–30 (2007): 175–80.

———. "Cultures of the Puerto Rican Queer Diaspora." In *Passing Lines: Sexuality and Immigration,* ed. Brad Epps, Keja Valens, and Bill Johnson González, 275–309. Cambridge, Mass.: David Rockefeller Center for Latin American Studies and Harvard University Press, 2005.

———. "De un pájaro, las dos alas: Travel Notes of a Queer Puerto Rican in Havana." *GLQ: A Journal of Lesbian and Gay Studies* 8, no. 1–2 (2002): 7–33.

————. "Leyendo el secreto abierto: 'Simón el mago,' *Frutos de mi tierra* y Tomás Carrasquilla." In *Tomás Carrasquilla: Nuevas aproximaciones críticas,* ed. Flor María Rodríguez-Arenas, 98–138. Medellín: Editorial Universidad de Antioquia, 2000.

————. "A Naked Puerto Rican Faggot from America: An Interview with Arthur Avilés." *CENTRO Journal* 19, no. 1 (Spring 2007): 314–29.

————. "Pop-Shock: Shifting Representations of Diasporic Puerto Rican Women's Queer Sexualities in U.S. Latina Cultural Texts." *Letras femeninas* 31, no. 1 (Summer 2005): 79–98.

————. "Pregones Theater's 2003 Asunción Playwrights Project." *Latin American Theatre Review* 37, no. 2 (Spring 2004): 141–46.

————. "Queer Ducks, Puerto Rican *Patos,* and Jewish *Feigelekh:* Birds and the Cultural Representation of Homosexuality." *CENTRO Journal* 19, no. 1 (Spring 2007): 192–229.

————. "Tomboy Tantrums and Queer Infatuations: Reading Lesbianism in Magali García Ramis's *Felices días, tío Sergio.*" In *Tortilleras: Hispanic and U.S. Latina Lesbian Expression,* ed. Lourdes Torres and Inmaculada Pertusa-Seva, 47–67. Philadelphia: Temple University Press, 2003.

————. "Trans/Bolero/Drag/Migration: Music, Cultural Translation, and Diasporic Puerto Rican Theatricalities." *WSQ: Women's Studies Quarterly* 36, no. 3–4 (Fall/Winter 2008): 190–209.

Lancaster, Roger N. "Guto's Performance: Notes on the Transvestism of Everyday Life." In *Sex and Sexuality in Latin America,* ed. Daniel Balderston and Donna Guy, 9–32. New York: New York University Press, 1997.

————. *Life Is Hard: Machismo, Danger, and the Intimacy of Power in Nicaragua.* Berkeley: University of California Press, 1992.

————. "Tolerance and Intolerance in Sexual Cultures in Latin America." In *Passing Lines,* ed. Brad Epps, Keja Valens, and Bill Johnson González, 255–74. Cambridge, Mass.: David Rockefeller Center for Latin American Studies and Harvard University Press, 2005.

Laó-Montes, Agustín. "Islands at the Crossroads: Puerto Ricanness Traveling between the Translocal Nation and the Global City." In *Puerto Rican Jam: Essays on Culture and Politics,* ed. Frances Negrón-Muntaner and Ramón Grosfoguel, 169–88. Minneapolis: University of Minnesota Press, 1997.

Laqueur, Thomas. *Solitary Sex: A Cultural History of Masturbation.* New York: Zone, 2003.

Latina Feminist Group. *Telling to Live: Latina Feminist Testimonios.* Durham, N.C.: Duke University Press, 2001.

Laureano Pérez, Javier E. "Nunca más: homofobia y violencia en la huelga de abril 2005 en la UPR." E-mail. April 28, 2005.

Laviera, Tato. *AmeRícan.* Houston: Arte Público Press, 1985.

————. *La Carreta Made a U-Turn.* 2nd ed. Houston: Arte Público Press, 1992 [1979].

Lavietes, Stuart. "Antonia Pantoja, Champion of Bilingualism, Dies at 80." *New York Times,* May 28, 2002, B6.

Lee, Albert. "Back Home in the Bronx: Arthur Avilés Makes his Neighborhood Safe for Dancing." *Dance Magazine* 75 (August 2001): 61–63.

Lennon, John J. *A Comparative Study of the Patterns of Acculturation of Selected Puerto Rican Protestant and Catholic Families in an Urban Metropolitan Area.* San Francisco: R and E Research Associates, 1976.

"Let the Summer Begin." *Village Voice,* May 24, 1994, SS3.

Levy, Emanuel. "Girl Meets Girl." *Advocate,* June 14, 1994, 93–94.

———. "*Go Fish.*" *Variety,* January 31, 1994, 66.

Lewis, Julinda. "Reviews: Performance Mix." *Dance Magazine* 64, no. 6 (June 1990): 68.

Lima, Lázaro. *The Latino Body: Crisis Identities in Literary and Cultural Memory.* New York: New York University Press, 2007.

Llamas, Ricardo. *Teoría torcida: Prejuicios y discursos en torno a "la homosexualidad."* Madrid: Siglo Veintiuno de España Editores, 1998.

Lo, Malinda. "*The L Word*'s Brush with 'Latino Culture.'" *AfterEllen.com.* February 13, 2006. www.afterellen.com/TV/2006/2/latinas.html.

Longsdorf, Amy. "Film Director's 'Portrait' Part of 'Conversation' at Open Space." *Allentown (Pa.) Morning Call* March 25, 1995. NewsBank Acces World News.

López, Erika. "*Erika Lopez's Tiny Fisted Tantrum Co. Presents NOTHING LEFT BUT THE SMELL: A Republican on Welfare.*" Performance. WOW Café, New York City, December 11, 2003.

———. *Flaming Iguanas: An Illustrated All-Girl Road Novel Thing.* New York: Simon and Schuster, 1997.

———. *Grandma López's Country-Mad Fried Chicken Book. Nothing Left But the Smell: A Republican on Welfare.* San Francisco: Tiny-Fisted Book Publishers, 2003.

———. "*Grandma López's Country-Mad Medicine Show: A Tonic for the Age. A Food Stamp Diatribe-in-Progress.*" Performance. Douglass College Center, Rutgers University, New Brunswick, New Jersey, November 20, 2002.

———. *Hoochie Mama: The Other White Meat.* New York: Simon and Schuster, 2001.

———. *Lap Dancing for Mommy: Tender Stories of Disgust, Blame, and Inspiration.* Seattle: Seal Press, 1997.

———. "Postcards from the Welfare Line: The Rise and Fall of Erika Lopez." *Junction-City/Progressive America.* www.junction-city.com/content/lopez.asp.

———. *They Call Me Mad Dog! A Story for Bitter, Lonely People.* New York: Simon and Schuster, 1998.

López, Iris. "Borinkis and Chop Suey: Puerto Rican Identity in Hawai'i, 1900 to 2000." In *The Puerto Rican Diaspora: Historical Perspectives,* ed. Carmen Teresa Whalen and Víctor Vázquez-Hernández, 43–67. Philadelphia: Temple University Press, 2005.

López Torregrosa, Luisita. *The Noise of Infinite Longing: A Memoir of a Family and an Island.* New York: Rayo/HarperCollins, 2004.

Louro, Guacira Lopes. *Um corpo estranho: Ensaios sobre sexualidade e teoria queer.* Belo Horizonte, Brazil: Autêntica, 2004.

Lozada, Angel. *No quiero quedarme sola y vacía.* San Juan: Isla Negra Editores, 2006.

———. *La patografía.* Mexico: Editorial Planeta, 1998.

Ludmer, Josefina. "Tretas del débil." In *La sartén por el mango,* ed. Patricia Elena González and Eliana Ortega, 47–54. Río Piedras: Ediciones Huracán, 1985.

Lugo Bertrán, Dorian. "*Brincando el charco:* Primer largometraje de Frances Negrón-Muntaner." *Nómada* (San Juan, P.R.) 3 (1997): 137–40.

Lugo Filippi, Carmen. "Milagros, calle Mercurio." In *Vírgenes y mártires,* Ana Lydia Vega and Carmen Lugo Filippi, 25–38. 2nd ed. Río Piedras: Editorial Antillana, 1983 [1981].

Lugo-Ortiz, Agnes. "Community at Its Limits: Orality, Law, Silence, and the Homosexual Body in Luis Rafael Sánchez's '¡Jum!' " In *¿Entiendes? Queer Readings, Hispanic Writings*, ed. Emilie Bergmann and Paul Julian Smith, 115–36. Durham, N.C.: Duke University Press, 1995.

———. "Nationalism, Male Anxiety, and the Lesbian Body in Puerto Rican Narrative." In *Hispanisms and Homosexualities*, ed. Sylvia Molloy and Robert McKee Irwin, 76–100. Durham, N.C.: Duke University Press, 1998.

———. "Sobre el tráfico simbólico de mujeres: Homosocialidad, identidad nacional y modernidad literaria en Puerto Rico (Apuntes para una relectura de *El puertorriqueño dócil* de René Marqués)." *Revista de Crítica Literaria Latinoamericana* 23, no. 45 (1997): 261–78.

Luibhéid, Eithne. *Entry Denied: Controlling Sexuality at the Border*. Minneapolis: University of Minnesota Press, 2002.

———. "Obvious Homosexuals and Homosexuals Who Cover Up: Lesbian and Gay Exclusion in U.S. Immigration." *Radical America* 26, no. 2 (October 1996): 33–40.

Luibhéid, Eithne, and Lionel Cantú Jr., eds. *Queer Migrations: Sexuality, U.S. Citizenship and Border Crossings*. Minneapolis: University of Minnesota Press, 2005.

Luis, William. *Dance between Two Cultures: Latino Caribbean Literature Written in the United States*. Nashville: Vanderbilt University Press, 1997.

———. "María C(h)ristina Speaks: Latina Identity and the Poetic Dialogue between Sandra María Esteves and Luz María Umpierre." *Hispanic Journal* 18, no. 1 (1997): 137–49.

Lumsden, Ian. *Machos, Maricones, and Gays: Cuba and Homosexuality*. Philadelphia: Temple University Press, 1996.

MacLean, Judy. "U.S. Seeks to Deport Man for Being Gay." *Advocate*, July 10, 1984, 9.

Maffi, Mario. *Gateway to the Promised Land: Ethnic Cultures on New York's Lower East Side*. New York: New York University Press, 1995.

Maine, Judith. "A Parallax View of Lesbian Authorship." In *Inside/Out: Lesbian Theories, Gay Theories*, ed. Diana Fuss, 173–84. New York: Routledge, 1991.

Manalansan, Martin F. *Global Divas: Filipino Gay Men in the Diaspora*. Durham, N.C.: Duke University Press, 2003.

———. "Queer Intersections: Sexuality and Gender in Migration Studies." *International Migration Review* 40, no. 1 (March 2006): 224–49.

Mandlove, Nancy. "In Response." Introduction to *. . . Y otras desgracias/And Other Misfortunes . . .*, by Luz María Umpierre, ix–xiii. Bloomington, Ind.: Third Woman Press, 1985.

Mariposa [María Fernández]. "Ode to the DiaspoRican." *CENTRO Journal* 12, no. 1 (Fall 2000): 66.

Marqués, René. *La carreta: drama en tres actos*. 18th ed. Río Piedras: Editorial Cultural, 1983 [1952].

———. *La mirada*. Río Piedras: Editorial Antillana, 1976. Translated by Charles Pilditch as *The Look*. New York: Senda Nueva de Ediciones, 1983.

———. *El puertorriqueño dócil y otros ensayos (1953–1971)*. 3rd ed. Río Piedras: Editorial Antillana, 1977.

Martínez, Elena M. "An Interview with Luz María Umpierre." *Christopher Street*, October 1991, 9–10.

———. *Lesbian Voices from Latin America: Breaking Ground*. New York: Garland Publishing, 1996.

———. "Luz María Umpierre: A Lesbian Puerto Rican Writer in America." *Christopher Street*, October 1991, 7–8.

Martínez, Manuel. *Chicago: Historia de nuestra comunidad puertorriqueña*. Chicago: Reyes and Sons, 1989.

Martínez–San Miguel, Yolanda. "Beyond Homonormativity: Queer Intimacies as Alternative Narratives in the Hispanic Caribbean." Paper presented at the 31st Caribbean Studies Association Conference, Port of Spain, Trinidad, May 29–June 2, 2006.

———. "Bitextualidad y bilingüismo: reflexiones sobre el lenguaje en la escritura latina contemporánea." *CENTRO Journal* 12, no. 1 (Fall 2000): 19–34.

———. "*Boricua* (Between) Borders: On the Possibility of Translating Bilingual Narratives." In *None of the Above: Puerto Ricans in the Global Era*, ed. Frances Negrón-Muntaner, 195–210. New York: Palgrave Macmillan, 2007.

———. *Caribe Two Ways: Cultura de la migración en el Caribe insular hispánico*. San Juan: Ediciones Callejón, 2003.

———. "Juan Antonio Ramos: Urbanizando la narrativa puertorriqueña." In *Narradores puertorriqueños del 70: guía biobibliográfica*, ed. Víctor Federico Torres, 161–65. San Juan: Editorial Plaza Mayor, 2001.

———. "Más allá de la homonormatividad: intimidades alternativas en el Caribe hispano." *Revista Iberoamericana* 74, no. 225 (October-December 2008): 1039–57.

Martorell, Antonio. "Nominación, dominación y desafío." *Piso 13 (Edición Gay)* (San Juan, P.R.) 2, no. 3 (1993): 10.

———. *La piel de la memoria*. Trujillo Alto, P.R.: Ediciones Envergadura, 1991. Translated by Andrew Hurley as *Memory's Tattoo*. San Juan: Editorial Plaza Mayor, 2005.

Maslin, Janet. "Girl Meets Girl, Laughter Included." *New York Times*, June 10, 1994, C6.

Matos-Cintrón, Nemir. *A través del aire y del fuego pero no del cristal*. Río Piedras: Atabex, 1981.

Matos-Cintrón, Nemir, and Yolanda Victoria Fundora. "Carta abierta a Manuel Ramos Otero (El Chú) en respuesta al artículo 'La luna ultrajada': 'Somos folkloristas y tradicionalistas.'" *Claridad* (San Juan, P.R.), February 19, 1982, 11.

———. *Las mujeres no hablan así*. Río Piedras: Atabex, 1981.

Mauceri, Marc, dir. *Lavender Limelight: Lesbians in Film*. Film. First Run Features, 1997.

Mayne, Judith. "A Parallax View of Lesbian Authorship." In *Inside/Out: Lesbian Theories, Gay Theories*, ed. Diana Fuss, 173–84. New York: Routledge, 1991.

McGehee, Helen. "Working for Martha Graham." *Dance Research* 3, no. 2 (Summer 1985): 56–64.

McNamara, Robert P. *The Times Square Hustler: Male Prostitution in New York City*. Westport, Conn.: Praeger, 1994.

Mele, Christopher. *Selling the Lower East Side: Culture, Real Estate, and Resistance in New York City*. Minneapolis: University of Minnesota Press, 2000.

Merced, Jorge. "Pregones Theater: Asunción Playwrights Project." *Ollantay Theater Magazine* 15, no. 29–30 (2007): 181–85.

Mercer, Kobena. "Black Hair/Style Politics." In *Welcome to the Jungle: New Positions in Black Cultural Studies*, 97–130. New York: Routledge, 1994.

Miller, John C. "Mohr, Nicholasa." In *Latin American Writers on Gay and Lesbian Themes: A Bio-Critical Sourcebook,* ed. David William Foster, 236–39. Westport, Conn.: Greenwood Press, 1995.

Miller, Sarah. "Images of Home: Local Filmmaker Captures Tent City's Puerto Rican Experience." *Philadelphia Weekly,* September 11, 1996, 11–13.

Mira, Alberto. *Para entendernos: Diccionario de cultura homosexual, gay y lésbica.* Barcelona: Ediciones de la Tempestad, 1999.

Mohanty, Chadra Talpade. *Feminism without Borders: Decolonizing Theory, Practicing Solidarity.* Durham, N.C.: Duke University Press, 2003.

Mohr, Nicholasa. *El Bronx Remembered: A Novella and Stories.* New York: HarperKeypoint, 1993 [1975].

———. *Nilda.* 2nd ed. Houston: Arte Público Press, 1986 [1972].

Moliner, María. *Diccionario de uso del español.* 2 vols. Madrid: Gredos, 1982.

Molloy, Sylvia. *At Face Value: Autobiographical Writing in Spanish America.* Cambridge: Cambridge University Press, 1991.

Montero, Oscar. "Angel Rodríguez Díaz: El retrato del otro." *El Mundo: Puerto Rico Ilustrado,* October 14, 1990, 10–11.

Moraga, Cherríe. *Loving in the War Years: Lo que nunca pasó por sus labios.* Boston: South End Press, 1983.

———. "Queer Aztlán: The Re-Formation of the Chicano Tribe." In *The Last Generation: Prose and Poetry,* 145–74. Boston: South End Press, 1993.

———. *Waiting in the Wings: Portrait of a Queer Motherhood.* Ithaca, N.Y.: Firebrand Books, 1997.

Moraga, Cherríe, and Gloria Anzaldúa, eds. *This Bridge Called My Back: Writings by Radical Women of Color.* 2nd ed. New York: Kitchen Table; Women of Color Press, 1983 [1981].

Morales, Ed. *Living in Spanglish: The Search for Latino Identity in America.* New York: St. Martin's Griffin, 2003.

Morales-Díaz, Enrique. "Identity of the 'Diasporican' Homosexual in the Literary Periphery." In *Writing Off the Hyphen: New Critical Perspectives on the Literature of the Puerto Rican Diaspora,* ed. José L. Torres-Padilla and Carmen Haydée Rivera, 295–312. Seattle: University of Washington Press, 2008.

Moreno, Hortensia. Editorial. "Raras rarezas." *Debate feminista* (Mexico) 8, no. 16 (1997): ix–xiv.

Mosse, George L. *Nationalism and Sexuality: Respectability and Abnormal Sexuality in Modern Europe.* New York: Howard Fertig, 1985.

Muñoz, José Esteban. *Disidentifications: Queers of Color and the Performance of Politics.* Minneapolis: University of Minnesota Press, 1999.

———. "No es fácil: Notes on the Negotiation of Cubanidad and Exilic Memory in Carmelita Tropicana's *Milk of Amnesia.*" *TDR: The Drama Review* 39, no. 3 (Fall 1995): 76–82.

Muñoz-Laboy, Miguel A. "Beyond 'MSM': Sexual Desire among Bisexually-Active Latino Men in New York City." *Sexualities* 7, no. 1 (2004): 55–80.

Murray, Stephen O., and Wayne R. Dynes. "Hispanic Homosexuals: A Spanish Lexicon." In *Latin American Male Homosexualities,* ed. Stephen O. Murray, 180–92. Albuquerque: University of New Mexico Press, 1995.

Negrón-Muntaner, Frances. *Boricua Pop: Puerto Ricans and the Latinization of American Culture.* New York: New York University Press, 2004.

———. "Drama Queens: Latino Gay and Lesbian Independent Media." In *The Ethnic Eye: Latino Media Arts,* ed. Chon Noriega and Ana López, 59–78. University of Minnesota Press, 1996.

———. "Echoing Stonewall and Other Dilemmas: The Organizational Beginnings of a Gay and Lesbian Agenda in Puerto Rico, 1972–1977." *CENTRO Journal* 4, no. 1 (1992): 77–95; 4, no. 2 (1992): 98–115.

———. "Insider/Outsider: Making Films in the Puerto Rican Community." *CENTRO Journal* 3, no. 1 (Winter 1990–91): 81–85.

———. "Jennifer's Butt." *Aztlán* 22, no. 2 (Fall 1997): 181–94.

———. "Magali García Ramis." *Hispamérica* 22, no. 64–65 (1993): 89–104.

———. "Of Lonesome Stars and Broken Hearts." In *New Latin American Cinema*, vol. 2, *Studies of National Cinemas*, ed. Michael T. Martin, 233–57. Detroit: Wayne State University Press, 1997.

———. "Surviving Cultures: A Dialogue on AIDS and Gay Latino Politics." *CENTRO Journal* 6, no. 1 and 2 (Spring 1994): 115–27.

———. "Twenty Years of Puerto Rican Activism: An Interview with Luis 'Popo' Santiago." *Radical America* 25, no. 1 (January–March 1991): 39–51. (Published September 1993.)

———. "Watching *Tongues Untie(d)* While Reading *Zami*: Mapping Boundaries in Black Gay and Lesbian Narratives." In *Feminism, Multiculturalism, and the Media: Global Diversities*, ed. Angharad N. Valdivia, 245–76. Thousand Oaks, Calif.: SAGE Publications, 1995.

———. "We Are Not a New York Suburb." Radio show. 1991.

———. "When I Was a Puerto Rican Lesbian." *GLQ: A Journal of Lesbian and Gay Studies* 5, no. 4 (1999): 511–26.

———, dir. *Brincando el charco: Portrait of a Puerto Rican*. Film. Women Make Movies, 1994.

———. *Homeless Diaries*. Video. 1996.

———, ed. *None of the Above: Puerto Ricans in the Global Era*. New York: Palgrave Macmillan, 2007.

———. *Shouting in a Whisper: Latino Poetry in Philadelphia, An Anthology*. Santiago de Chile: Asterion, 1994.

———, prod. *Just Like You Imagined?* Co-written by Frances Negrón-Muntaner and Verena Fadden. Directed by David Frankel. Video. Scenarios, USA, 2000. Online at www.scenariosusa.org.

Negrón-Muntaner, Frances, and Peter Biella, dir. *AIDS in the Barrio: Eso no me pasa a mí*. Video. Cinema Guild, 1989.

Negrón-Muntaner, Frances, and Ramón Grosfoguel, eds. *Puerto Rican Jam: Essays on Culture and Politics*. Minneapolis: University of Minnesota Press, 1997.

Negrón-Muntaner, Frances, and Rita González. "Boricua Gazing: An Interview with Frances Negrón-Muntaner." *Signs* 30, no. 1 (Autumn 2004): 1345–60.

"New Virginia Law Causes Some Gays to Consider Leaving State." *Gay and Lesbian Times*, May 27, 2004, 28–29.

Nieves, Evelyn. "Fund Provides Window into the American Dream." *New York Times*, June 14, 1992, 53.

Obejas, Achy. *Memory Mambo: a novel*. Pittsburgh: Cleis Press, 1996.

Ocasio Rivera, Juan Antonio. "Visions of Struggle from Exile: The Puerto Rican Diaspora and the Struggle For Independence." *Upside Down World* April 17, 2007. http://upsidedownworld.org/main/content/view/703/60/.

Ochoa, Marcia. "Perverse Citizenship: Divas, Marginality, and Participation in 'Loca-lization.'" *WSQ: Women's Studies Quarterly* 36, no. 3–4 (Fall/Winter 2008): 146–69.

Olalquiaga, Celeste. *Megalopolis: Contemporary Cultural Sensibilities*. Minneapolis: University of Minnesota Press, 1992.

Oliver, Jorge. *Pride in Puerto Rico.* Film. San Francisco: Frameline, 1999.

Omi, Michael, and Howard Winant. *Racial Formation in the United States: From the 1960s to the 1980s.* New York: Routledge, 1986.

O'Neil, Brian. "Carmen Miranda: The High Price of Fame and Bananas." In *Latina Legacies: Identity, Biography, and Community,* ed. Vicki L. Ruiz and Virginia Sánchez Korrol, 193–208. New York: Oxford University Press, 2005.

Ong, Walter J. *Orality and Literacy: The Technologizing of the Word.* London: Methuen, 1982.

Orlan. Talk presented as part of the Penny W. Stamps Distinguished Visitor Series. University of Michigan, Ann Arbor. March 30, 2006. Available through iTunes.

Ortega, Julio. "Teoría y práctica del discurso popular (Luis Rafael Sánchez y la nueva escritura puertorriqueña)." In *Reapropiaciones: Cultura y nueva escritura en Puerto Rico,* 9–52. Río Piedras: Editorial de la Universidad de Puerto Rico, 1991.

Ortega, Ralph. "Antonia Pantoja, Bilingual Ed Icon." *New York Daily News,* May 29, 2002, 32.

Ostriker, Alicia Suskin. *Stealing the Language: The Emergence of Women's Poetry in America.* Boston: Beacon Press, 1986.

Otalvaro-Hormillosa, Sonia (Gigi). "The Homeless Diaspora of Queer Asian Americans." *Social Justice* 26, no. 3 (Fall 1999): 103–22.

Otero Garabís, Juan. *Nación y ritmo: "Descargas" desde el Caribe.* San Juan: Ediciones Callejón, 2000.

Our Latin Thing/Nuestra Cosa. Film. Leon Gast, dir. Jerry Masucci, prod. Movies & Pictures International, 1971.

Padilla, Félix M. *Latino Ethnic Consciousness: The Case of Mexican Americans and Puerto Ricans in Chicago.* Notre Dame, Ind.: University of Notre Dame Press, 1985.

———. *Puerto Rican Chicago.* Notre Dame, Ind.: University of Notre Dame Press, 1987.

Palés Matos, Luis. "Majestad negra." In *Poesía (1915–1956),* 219–20. 5th rev. ed. San Juan: Editorial de la Universidad de Puerto Rico, 1974 [1937].

Pantoja, Antonia. *Memoirs of a Visionary: Antonia Pantoja.* Houston: Arte Público Press, 2002.

Pattatucci-Aragón, Angela. "Contra la corriente (Against the Current)." *Journal of Lesbian Studies* 5, no. 3 (2001): 1–13.

Patton, Cindy. *Globalizing AIDS.* Minneapolis: University of Minnesota Press, 2002.

———. *Inventing AIDS.* New York: Routledge, 1990.

Patton, Cindy, and Benigno Sánchez-Eppler, eds. *Queer Diasporas.* Durham, N.C.: Duke University Press, 2000.

Paz Brownrigg, Coya. "Linchocracia: Performing 'America' in *El Clamor Público.*" *California History* 84, no. 2 (Winter 2006): 40–53, 71–72.

Pedreira, Antonio S. *Insularismo.* Vol. 3 of Complete Works. Río Piedras: Editorial Edil, 1969 [1934].

Peña, Susana. "*Pájaration* and Transculturation: Language and Meaning in Miami's Cuban American Gay Worlds." In *Speaking in Queer Tongues: Globalization and Gay Language,* ed. William L. Leap and Tom Boellstorff, 231–50. Urbana: University of Illinois Press, 2004.

———. "Visibility and Silence: Mariel and Cuban American Gay Male Experience and Representation." In *Queer Migrations: Sexuality, U.S. Citizenship, and Border Crossings,* ed. Eithne Luibhéid and Lionel Cantú Jr., 125–45. Minneapolis: University of Minnesota Press, 2005.

Pérez, Gina M. *The Near Northwest Side Story: Migration, Displacement, and Puerto Rican Families.* Berkeley: University of California Press, 2004.

Pérez-Erdelyi, Mireya. "Luz María Umpierre: Poeta puertorriqueña." Interview. *Chasqui* 16, no. 2–3 (1987): 61–68.

Pérez Firmat, Gustavo. *Life on the Hyphen: The Cuban-American Way.* Austin: University of Texas Press, 1994.

Perivolaris, John Dimitri. *Puerto Rican Cultural Identity and the Work of Luis Rafael Sánchez.* Chapel Hill: U.N.C. Department of Romance Languages, 2000.

Perlongher, Néstor. *O negócio do michê: A prostituição viril em São Paulo.* São Paulo: Editora Brasiliense, 1987.

Pierson, John. *Spike, Mike, Slackers and Dykes: A Guided Tour across a Decade of American Independent Cinema.* New York: Hyperion, 1995.

Pietri, Pedro. "Suicide Note from a Cockroach in a Low Income Housing Project." In *Puerto Rican Obituary/Obituario puertorriqueño,* 34–45. San Juan: Isla Negra, 2000.

Piñero, Miguel. "A Lower East Side Poem." In *La Bodega Sold Dreams,* 7–8. Houston: Arte Público Press, 1985.

Plath, Sylvia. "Lady Lazarus" [1962]. In *The Collected Poems,* 244–47. New York: HarperPerennial, 1992.

Platizky, Roger. "From Dialectic to Deliverance: Luz María Umpierre's *The Margarita Poems.*" In *The Margarita Poems,* by Luz María Umpierre, 12–15. Bloomington, Ind.: Third Woman Press, 1987.

Pollack, Barbara, and Charles Humphrey Woodford. *Dance Is a Moment: A Portrait of José Limón in Words and Pictures.* Pennington, N.J.: Princeton Book Co., 1993.

Pons, Joey, and Moisés Agosto-Rosario. *Poemas de lógica inmune.* 2nd. ed. San Juan: Publivisiones Pons, 1991.

Portes, Alejandro, and Rubén Rumbaut. *Immigrant America: A Portrait.* Berkeley: University of California Press, 1996.

———. *Legacies: The Story of the Second Generation.* Berkeley: University of California Press, 2001.

Pramaggiore, Maria. "Fishing for Girls: Romancing Lesbians in New Queer Cinema." *College Literature* 24, no. 1 (Fall 1997): 59–75.

Pratt, Mary Louise. *Imperial Eyes: Travel Writing and Transculturation.* London: Routledge, 1992.

Prida, Dolores. *Beautiful Señoritas & Other Plays.* Houston: Arte Público Press, 1991.

Prosper-Sánchez, Gloria D. "Transing the Standard: The Case of Puerto Rican Spanish." In *None of the Above: Puerto Ricans in the Global Era,* ed. Frances Negrón-Muntaner, 183–94. New York: Palgrave Macmillan, 2007.

Puar, Jasbir Kaur. "Transnational Sexualities: South Asian (Trans)nation(alism)s and Queer Diasporas." In *Q & A: Queer in Asian America,* ed. David L. Eng and Alice Y. Hom, 405–22. Philadelphia: Temple University Press, 1998.

El pueblo se levanta/The People Are Rising. Film. New York: Third World Newsreel, 1970.

Quiñones Santiago, Juan C. "Ideología y discurso en *La novelabingo* de Manuel Ramos Otero." Ph.D. diss., Universidad de Puerto Rico, Río Piedras, 2004.

Quintero Herencia, Juan Carlos. *La máquina de la salsa: Tránsitos del sabor.* San Juan: Ediciones Vértigo, 2005.

———. "Notes toward a Reading of Salsa." In *Everynight Life: Culture and Dance in Latin/o America*, ed. Celeste Fraser Delgado and José Esteban Muñoz, 189–222. Durham, N.C.: Duke University Press, 1997.

Quintero Rivera, Angel G. *Salsa, sabor y control: sociología de la música tropical.* Mexico: Siglo Veintiuno Editores, 1998.

Quiroga, José. *Cuban Palimpsests.* Minneapolis: University of Minnesota Press, 2005.

———. *Tropics of Desire: Interventions from Queer Latino America.* New York: New York University Press, 2000.

Ramírez, Rafael L. *What It Means to Be a Man: Reflections on Puerto Rican Masculinity.* Trans. Rosa E. Casper. New Brunswick, N.J.: Rutgers University Press, 1999.

Ramírez Mercado, Sergio. "Lecciones de la imaginación." *Ideay* (Nicaragua). n.d. www.ideay.net.ni/servicios/pluma/editorial.php?tipo=1&cod=189&ant=16.

Ramos, Juan Antonio. *Papo Impala está quitao.* Río Piedras: Ediciones Huracán, 1983.

Ramos, Juanita, ed. *Compañeras: Latina Lesbians (An Anthology).* 3rd. ed. New York: Latina Lesbian History Project, 2004 [1987].

Ramos Otero, Manuel. *Concierto de metal para un recuerdo y otras orgías de soledad.* San Juan: Editorial Cultural, 1971.

———. *El cuento de la Mujer del Mar.* Río Piedras: Ediciones Huracán, 1979.

———. *Cuentos de buena tinta.* San Juan: Instituto de Cultura Puertorriqueña, 1992.

———. "De la colonización a la culonización." *Cupey* 8, no. 1–2 (1991): 63–79.

———. "La ética de la marginación en la poesía de Luis Cernuda." *Cupey* 5, no. 1–2 (1988): 16–29.

———. "Ficción e historia: Texto y pretexto de la autobiografía." *El mundo (Puerto Rico Ilustrado)* (San Juan, P.R.), October 14, 1990, 20–23.

———. *Invitación al polvo.* Madrid: Editorial Plaza Mayor, 1991.

———. *El libro de la muerte.* Río Piedras: Editorial Cultural; Maplewood, N.J.: Waterfront Press, 1985.

———. "La luna ultrajada." *Claridad* (San Juan, P.R.), February 5, 1982, 8–11.

———. *La novelabingo.* New York: Editorial El Libro Viaje, 1976.

———. *Página en blanco y staccato.* 2nd ed. Madrid: Editorial Playor, 1988 [1987].

Ramos Otero, Manuel, Manuel Puig, and Olga Nolla. "Escritura y ensoñación. Transcripción de la actividad celebrada el 28 de septiembre de 1988." *Cupey* 5, no. 1–2 (1988): 62–77.

Ramos Rosado, Marie. *La mujer negra en la literatura puertorriqueña: Cuentística de los setenta (Luis Rafael Sánchez, Carmelo Rodríguez Torres, Rosario Ferré y Ana Lydia Vega).* San Juan: Editorial de la Universidad de Puerto Rico, 1999.

Ramos-Zayas, Ana Yolanda. "All This Turning White Now: Latino Constructions of 'White Culture' and Whiteness in Chicago." *CENTRO Journal* 13, no. 2 (Fall 2001): 72–95.

———. *National Performances: The Politics of Class, Race, and Space in Puerto Rican Chicago.* Chicago: University of Chicago Press, 2003.

Reaven, Marci, and Beni Matías, dirs. *The Heart of Loisaida.* Film. New York: Cinema Guild, 1979.

Reddy, Chandan. "Asian Diasporas, Neoliberalism, and Family: Reviewing the Case for Homosexual Asylum in the Context of Family Rights." *Social Text* 84–85 (Fall–Winter 2005): 101–19.

Reid-Pharr, Robert F. *Black Gay Man: Essays.* New York: New York University Press, 2001.

———. "Makes Me Feel Mighty Real: *The Watermelon Woman* and the Critique of Black Visuality." In *F Is for Phony: Fake Documentary and Truth's Undoing,* ed. Alexandra Juhasz and Jesse Lerner, 130–42. Minneapolis: University of Minnesota Press, 2006.

Retzloff, Tim. "Eliding Trans Latino/a Queer Experience in U.S. LGBT History: José Sarria and Sylvia Rivera Reexamined." *CENTRO Journal* 19, no. 1 (Spring 2007): 140–61.

Reyes, Israel. "Modernism and Migration in Manuel Ramos Otero's *El cuento de la Mujer del Mar.*" *Journal of the Midwest Modern Language Association* 29, no. 1 (Spring 1996): 63–75.

———. "Recuerdos 'parciales' y el *closet* de la literatura: Ficción y autobiografía de Judith Ortiz Cofer." *Revista Iberoamericana* 71, no. 212 (July–September 2005): 847–63.

Rich, Adrienne. "Diving into the Wreck." In *Diving into the Wreck: Poems 1971–1972,* 22–24. New York: Norton, 1973.

Rich, B. Ruby. "Goings and Comings." *Sight and Sound* 4, no. 7 (July 1994): 14–16.

Riggs, Marlon, dir. *Tongues Untied.* Video. San Francisco: Frameline, 1989.

Rinaldo, Rachel. "Space of Resistance: The Puerto Rican Cultural Center and Humboldt Park." *Cultural Critique* 50 (Winter 2002): 135–74.

Ríos Avila, Rubén. "Caribbean Dislocations: Arenas and Ramos Otero in New York." In *Hispanisms and Homosexualities,* ed. Sylvia Molloy and Robert McKee Irwin, 101–19. Durham, N.C.: Duke University Press, 1998.

———. "The End of Gay Culture?" Talk presented at the University of Michigan, Ann Arbor, March 10, 2006.

———. "Gaiety Burlesque: Homosexual Desire in Puerto Rican Literature." *Piso 13 (Edición Gay)* (San Juan, P.R.) 2, no. 3 (1993): 8–9. Reprinted in *Polifonía salvaje: Ensayos de cultura y política en la postmodernidad,* ed. Irma Rivera Nieves and Carlos Gil, 138–46. San Juan: Editorial Postdata and Editorial de la Universidad de Puerto Rico, 1995.

———. "Migrant Hybridity." *Postdata* (San Juan, P.R.), 13 (May 1998): 45–47.

———. *La raza cómica: del sujeto en Puerto Rico.* San Juan: Ediciones Callejón, 2002.

———. "El show de Cristina." Interview with Cristina Hayworth. *Piso 13* (Edición Gay) (San Juan, P.R.) 2, no. 3 (1993): 13.

Rivera, Carmen Haydée. "Language Is Our Only Homeland: An Interview with Luz María Umpierre." *CENTRO Journal* 20, no. 1 (Spring 2008): 13–21.

Rivera, Carmen S. *Kissing the Mango Tree: Puerto Rican Women Rewriting American Literature.* Houston: Arte Público Press, 2002.

Rivera, Raquel Z. *New York Ricans from the Hip Hop Zone.* New York: Palgrave Macmillan, 2003.

Rivera, Sylvia. "Queens in Exile, the Forgotten Ones." In *GenderQueer: Voices from Beyond the Sexual Binary,* ed. Joan Nestle, Clare Howell, and Riki Wilchins, 67–85. Los Angeles: Alyson Publications, 2002.

———. "Sylvia Rivera's Talk at LGMNY, June 2001." *CENTRO Journal* 19, no. 1 (Spring 2007): 116–23.

Rivera Lassén, Ana Irma, and Elizabeth Crespo Kebler, eds. *Documentos del feminismo en Puerto Rico: Facsímiles de la historia.* San Juan: Editorial de la Universidad de Puerto Rico, 2001.

Rivera-Servera, Ramón H. "Grassroots Globalization, Queer Sexualities, and the Performance of Latinidad." Ph.D. diss., University of Texas, Austin, 2003.

———. "Latina/o Queer Futurities: Arthur Aviles Takes on the Bronx." *Ollantay Theater Magazine* 15, no. 29–30 (2007): 127–46.

Rivero, Eliana. "De maravillas, oraciones y sofritos: La poeta cautiva." Introduction. In *En el país de las maravillas,* by Luz María Umpierre, i–iv. Bloomington, Ind.: Third Woman Press, 1982.

Rodríguez, Clara E. *Puerto Ricans: Born in the U.S.A.* Boulder, Colo.: Westview Press, 1991.

Rodríguez, Dinah E. "Un cine sospechoso: Conversando con Frances Negrón-Muntaner." Interview. *Revista de Crítica Literaria Latinoamericana* 23, no. 45 (1997): 411–20.

Rodríguez, Juana María. "Getting F**ked in Puerto Rico: Metaphoric Provocations and Queer Activist Interventions." In *None of the Above: Puerto Ricans in the Global Era,* ed. Frances Negrón-Muntaner, 129–46. New York: Palgrave Macmillan, 2007.

———. *Queer Latinidad: Identity Practices, Discursive Spaces.* New York: New York University Press, 2003.

Rodríguez Allende, José D. "El movimiento homosexual puertorriqueño y su impacto social (1950–1997)." Master's thesis, Universidad de Puerto Rico, Río Piedras, 2000.

Rodríguez de Laguna, Asela, ed. *Images and Identities: The Puerto Rican in Two World Contexts.* New Brunswick, N.J.: Transaction Books, 1987.

Rodríguez-Díaz, Angel. "Approximations to Death and the Representation of AIDS." *CENTRO Journal* 6, no. 1–2 (Spring 1994): 177–78.

Rodríguez Jr., Abraham. *Spidertown.* New York: Penguin, 1993.

Rodríguez Juliá, Edgardo. *Una noche con Iris Chacón.* San Juan: Editorial Antillana, 1986.

———. *Las tribulaciones de Jonás.* Río Piedras: Ediciones Huracán, 1981.

Rodríguez Madera, Sheilla Lee. "Subjects in Transit: The Transgender Phenomenon in Puerto Rico." Ph.D. diss., Universidad de Puerto Rico, Río Piedras, 2003.

Rodríguez-Matos, Carlos Antonio. "Acts of Love: Introduction to the Study of Puerto Rican Homosexual and Lesbian Poetry." *Desde este lado/From This Side* 1, no. 2 (Fall 1990): 27–33.

———. "Agosto, Moisés." In *Latin American Writers on Gay and Lesbian Themes: A Bio-Critical Sourcebook,* ed. David William Foster, 4–5. Westport, Conn.: Greenwood Press, 1994.

———. "Fernández-Fragoso, Víctor." In *Latin American Writers on Gay and Lesbian Themes: A Bio-Critical Sourcebook,* ed. David William Foster, 154–56. Westport, Conn.: Greenwood Press, 1994.

———. "Matos-Cintrón, Nemir." In *Latin American Writers on Gay and Lesbian Themes: A Bio-Critical Sourcebook,* ed. David William Foster, 216–17. Westport, Conn.: Greenwood Press, 1994.

———. "Mena-Santiago, William Manuel." In *Latin American Writers on Gay and Lesbian Themes: A Bio-Critical Sourcebook,* ed. David William Foster, 220–21. Westport, Conn.: Greenwood Press, 1994.

———. "Negrón-Muntaner, Frances." In *Latin American Writers on Gay and Lesbian Themes: A Bio-Critical Sourcebook,* ed. David William Foster, 288–90. Westport, Conn.: Greenwood Press, 1994.

———. "Por el río a la mar, todo por Margarita." In *The Margarita Poems,* by Luz María Umpierre, 8–11. Bloomington, Ind.: Third Woman Press, 1987.

————. "To Be Gay, Puerto Rican, and a Poet." *ANQ* 10, no. 3 (Summer 1997): 25–37.

————. "Villanueva, Alfredo." In *Latin American Writers on Gay and Lesbian Themes: A Bio-Critical Sourcebook,* ed. David William Foster, 447–50. Westport, Conn.: Greenwood Press, 1994.

————, ed. *POESídA: An Anthology of AIDS Poetry from the United States, Latin America and Spain.* Jackson Heights, N.Y.: Ollantay Center for the Arts, 1995.

Rodríguez Ramírez, René. "El cuerpo nacional o lo nacional en el cuerpo: El performance identitario en la narrativa contemporánea puertorriqueña." Ph.D. diss., Rutgers University, New Brunswick, N.J., 2006.

Román, David. "Teatro Viva! Latino Performance and the Politics of AIDS in Los Angeles." In *Acts of Intervention: Performance, Gay Culture, and AIDS,* 177–201. Bloomington: Indiana University Press, 1998.

Romney, Jonathan. "Angling for Controversy." *New Statesman and Society* July 15, 1994: 32–34.

Romo-Carmona, Mariana. *Living at Night.* Duluth, Minn.: Spinsters Ink, 1997.

————. *Speaking Like an Immigrant.* New York: Latina Lesbian History Project, 1998.

————, ed. *Conversaciones: Relatos por padres y madres de hijas lesbianas e hijos gay.* San Francisco: Cleiss Press, 2001.

Ronell, Avital. *Stupidity.* Urbana: University of Illinois Press, 2002.

Roque Ramírez, Horacio N. "*Mira, yo soy boricua y estoy aquí:* Rafa Negrón's Pan Dulce and the Queer Sonic Latinaje of San Francisco." *CENTRO Journal* 19, no. 1 (Spring 2007): 274–313.

Rosado, José O. "La homofobia que nos arropa." *Claridad* (San Juan, P.R.), July 12–18, 2007, 24.

————. "Homofóbicos al ataque." *Claridad* (San Juan, P.R.), July 19–25, 2007, 25.

Roscoe, Jane, and Craig Hight. *Faking It: Mock-Documentary and the Subversion of Factuality.* Manchester, U.K.: Manchester University Press, 2001.

Rose, David James. "Coming Out, Standing Out." *Hispanic* 21 (June 1994): 44–48.

Rosenthal, Mel. *In the South Bronx of America.* Willimantic, Conn.: Curbstone Press, 2000.

Rowlett, Lori. "Symbols." In *Encyclopedia of Lesbian, Gay, Bisexual, and Transgender History in America,* ed. Marc Stein, 166–67. New York: Charles Scribner's Sons, 2004.

Russo, Vito. *The Celluloid Closet: Homosexuality in the Movies.* New York: Harper & Row, 1987.

Said, Edward. "Reflections on Exile." In *Reflections on Exile and Other Essays,* 173–86. Cambridge, Mass.: Harvard University Press, 2002.

Salessi, Jorge. *Médicos maleantes y maricas: Higiene, criminología y homosexualidad en la construcción de la nación argentina (Buenos Aires: 1871–1914).* Rosario, Argentina: Beatriz Viterbo Editora, 1995.

Sánchez, Luis Rafael. *La guagua aérea.* Río Piedras: Editorial Cultural, 1994.

————. *La guaracha del Macho Camacho.* Buenos Aires: Ediciones La Flor, 1976.

————. *La importancia de llamarse Daniel Santos.* Mexico: Editorial Diana, 1989.

————. "¡Jum!" In *En cuerpo de camisa,* 53–60. 5th ed. Río Piedras: Editorial Cultural, 1990 [1966]. Translated by Rose M. Sevillano as "Hum!" *Grand Street* 61 (Summer 1997): 130–35.

Sánchez González, Lisa. *Boricua Literature: A Literary History of the Puerto Rican Diaspora.* New York: New York University Press, 2001.

Sánchez Korrol, Virginia E. *From Colonia to Community: The History of Puerto Ricans in New York City.* Berkeley: University of California Press, 1994.

Sandlin, Betsy A. "Julia de Burgos as a Cultural Icon in Works by Rosario Ferré, Luz María Umpierre, and Manuel Ramos Otero." Ph.D. diss., University of North Carolina, Chapel Hill, 2003.

———. "Manuel Ramos Otero's Queer Metafictional Resurrection of Julia de Burgos." In *Writing Off the Hyphen: New Critical Perspectives on the Literature of the Puerto Rican Diaspora,* ed. José L. Torres-Padilla and Carmen Haydée Rivera, 313–31. Seattle: University of Washington Press, 2008.

Sandoval, Chela. *Methodology of the Oppressed.* Minneapolis: University of Minnesota Press, 2000.

Sandoval-Sánchez, Alberto. "Imagining Puerto Rican Queer Citizenship: Frances Negrón-Muntaner's *Brincando el charco.*" In *None of the Above: Puerto Ricans in the Global Era,* ed. Frances Negrón-Muntaner, 147–64. New York: Palgrave Macmillan, 2007.

———. *José, Can You See? Latinos On and Off Broadway.* Madison: University of Wisconsin Press, 1999.

———. "Politicizing Abjection: Towards the Articulation of a Latino AIDS Queer Identity." In *Passing Lines,* ed. Brad Epps, Keja Valens, and Bill Johnson González, 311–19. Cambridge, Mass.: David Rockefeller Center for Latin American Studies and Harvard University Press, 2005.

———. "Puerto Rican Identity Up in the Air: Air Migration, Its Cultural Representations, and Me 'Cruzando El Charco.' " In *Puerto Rican Jam: Essays on Culture and Politics,* ed. Frances Negrón-Muntaner and Ramón Grosfoguel, 189–208. Minneapolis: University of Minnesota Press, 1997.

Sandoval-Sánchez, Alberto, and Nancy Saporta-Sternbach. *Stages of Life: Transcultural Performance and Identity in U.S. Latina Theater.* Tucson: University of Arizona Press, 2001.

Santiago, Silviano. *The Space In-Between: Essays on Latin American Culture.* Durham, N.C.: Duke University Press, 2001.

Santiago-Ortiz, Vilma. *Medicalizing Ethnicity: The Construction of Latino Identity in a Psychiatric Setting.* Ithaca, N.Y.: Cornell University Press, 2001.

Santos-Febres, Mayra. "Hebra rota." In *Pez de vidrio,* 63–71. Río Piedras: Ediciones Huracán, 1996.

———. "La memoria como viaje o reseña de *Brincando el charco* de Frances Negrón." *Claridad* (San Juan, P.R.), November 10–16, 1995, 20.

———. "Salsa as Translocation." In *Everynight Life: Culture and Dance in Latin/o America,* ed. Celeste Fraser Delgado and José Esteban Muñoz, 175–88. Durham, N.C.: Duke University Press, 1997.

———. *Sirena Selena vestida de pena.* Barcelona: Mondadori, 2000. Translated by Stephen Litle as *Sirena Selena.* New York: Picador USA, 2000.

Sarduy, Severo. *La simulación.* Caracas: Monte Avila Editores, 1982.

Schechner, Richard. *Performance Studies: An Introduction.* London: Routledge, 2002.

Sedgwick, Eve Kosofsky. *Epistemology of the Closet.* Berkeley: University of California Press, 1990.

Seideman, Steven. *Difference Troubles: Queering Social Theory and Sexual Politics.* Cambridge: Cambridge University Press, 1997.

Shepard, Benjamin. "Sylvia and Sylvia's Children: A Battle for a Queer Public Space." In *That's Revolting! Queer Strategies for Resisting Assimilation,* ed. Mattilda, a.k.a. Matt Bernstein Sycamore, 97–112. Brooklyn: Soft Skull Press, 2004.

Siegal, Nina. "At a Long-Vacant Plant, Dabs of Life." *New York Times,* April 10, 2000, B3.

———. "Hope Is Artists' Medium in a Bronx Neighborhood: Dancers, Painters, and Sculptors Head to Hunts Point." *New York Times,* December 27, 2000, E1.

Siegel, Marcia B. "The Harsh and Splendid Heroines of Martha Graham." In *Moving History/Dancing Cultures: A Dance History Reader,* ed. Ann Dils and Ann Cooper Albright, 307–14. Middletown, Conn.: Wesleyan University Press/University Press of New England, 2001.

Sifuentes-Jáuregui, Ben. *Transvestism, Masculinity, and Latin American Literature: Genders Share Flesh.* New York: Palgrave Macmillan, 2002.

Silén, Iván. *Los poemas de Filí-Melé.* New York: El Libro Viaje, 1976.

Simounet, Alma. "Delegitimizing Oppressive Culture: The Voice of Counter-Discourse in Umpierre's Poetic Work." *CENTRO Journal* 20, no. 1 (Spring 2008): 22–35.

Sloane, Jeannine. "Rose Troche — Recreating a Contemporary Image of Lesbians in Film and Television" (2005). New York. http://rosetroche.tripod.com/index.html.

Smith, Patricia Juliana. "Troche, Rose." In *glbtq: An Encyclopedia of Gay, Lesbian, Bisexual, Transgender, and Queer Culture,* ed. Claude J. Summers. Chicago: 2002, updated 2005. www.glbtq.com/arts/troche_r.html.

Solberg, Helena, dir. *Carmen Miranda: Bananas Is My Business.* Film. New York: Fox Lorber Home Video, 1994.

Solomon, Melissa. "Flaming Iguanas, Dalai Pandas, and Other Lesbian Bardos (A Few Perimeter Points)." In *Regarding Sedgwick: Essays on Queer Culture and Critical Theory,* ed. Stephen M. Barber and David L. Clark, 201–16. New York: Routledge, 2002.

Solomons, Gus J. "Go Go Latino." *Village Voice,* February 12, 1991, 84.

Sommer, Doris. *Foundational Fictions: The National Romances of Latin America.* Berkeley: University of California Press, 1991.

Sontag, Susan. *AIDS and Its Metaphors.* New York: Farrar, Straus, Giroux, 1989.

Sosa, Irene, dir. *Sexual Exiles.* Film. 1999.

Soto, Pedro Juan. *Spiks.* 7th ed. Río Piedras: Editorial Cultural, 1985.

———, ed. *En busca de J. I. de Diego Padró.* Río Piedras: Editorial de la Universidad de Puerto Rico, 1990.

Sotomayor, Aurea María. *De lengua, razón y cuerpo (nueve poetas contemporáneas puertorriqueñas): Antología y ensayo crítico.* San Juan: Instituto de Cultura Puertorriqueña, 1987.

———. "Genealogías o el suave desplazamiento de los orígenes en la narrativa de Manuel Ramos Otero." *Nómada* (San Juan, P.R.) 1 (1995): 92–106.

Souza, Caridad. "Esta risa no es de loca." In *Telling to Live: Latina Feminist Testimonios,* by the Latina Feminist Group, 114–22. Durham, N.C.: Duke University Press, 2001.

Spacks, Patricia Meyer. *Gossip.* New York: Alfred A. Knopf, 1985.

Spivak, Gayatri Chakravorty. "Can the Subaltern Speak?" In *Marxism and the Interpretation of Culture,* ed. Cary Nelson and Lawrence Grossberg, 271–313. Urbana: University of Illinois Press, 1988.

Stein, Marc. *City of Sisterly and Brotherly Love: Lesbian and Gay Philadelphia, 1945–1972.* Chicago: University of Chicago Press, 2000.

Stewart, William. *Cassell's Queer Companion: A Dictionary of Lesbian and Gay Life and Culture.* London: Cassell, 1995.

Stukin, Stacie. "Lesbian Directors Hit the Big Time." *Advocate,* April 2, 2002, 58–59.

———. "Rose to the Occasion." *Advocate,* March 18, 2003, 56.

Stychin, Carl F. " 'A Stranger to its Laws': Sovereign Bodies, Global Sexualities, and Transnational Citizens." *Journal of Law and Society* 27, no. 4 (December 2000): 601–25.

Suárez, Juan A. "The Puerto Rican Lower East Side and the Queer Underground." *Grey Room* 32 (Summer 2008): 6–37.

Sulcas, Roslyn. "Reviews: Festival International de Danse." *Dance Magazine* 67, no. 3 (March 1993): 97–99.

Sullivan, Laura L. "Chasing Fae: *The Watermelon Woman* and Black Lesbian Possibility." *Callaloo* 23, no. 1 (Winter 2000): 448–60.

Supree, Burt. "Belly Up: Arthur Avilés and Jody Oberfelder-Riehm." *Village Voice*, June 19, 1990, 111–12.

Sutton, Lorraine. *SAYcred LAYdy*. New York: Sunbury Press, 1975.

Swartz, Mark Evan. *Oz before the Rainbow: L. Frank Baum's The Wonderful Wizard of Oz on Stage and Screen to 1939*. Baltimore: Johns Hopkins University Press, 2000.

Tobias, Tobi. "Heaven Can Wait." *New York* December 12, 1994: 98.

Toro-Morn, Maura I. "Boricuas en Chicago: Gender and Class in the Migration and Settlement of Puerto Ricans." In *The Puerto Rican Diaspora: Historical Perspectives*, ed. Carmen Teresa Whalen and Víctor Vázquez-Hernández, 128–50. Philadelphia: Temple University Press, 2005.

Torre, Carlos Antonio, Hugo Rodríguez Vecchini, and William Burgos, eds. *The Commuter Nation: Perspectives on Puerto Rican Migration*. Río Piedras: Editorial de la Universidad de Puerto Rico, 1994.

Torres, Andrés, and José E. Velázquez, eds. *The Puerto Rican Movement: Voices From the Diaspora*. Philadelphia: Temple University Press, 1998.

Torres, Arlene. "La gran familia puertorriqueña 'ej prieta de beldá' (The Great Puerto Rican Family Is Really Really Black)." In *Blackness in Latin America and the Caribbean: Social Dynamics and Cultural Transformations*, vol. 2, ed. Norman E. Whitten Jr. and Arlene Torres, 285–306. Bloomington: Indiana University Press, 1998.

Torres, Daniel. "El 'hombre de papel' en *Invitación al polvo* de Manuel Ramos Otero." *Chasqui* 29, no. 1 (May 2000): 33–49.

———. *Verbo y carne en tres poetas de la lírica homoerótica en Hispanoamérica*. Santiago de Chile: Editorial Cuarto Propio, 2005.

Torres, Lourdes. "Boricua Lesbians: Sexuality, Nationality, and the Politics of Passing." *CENTRO Journal* 19, no. 1 (Spring 2007): 230–49.

Torres-Saillant, Silvio. "The Latino Autobiography." In *Latino and Latina Writers*, vol. 1, ed. Alan West-Durán, María Herrera-Sobek, and César A. Salgado, 61–79. New York: Scribner's, 2004.

Trelles, Luis. "*La guagua* por poco se estrella." *Diálogo* (Río Piedras, P.R.), September 1993, 43.

Trelles Hernández, María D. "Silencio en la corte: La aplicación e implicaciones del derecho a la intimidad en las agencias de ley y orden público." *Revista Jurídica de la Universidad de Puerto Rico* 72 (2003): 971–1007.

Troche, Rose, dir. *Bedrooms and Hallways*. Film. First Run Features, 1999.

———. *Go Fish*. Film. Samuel Goldwyn/MGM/UA Home Video, 1994.

———. *The Safety of Objects*. Film. MGM Home Entertainment, 2001.

———, co-executive prod., segment dir., and writer. *The L Word*. TV series. Showtime Entertainment, 2004–06.

———, segment dir. *Six Feet Under*. TV series. HBO, 2001.

Troyano, Alina. *I, Carmelita Tropicana: Performing between Cultures.* Ed. Chon A. Noriega. Boston: Beacon Press, 2000.

Troyano, Ela, dir. *Carmelita Tropicana: Your Kunst Is Your Waffen.* Film. First Run/Icarus Films, 1994.

———. *Once Upon a Time in the Bronx.* Video. Independent Television Service, 1994.

Trujillo, Carla, ed. *Chicana Lesbians: The Girls Our Mothers Warned Us About.* Berkeley: Third Woman Press, 1991.

Turner, Guinevere, and Rose Troche. *Go Fish.* Woodstock, N.Y.: Overlook Press, 1995.

Umpierre, Luz María. "La ansiedad de la influencia en Sandra María Esteves y Marjorie Agosín." *Revista Chicano-Riqueña* 11, no. 3–4 (1983): 139–47.

———. "An Anti-Pro." Prologue. *Third Woman* 1, no. 2 (1982): 5.

———. "The Breaking of Form in Lorraine Sutton's *SAYcred LAYdy.*" In *La escritora hispánica: Actas de la Decimotercera Conferencia Anual de Literatura Hispánicas en Indiana University of Pennsylvania,* ed. Nora Erro-Orthmann and Juan Mendizábal, 287–91. Miami: Ediciones Universal, 1990.

———. "El diálogo poético como forma de apoyo y sobrevivencia: Mi relación con Sandra María Esteves." In *Entre mujeres: Colaboraciones, influencias e intertextualidades en la literatura y el arte latinoamericanos,* ed. María Claudia André and Patricia Rubio, 109–17. Santiago, Chile: RIL, 2005.

———. *En el país de las maravillas (Kempis puertorriqueño).* Bloomington, Ind.: Third Woman Press, 1982.

———. *For Christine: Poems and One Letter.* Chapel Hill, N.C.: Professional Press, 1995.

———. *Ideología y novela en Puerto Rico: un estudio de la narrativa de Zeno, Laguerre y Soto.* Madrid: Playor, 1983.

———. Interview with Cherríe Moraga. *The Americas Review* 14, no. 2 (1986): 54–67.

———. "Lesbian Tantalizing in Carmen Lugo Filippi's 'Milagros, Calle Mercurio.'" In *¿Entiendes? Queer Readings, Hispanic Writings,* ed. Emilie Bergmann and Paul Julian Smith, 306–14. Durham, N.C.: Duke University Press, 1995.

———. *The Margarita Poems.* Bloomington, Ind.: Third Woman Press, 1987.

———. "Metapoetic Code in Julia de Burgos' *El mar y tú:* Towards a Re-Vision." In *Retrospect: Essays on Latin American Literature,* ed. Elizabeth S. Rogers and Timothy J. Rogers, 85–94. York, S.C.: Spanish Literature Publications, 1987.

———. *Nuevas aproximaciones críticas a la literatura puertorriqueña contemporánea.* Río Piedras: Editorial Cultural, 1983.

———. *Pour toi/For Moira.* Folio. San Juan: Mariita Rivadulla & Associates, 2005.

———. *Una puertorriqueña en Penna.* [Puerto Rico]: Master Typesetting of P.R., 1979.

———. "La veintiuna." In *Cuentos: Stories by Latinas,* ed. Alma Gómez, Cherríe Moraga, and Mariana Romo-Carmona, 88–91. New York: Kitchen Table/Women of Color Press, 1983.

———. "Whose Taboos? Theirs, Yours, or Ours?" *Letras femeninas,* 22, no. 1–2 (Spring–Fall 1996): 263–68.

———. *... Y otras desgracias/And Other Misfortunes....* Bloomington, Ind.: Third Woman Press, 1985.

U.S. Commission on Civil Rights, Western Regional Office. *Puerto Ricans in California.* Washington, D.C.: U.S. Government Printing Office, 1980.

Vachon, Christine, and Austin Bunn. *A Killer Life: How an Independent Film Producer Survives Deals and Disasters in Hollywood and Beyond.* New York: Simon and Schuster, 2006.

Vachon, Christine, and David Edelstein. *Shooting to Kill: How an Independent Producer Blasts through the Barriers to Make Movies That Matter.* New York: Avon Books, 1998.

Vaquero, María, and Amparo Morales. *Tesoro lexicográfico del español de Puerto Rico.* Academia Puertorriqueña de la Lengua Española. San Juan: Editorial Plaza Mayor, 2005.

Varo, Carlos. *Rosa Mystica.* Barcelona: Seix Barral, 1987.

Vásquez, Eva C. *Pregones Theatre: A Theatre for Social Change in the South Bronx.* New York: Routledge, 2003.

Vázquez, Carmen. "Citizen Queer." In *This Is What Lesbian Looks Like: Dyke Activists Take on the 21st Century,* ed. Kris Kleindienst, 268–78. Ithaca, N.Y.: Firebrand Books, 1999.

———. "The Land That Never Has Been Yet: Dreams of a Gay Latina in the United States." In *The Third Pink Book: A Global View of Lesbian and Gay Liberation and Oppression,* ed. Aart Hendricks, Rob Tielman, and Evert van der Veen, 217–24. Buffalo, N.Y.: Prometheus Books, 1993.

Vázquez-Hernández, Víctor. "From Pan-Latino Enclaves to a Community: Puerto Ricans in Philadelphia, 1910–2000." In *The Puerto Rican Diaspora: Historical Perspectives,* ed. Carmen Teresa Whalen and Víctor Vázquez-Hernández, 88–105. Philadelphia: Temple University Press, 2005.

Vega, Ana Lydia. "Muerto pero decente." *El Nuevo Día* (San Juan, P.R.), July 6, 2007. Accessed electronically.

Vega, Bernardo. *Memoirs of Bernardo Vega: A Contribution to the History of the Puerto Rican Community in New York.* Trans. Juan Flores. New York: Monthly Review Press, 1984.

Vélez, Isabel E. "Crossing El Río: Sexuality and Puerto Rican Migration." Ph.D. diss. in progress, University of California, Santa Cruz. http://clnet.ucla.edu/people/velez.i.html.

Vidal-Ortiz, Salvador. "Sexuality and Gender in Santería: LGBT Identities at the Crossroads of Santería Religious Practices and Beliefs." In *Gay Religion,* ed. Scott Thumma and Edward R. Gray, 115–37. Walnut Creek, Calif.: AltaMira Press, 2005.

———. "Sexuality Discussions in Santería: A Case Study of Religion and Sexuality Negotiation." *Sexuality Research and Social Policy* 3, no. 3 (September 2006): 52–66.

Villa, Raúl Homero. *Barrio-Logos: Space and Place in Urban Chicano Literature and Culture.* Austin: University of Texas Press, 2000.

Villanueva-Collado, Alfredo. "René Marqués, Angel Lozada, and the Constitution of the (Queer) Puerto Rican National Subject." *CENTRO Journal* 19, no. 1 (Spring 2007): 178–91.

Vivas Maldonado, José Luis. *A vellón las esperanzas o Melania (Cuentos de un puertorriqueño en Nueva York).* Long Island City, N.Y.: Las Américas, 1971.

Vosburg, Nancy. "Luz María Umpierre-Herrera." In *Contemporary Lesbian Writers of the United States: A Bio-Bibliographical Critical Sourcebook,* ed. Sandra Pollack and Denise D. Knight, 549–55. Westport, Conn.: Greenwood Press, 1993.

Warner, Michael, ed. *Fear of a Queer Planet: Queer Politics and Social Theory.* Minneapolis: University of Minnesota Press, 1993.

West Side Story. Film. Robert Wise and Jerome Robbins, dir. MGM, 1961.

Whalen, Carmen Teresa. "Bridging Homeland and Barrio Politics: The Young Lords in Philadelphia." In *The Puerto Rican Movement: Voices from the Diaspora,* ed. Andrés Torres and José E. Velázquez, 107–23. Philadelphia: Temple University Press, 1998.

———. *From Puerto Rico to Philadelphia: Puerto Rican Workers and Postwar Economies.* Philadelphia: Temple University Press, 2001.

Whalen, Carmen Teresa, and Víctor Vázquez-Hernández, eds. *The Puerto Rican Diaspora: Historical Perspectives.* Philadelphia: Temple University Press, 2005.

Williams, Raymond. *The Sociology of Culture.* New York: Schocken Books, 1981.

Willis, Holly. "Fish Stories." *Filmmaker* 2, no. 3 (Spring 1994): 18–20.

Wilmington, Michael. "Roll 'Em: Women in the Director's Chair Begins at Locations around the City." *Chicago Tribune* March 9, 1995. NewsBank Acces World News.

Wilson, Andrew R., ed. *The Chinese in the Caribbean.* Princeton, N.J.: Marcus Wiener Publishers, 2004.

Wilson, August. *Fences.* New York: Plume, 1986.

Winokur, Mark. "Body and Soul: Identifying (with) the Black Lesbian Body in Cheryl Dunye's *The Watermelon Woman.*" In *Recovering the Black Female Body: Self-Representations by African American Women,* ed. Michael Bennett and Vanessa D. Dickerson, 231–52. New Brunswick, N.J.: Rutgers University Press, 2001.

Wittig, Monique. *Le corps lesbien.* Paris: Editions de minuit, 1973. Trans. David Le Vay as *The Lesbian Body.* New York: Avon, 1976.

The Wizard of Oz. Film. Victor Fleming, dir. MGM, 1939.

Xavier, Emanuel. *Christ-Like.* New York: Painted Leaf Press, 1999.

———. *Pier Queen.* New York: Pier Queen Productions, 1997.

Young, Allen. *Gays under the Cuban Revolution.* San Francisco: Grey Fox, 1981.

Zavala, Iris M. *El bolero: historia de un amor.* Madrid: Celeste, 2000.

Zenón Cruz, Isabelo. *Narciso descubre su trasero (El negro en la cultura puertorriqueña).* 2 vols. Humacao, P.R.: Editorial Furidi, 1974–75.

Zimmer, Elizabeth. "Dance: Arthur Avilés and Stephane Vambre." *Village Voice,* January 3, 1995, S2.

———. "West Side Stories." *Village Voice,* September 7, 1993, 80.

Publication History

Part of the Introduction, part of chapter 2, and part of chapter 4 were previously published in "Cultures of the Puerto Rican Queer Diaspora," in *Passing Lines: Sexuality and Immigration*, ed. Brad Epps, Keja Valens, and Bill Johnson González (Cambridge, Mass.: David Rockefeller Center for Latin American Studies and Harvard University Press, 2005), 275–309. Reprinted with permission of the David Rockefeller Center for Latin American Studies, Harvard University.

An earlier version of chapter 5 appeared as "Dancing *La Vida Loca*: The Queer Nuyorican Performances of Arthur Avilés and Elizabeth Marrero," in *Queer Globalizations: Citizenship and the Afterlife of Colonialism*, ed. Arnaldo Cruz-Malavé and Martin Manalansan IV (New York: New York University Press, 2002), 162–75. Reprinted with permission from New York University Press.

In chapter 1, excerpts from "¡Jum!" are from Luis Rafael Sánchez, *En cuerpo de camisa* (Río Piedras: Editorial Cultural, 1966). Reprinted with permission from Luis Rafael Sánchez.

In chapter 2, excerpts from "against muñoz pamphleteering" are from Tato Laviera, *La Carreta Made a U-Turn* (Houston: Arte Público Press, 1992). Copyright 1992 Arte Público Press, University of Houston. Reprinted with permission from Arte Público Press, University of Houston.

In chapter 3, excerpts from "A la Mujer Borrinqueña" are from Sandra María Esteves, *Yerba Buena* (Greenfield Center, N.Y.: Greenfield Review, 1980). Copyright 1980 Sandra María Esteves. Reprinted with permission from Sandra María Esteves.

In chapter 3, excerpts from "In Response" are from Luz María Umpierre, *... Y otras desgracias / And Other Misfortunes...* (Bloomington, Ind.: Third Woman Press, 1985), and excerpts from "Immanence," "No Hatchet Job," "Madre," "Ceremonia Secreta," and "The Mar/Garita Poem" are from Luz María Umpierre, *The Margarita Poems* (Bloomington, Ind.: Third Woman Press, 1987). Reprinted with permission from Dr. Luz María Umpierre, www.luzmaumpierre.com.

In chapter 3, excerpts from "Me robaron el cuerpo" and "Vuelo en las aletas de tu crica en pleamar" by Nemir Matos-Cintrón are from Nemir Matos-Cintrón and Yolanda Fundora, *Las mujeres no hablan así* (Río Piedras: Editorial Atabex, 1981). Reprinted with permission from Nemir Matos-Cintrón.

Index

Abbe, Elfrieda, 99
abjection, 47, 80–81, 90
Acid, 151–52
Acosta, Juan David, 99, 100, 186n12
activism, AIDS, 97–99, 103, 131, 135
activism, feminist, 68
activism, LGBT, xv, xxiii–xxiv, 36–37, 67, 95, 131
activism, Puerto Rican anticolonial, xviii, 98, 186n13
African Americans: in Chicago, 109, 114; and dance, 134–35; and language, 142; lesbian and gay in Philadelphia, 70, 106; links with Puerto Ricans, xxii, xxvii, 50, 100, 106, 114–15, 133, 140; passing as, 127; style, seventies, 166
Afro-Diasporic culture, 140, 151. *Also see* blackness
"against muñoz pamphleteering" (Laviera), 56
Agosín, Marjorie, 69, 76, 91
Agosto, Moisés, xxiii, 103
Ah mén! (Cardona), 10
AIDS. *See* HIV/AIDS
AIDS in the Barrio (Negrón-Muntaner), 96–99, 131
Aïnouz, Karim, 102
"A la Mujer Borrinqueña" (Esteves), 73
Alarcón, Norma, 76
Albizu Campos, Pedro, 88
Albright, Ann Cooper, 156
alcohol, 33, 49
alcoholism, 61
Alfaro, Luis, 131, 168, 190n2
Algarín, Miguel, 38, 47, 97, 138, 182n64
"¡Algo en la cocina" (Avilés), 160–61
"Alrededor del mundo con la señorita Mambresi" (Ramos Otero), 29–30, 32
Alvarez, Aldo, xxiii, 186n3
Alvarez, Julia, 69, 76, 77, 153
American-Rican identity, 139
AmeRícans (Laviera), 139
Anderson, Benedict, xvi
Andino, Sandra, 103
Animal fiero y tierno (Dávila), 82

anthologies, 103. Also see *Chicana Lesbians, Compañeras, Telling to Live, This Bridge Called My Back*
anticolonialism, 64, 91
anorexia, 82
Anthes, John, 59, 62
Anzaldúa, Gloria, xiv, 23, 62, 63, 68, 75; border/mestiza sensibility, 25–26; critique of Western rationalism, 91; and lesbian of color feminism, 68, 76–77, 116, 123, 127
Aparicio, Frances, 48, 71, 186n11
"Apartamiento vasto" (Ramos Otero), 58
Aponte-Parés, Luis, 88, 174n12–13
aporrear, 178n37
architecture, 87–88
Arenas, Reinaldo, xviii, 20, 38, 54, 179n3
"A Rizos de Oro" (Umpierre), 73
Arlen, Harold, 160–61
Arrillaga, María, *Yo soy Filí Melé*, 34
Arroyo, Rane, xxiv, 89, 123
Arroyo, Jossianna, 2, 29, 174n12, 176n10, 177n24, 178n51, 179n4
Arthur Avilés Typical Theatre, 132, 135, 136, 137; and *Arturella*, 147, 148; meaning of name, 135; and *Súper Maéva de Oz*, 156–67
Article 103, 174n25
Arturella (Avilés), xxvii, 54, 137, 147–56; Afro-diasporic culture in, 151; as parody of Broadway, 151; characters in, 144, 150; drag in, 151, 153–56; representation of the ghetto in, 140; use of kurokos, 158; compared to *Maéva de Oz*, 162, 166; Marrero, performance style, 152–53; nudity in, 154–56, 166; as postmodern fairytale, 159–60; schizophrenia in, 153, 156–59, 164–65; transcription of, 173n4; as critique of Western rational thought, 153; and *West Side Story*, 149, 151, 152
assimilation: cultural, 136–40; linguistic, 120
Astor del Valle, Janis, xxiv, 133, 161–62, 168
autobiographical fiction, 23–24; and Ramos Otero, 20–28

Lawrence La Fountain–Stokes is assistant professor of Latina/o studies, American culture, and Romance languages and literatures at the University of Michigan, Ann Arbor. He is author of *Uñas pintadas de azul/Blue Fingernails*.

CULTURAL STUDIES OF THE AMERICAS

(*continued from page ii*)

Made in the USA
Middletown, DE
05 July 2022